Praise for

THE KINGDOM OF PREP

"A buoyant and persuasive account of how the company's fluctuating fortunes reflect Americans' shifting attitudes toward dress, shopping, and identity."

—***The New Yorker***

"Ms. Bullock is a crackerjack writer who can keep a narrative moving."

—***Wall Street Journal***

"An insightful, candid, and engrossing story about the American Dream, rollneck sweaters, and the incredible value of the stories we tell through what we wear."

—***Town & Country***

"Smart, funny. . . . A lively and fascinating read, no matter what you wear."

—***People***

"Maggie Bullock's very soul wears a J.Crew sweater. *The Kingdom of Prep* is the maddest, wildest, sharpest book about fashion of the past decade—it dissects the industry with warm wit and devastating precision."

—E. Jean Carroll, author of *What Do We Need Men For? A Modest Proposal*

"*The Kingdom of Prep* is a fashion-biz chronicle that reads like a page-turner. But it's also the story of American style writ large—and how what we wear reflects our national character. You'll never look at a rollneck sweater in the same way again." **—Véronique Hyland, author of *Dress Code: Unlocking Fashion from the New Look to Millennial Pink***

"*The Kingdom of Prep* dives deep into the allure of an empire originally built on broken-in basics and fireside photo shoots, offering a guided tour through catalogue booms, billion-dollar investment deals, models, fashion shows, and true style stardom in the Mickey Drexler and Jenna Lyons era. In this entertaining, behind-the-scenes insider account, Maggie Bullock shows us how J.Crew captured—then lost, then captured again—the zeitgeist of American privilege and membership to a club that defies definition, yet is ever present in our psyche." **—Marisa Meltzer, author of *This Is Big: How the Founder of Weight Watchers Changed the World—and Me***

The KINGDOM *of* PREP

THE INSIDE STORY OF THE
RISE AND (NEAR) FALL OF J.CREW

Maggie Bullock

DEYST.

An Imprint of WILLIAM MORROW

DEYST.

HarperCollins books may be purchased for educational, business, or sales promotional use. For information, please email the Special Markets Department at SPsales@harpercollins.com.

A hardcover edition of this book was published in 2023 by Dey Street, an imprint of William Morrow.

FIRST DEY STREET PAPERBACK EDITION PUBLISHED 2024.

Designed by Jennifer Chung
Fabric texture © m.jrn/shutterstock

Library of Congress Cataloging-in-Publication Data has been applied for.

ISBN 978-0-06-304265-0

24 25 26 27 28 LBC 5 4 3 2 1

For my boys, Nick, Finn, and Max—always

CONTENTS

PART ONE

PART ONE

INTRODUCTION

On May 4, 2020, six weeks into the first global pandemic in a century, J.Crew filed for Chapter 11 bankruptcy protection. Within hours, true believers came out of the woodwork. On digital platforms that could not have been fathomed back when the company printed its first catalogue in 1983, tributes piled up. They read like sympathy cards to an old friend.

> "*My email is literally lovesjcrew. We're pulling for you.*"
>
> "*We've been best friends for a long time now and I refuse to break up.*"
>
> "*Forever a J.Crew girl.*"

What was it about J.Crew? I had been pondering this question since 2019, when *Vanity Fair* assigned me the task of figuring out why the golden brand of the Obama era had been reduced to "rearranging deck chairs on the *Titanic*," as the *Washington Post* had recently put it. The pandemic shutdown was not the cause of J.Crew's problems—more like a final straw. The company had suffered extensive preexisting conditions for years: Crushing debt. A spin cycle of failed execs. Irate customers decrying problems of quality, fit, pricing. Lackluster clothes. And a major identity crisis. How could this happen to a company people once *loved*?

This was the right assignment for me, for a few reasons. I'd spent my career covering beauty, fashion, and culture, mostly as an editor at *Elle* and *Vogue*. And for most of that time, I kept a J.Crew shopping cart bookmarked on my laptop, ready to press "Buy Now" whenever the right sale code struck. Not everyone is susceptible to the magic J.Crew once embodied: the delicate brine of a clambake wafting in the air; the particular romance of a misty morning at a rustic lakehouse. Lots of people see no particular allure in a rumpled chambray shirt, or the well-trod cliché of a bateau stripe. I happen to be the kind of person who *is* susceptible.

But by the time *Vanity Fair* came calling, I was also like any other customer, occasionally buying summer sandals at 60 percent off in what appeared to be a never-ending fire sale, wondering what the hell had gone wrong with the company that once handily provided the basic building blocks of my wardrobe. Walking into any J.Crew store at that point was confusing. The brand that once arguably had the most clear-cut identity and aesthetic in mass retail seemed to have no discernible identity at all. The clothes were an uninspired mishmash of trends in noticeably subpar fabrics. Even the racks themselves seemed somehow dejected. Was I imagining it, or was that heart-printed frock a little *slumped* on its hanger, as if it, too, was depressed by this recent state of affairs?

Why couldn't J.Crew get it together? Was it simply another casualty of the "retail apocalypse" that had been steamrolling once-great American brands for years, leaving tumbleweeds bumbling down the corridors of American malls? Or was this condition more specific to J.Crew?

What I found were two things: Yes, of course it was the retail apocalypse. J.Crew is, in fact, an almost perfect microcosm of how shopping itself has evolved over the past forty years—and how we as consumers have evolved, too. Its story, as you'll soon see, connects the dots from the catalogue boom of the '80s to the specialty retail bonanza of the '90s, through the birth of online shopping, and into an era in which we shop from phones that never leave our hands—tracing our longing, and our consumption, from a time when it was a small thrill to drop an order form in the mail and wait for that rollneck sweater to arrive on the doorstep, all the way up to the impatient present, when a sweater ordered Monday morning with a single swipe of the finger could be drone-dropped into our hands by Tuesday afternoon. All the forces that have been working against the brands that once dressed America—the rise of new technologies, the often-disastrous interventions of venture capital—have been working hard against J.Crew, too.

But perhaps I should say . . . yes, *and*. As I began to peel back the 100 percent cotton layers of J.Crew, I discovered that it was a story of not one but *two* cults of personality. Everybody knows about one of these: Mickey and Jenna. As in Mickey Drexler, the "merchant prince"—the most famous clothing retail exec of the past fifty years, the man who helmed the monstrous rise of Gap in the '80s, birthed Old Navy in the '90s, and reinvented J.Crew as the great American mass retailing success of the aughts. As in Jenna Lyons, the one-of-a-kind fashion star—the woman who spent her career toiling in obscurity at one catalogue brand, yet somehow became a bona fide celebrity. He was the P. T. Barnum of retail; she was the walking fashion illustration in a Schiaparelli-pink evening skirt and a jean jacket, standing on the steps of the Met Gala—the *J* in her own J.Crew. Together they built a J.Crew where any mall-going American with sufficient disposable income could purchase a sequin-studded cardigan worthy of a First Lady.

But almost nobody outside of J.Crew's inner circle remembers the other pairing—also of an older male business eye and a younger female creative—that built the brand that Mickey and Jenna revived: J.Crew's father-daughter founders, Arthur Cinader and Emily Cinader (now Emily Scott). Here was a duo just as fascinating—as *specific*—as that of Mickey and Jenna. Arthur erected the business of J.Crew and agonized over every comma in its catalogue copy. Emily, as gorgeous as the models in her own pages, honed a uniform of East Coast minimalism—prep, minus the schlock—in images that sold us not just sweaters but membership to the world those sweaters beckoned to.

So, what was it about J.Crew? Two wildly different—yet oddly parallel—duos molded a brand that embodied at least two zeitgeists:

First, as the understated, feel-good catalogue of the '80s and '90s; and again, as the exuberant, rule-breaking Obama house brand of the 2000s and 2010s. Each of these duos would lead J.Crew to a golden period. Each would lead J.Crew to crash and burn, too.

For all of the prepandemic chaos evident within the walls of J.Crew, I could understand why people still loved this brand. I had loved it, too, for ages. Ever since boarding school.

I know what you're thinking: *boarding school.* A whole meal's worth of associations in one small bite. But this was no tradition in my family; my parents were achievers from the American South, first in their line of blue-collar Presbyterians to earn college degrees. I arrived at that school, in a leafy enclave of Long Island, with a thick North Carolina accent. I didn't know a "green" could be a place, not a hue. I'd never heard of a WASP, possibly never seen one in the flesh. My idea of a preppy was that parody of the species, Alex P. Keaton, clutching his briefcase on the way to high school.

In my memory, there was one item, and one item only, that signified belonging on that campus, and to my untrained eye it held no special charm. Unlike my acid-wash Guess jeans, with their cunning zips at the ankle and that coveted upside-down triangle on the back pocket—baby's first status symbol—the J.Crew rollneck sweaters these floppy-haired kids wore to crisscross the "green" looked exceedingly plain. Unlike the Gap sweatshirts and Polo ponies of the era, which broadcast their provenance, the rollneck had no visible branding. It was just a solid-color, square-shape, boxy sweater with a collar that rolled over into a little donut-like ridge. Ho-hum. But as I watched the girls in my dorm pull the sleeves of their rollnecks down over their knuckles in a sort of cozy, pregrunge slouch, so at ease laughing with boys in *their* rollneck sweaters, I felt the power of those Guess jeans drain away.

The first time I wore a (borrowed) rollneck to the dining hall was the first time I experienced the power of wearing a garment that had social acceptance knit into its very fibers. I'm sure no one else noticed. But to me that sweater felt like a password, a secret handshake; in it, I felt as if my rough edges—my outsider's accent, my general grasping cluelessness—were ground down. I felt like one of *them*.

What is it about J.Crew? For four decades, the company sold a certain slice of America its T-shirts and chinos, plus a kind of aspiration that's harder to put into words. In recent years, though, I've wondered if the answer to that question—*What is it about J.Crew?*—is also, in part, the answer to the question *What's the matter with J.Crew?* Despite its own extensive efforts to "twist" the preppy look, J.Crew is fundamentally a brand built on prep: for more than a century, the bedrock of straightforward, unfettered "American" style. Also: the leisure uniform of the establishment. A look of belonging that generations were born into, and countless others adopted to get a leg up. To those striving to belong, to level up in the world, prep has long been a useful shortcut.

Now that we've witnessed waves of pink pussy hats and Black Lives Matter T-shirts taking to the streets of a nation more fractured, more class-conscious, more awake to the problems inherent in being American than ever before—if the J.Crew catalogue of yore is still somehow analogous in many minds to *The Official Preppy Handbook*, what the societal backstory was once a boon to J.Crew's value proposition now seems like heavy baggage to carry.

When I began writing this book—one month before the bankruptcy news, when there was no apparent fix-it plan in place for this ailing company—I wondered: Was it time to let the old friend go? Or could this brand feel special, covetable, or even just *dependable* again? Is it possible to cherry-pick what is best about J.Crew and leave the rest behind?

CHAPTER 1

"How to Be Really Top-Drawer"

October 1980. Twenty-one-year-old Lisa Birnbach bumped her suitcase up the stairs of yet another radio station in yet another new town, hiked up her knee socks, smoothed her wraparound plaid skirt, and prepared to do another interview. *How many books have you sold so far, Lisa?* the interviewers always wanted to know. Hang on, lemme check, she'd tell them, and borrow someone's phone to call her publisher back in New York for the latest count. Every day, the numbers for *The Official Preppy Handbook* shot higher. "It was like a telethon," Birnbach recalls.

The book in question was a handy step-by-step guide to the Locust Valley lockjaw set, a road map that made public the previously clandestine route to becoming a well-bred Muffy or a Skip. This was a joke, of course. That kind of quantum leap wasn't something you could learn to execute from a manual, particularly not a madras-print, pocket-size novelty book sold for $3.95 in those little holders by the bookstore cash register. Everybody knew that the only way to *really* be a Muffy—to gain access to that good-looking life of American privilege—was to be born one.

But if *The Official Preppy Handbook* was a joke, it was more than that, too. Today, it is often inaccurately remembered as nothing more than an unctuous catalogue of funny stuff from the '80s—indeed, that was the publisher's original idea: to catalogue all the *stuff* that went with prep. "But I was bent on explaining the context of everything," Birnbach told me. "To me the stuff was only interesting if you knew *why* the stuff." So, with the satirical bite of *Spy* magazine—where, indeed, Birnbach would later work—the book dissected the gin-and-tonic-swilling WASP as if it were the winged species, mercilessly pinned beneath an entomologist's magnifying glass. It documented everything from drinking habits to decorating ephemera—admissions offices, toga parties, dressage, cotillions, yacht clubs—in countless little boxes, charts, and diagrams. And, yes, all the trappings were noted: Tretorn sneakers, signet rings, ribbon belts. Shocking-pink Lilly Pulitzer bikinis. Popped-collar Lacoste shirts. Pricey? Not necessarily. But each item was exceedingly *particular*: A Fair Isle sweater, "blue with yellow yoke—her mother's, bought in Edinburgh in 1962."[1]

Worn in assemblage, these prosaic pieces made up a uniform that had been embedded deep in the American consciousness for more than a century: They telegraphed "good taste" and "breeding," access, belonging—a certainty of one's place in the world. Before the *Handbook*, you knew it if you saw it, but pop culture lacked a single word to encapsulate what and whom it represented. Birnbach and her three cowriters gave us *preppy*.

The term had popped up here and there since the late 1800s, to describe the jacket-and-tie dress codes of the college prep set (Deerfield, Choate, Exeter). It had its mainstream debut in 1970, when Ali MacGraw hurled it as an epithet at Ryan O'Neal in *Love Story*:

"What makes you so sure I went to prep school?" demands Oliver Barrett IV, a sensitive, brawny young scion whose surname is etched on the side of a hulking limestone building at Harvard. Jenny Cavalleri, the daughter of an Italian baker, who made it to Radcliffe on wits alone, sticks her nose skyward and retorts: "You look stupid and rich."

But what with all the interclass marriage and mysterious consumptive illness in *Love Story*—and those bewitching striped campus scarves and camel hair polo coats—it's unlikely that the etymology of *preppy* was a major takeaway. By the late '70s the word was still so unfamiliar that when Birnbach was editing her manuscript, she was unsure of its correct spelling. When she got an early proof of the book's cover, the publisher had gone with *y* instead of *ie*. She had to go back and retype every usage.

She was certain the *Handbook* would be a flash in the pan, a stocking stuffer for the kind of people who already held the keys to the kingdom of prep—and how big an audience could that be, really? Would even those people embrace it? The *Handbook* didn't exactly frame *preppy* as a compliment. (See: "20 verbal expressions for vomiting," in a chapter about campus partying, or the memorable chapter 3 discussion, "Prep Sex: A contradiction in terms."[2]) One of the book's biggest influences had been *Animal House*, the monster movie hit of 1978 that set up Ivy League snobs as a bunch of clueless, out-of-touch miscreants whose madras shorts and Crayola-colored crewnecks served as a visual shorthand for "overgrown brat."

But what many people didn't realize was that *Animal House* was a takedown of prep from within—made by a bunch of humorists who cut their teeth at the *Harvard Lampoon*, once described as "a campus joke machine founded in 1876 which today makes its home in a castle."[3] Those toga party scenes came straight out of a snide stereotype Harvard kids had about the unevolved social scene at hard-partying (also Ivy) Dartmouth. The movie was a classic insiders' exercise. As Birnbach herself has noted, sarcasm is the cornerstone of the preppy sense of humor. Rich kids love poking fun at their own privilege, so long as they don't lose any of it in the process.

Birnbach was a smart-mouthed private school kid who grew up in Manhattan, graduated from Brown. She'd spent a few summers in East

Hampton, but was not the kind of girl who "summered" there. And as her surname clearly indicated, she was Jewish. By the late '70s, that "J" had penetrated the upper crust of Hollywood and finance but still prohibited membership at certain deep-establishment country clubs. Most of Birnbach's speaking events and interviews sailed by without incident, but occasionally someone would pop up who "wanted me to know that I wasn't really preppy because I was Jewish," she says. She likes to call herself an "insider-outsider." Arguably that status gave the book both its authority and its bite: Birnbach was at ease inside the snow globe but was not inured to how bizarro things looked inside its walls. "Being an outsider makes you see what an insider doesn't," she says—a notion that will come up time and again in *this* book.

The *Handbook* turned out to be an unironic hit. As Tommy Hilfiger, another insider-outsider who made a fortune on the aesthetic, would note, "Preppy travels so well."[4] The French rushed to define their own old-money subculture, *bon chic, bon genre*—that is, "good style, good attitude"—or BCBG. Brits dubbed their lot the "Sloane Rangers," after the elite London stomping grounds, and celebrated them in a handbook of their own, with "supersloan" Princess Di on the cover. In the United States, *The Official Preppy Handbook* enjoyed thirty-eight weeks on the *New York Times* bestseller list, selling 2 million copies. Critics were flummoxed. "Why do preppies transfix Americans?" wrote a reviewer in the *Washington Post*. "We grab for details about their lives as if they were Triscuits at a tailgate picnic."[5]

Well, of course we did: preppies embodied that most ephemeral quality, "having it." The fact that their clothes were not gilded or ornate but just simple, functional togs was all part of a nonchalance about wealth. "The thing about money is that it's nice that you have it," wrote Birnbach et al., irony dripping from every syllable. "You're not excited to get it. You don't talk about it. It's like the golden retriever by the chair—when you reach out for it it's there."[6] That kind of ease was utterly foreign—baffling, even—to anyone who didn't "have it" or, more to the point, inherit it. But before the term *prep,* there wasn't a shorthand for all that.

Prep was a new word for a very old theme. Strivers had long masked the anxiety of improving one's station in life by adopting the look of belonging, the look that made them fit in at the country club, the sorority house. You could argue this need to be part of the crowd was anything but frivolous: It was a biological need, pure survival instinct—a way to feel somehow safe. To know where you stood. In the case of J.Crew, we'll see how the need for belonging—in a cocktail shaker of societal aspiration and throbbing ambition—motivated the leaders of the company. But we're not quite there yet . . .

In the most palatable way possible, in a format anybody could digest, the *Handbook* directly addressed an uncomfortable truth about the American caste system. Insiders saw an ironic take on their own rites of passage. Outsiders saw the gatekeepers they envied, or emulated, or loved—or loved to hate. And doubtless a healthy proportion of readers were those insider-outsiders like Birnbach herself, who occupied a wobbly liminal space: close enough to be drawn in, not close enough for true membership. To them the *Handbook* was a way into—a way of understanding—something elusive that had been baked into American culture for generations.

PREP GOT ITS START IN THE KIND OF SEPIA-TONE SCENE WE NOW associate with Hollywood backlots. Picture it: 1818. The unpaved streets of lower Manhattan, on the corner of Catherine and Cherry Streets, just around the corner from the city's stinking, bustling seaport—where a throng of seamen, longshoremen, and market vendors descended every day, and goods arrived around the clock to be hustled onto the railway network that was starting to stretch across a voracious new nation. The merchant Henry Sands Brooks, seeing strivers with money in their pockets and a new need for the look of "respectability"—but with neither personal tailors nor the time to sit around waiting for a suit to be custom made by one—opens his emporium, determined to sell a new kind of clothing: ready-made.

What we now know as prep is usually thought of as an elitist country club tradition. That's accurate, but it's not the whole story. The flip side of prep—lesser known but no less ingrained—is that at various points in time, it has also been a deeply egalitarian mode of dress. The pendulum of whose clothes these are, and what they imply, swung dramatically during the twentieth century.

The ready-to-wear that Brooks pioneered would be one of the great American innovations of the nineteenth century—both as an industry, and as a leg up in society—arriving more than a century before mass-produced clothing was widely available in Europe. "Ready-to-wear placed gentlemanliness within the reach of men who once inhabited the outer reaches of society, enabling them to subscribe to its tenets and tout its virtues," wrote Jenna Weissman Joselit in her book *A Perfect Fit: Clothes, Character, and the Promise of America.*[7]

Indeed, Brooks Brothers' two biggest breakthroughs—still fundamental to the way we dress today—were defined by their ability to be ready-made, and delivered a one-two punch to the rigid, high-and-tight uniform of the Victorian-era gentleman. First, at the turn of the twentieth century, came the No. 1 Sack Suit—its unstructured shoulder and looser shape considered hair-raising at the time. Shortly thereafter, Brooks devised the oxford-cloth button-down shirt, with a built-in collar that eliminated the stiff, detachable clerical-looking collars men had long worn.[8] In menswear circles, the shirt is still referred to as the OCBD. (There's a reason preppy has a reputation for being stuck in amber.)

But by the 1910s and '20s, the prep pendulum had taken its first major swing. The Brooks Brothers look, originally intended to make the look of belonging attainable to the American everyman, had been adopted by fashionable youth, eager to shake out the starch of their fathers' generation. Brooks Brothers was de rigueur at prep schools and colleges of the Northeast; an army of Brooks' traveling salesmen frequented these campuses to peddle diagonal-stripe "repp" ties (first adopted from British military uniforms) and soft-shouldered tweed jackets—the original sport coat, originally marketed as the "odd jacket" because it was sold without matching trousers. This, too, was radical in its day.

If the look had a name at all, it was referred to as "campus" or "collegiate" dress. Mostly it was just considered "our clothes." In the 1920s, the young swains of the Ivy League obsessed over every detail. Campus style was a sport unto itself—a high-stakes game of peacocking and peak conformity. "One's identity *was* in the details: What a man wore, how his tie was tied, where his hair was parted and what club he joined were of paramount importance," write designers Jeffrey Banks and Doria de La Chapelle in *Preppy: Cultivating Ivy Style*. "The roll of a collar, the width of a lapel, the vent of a jacket, and the vital question of whether a shirt cuff should possess one button or two, and a sport coat two buttons or three—quirky little elements that helped form the preppy canon."[9]

Nowhere was this game more intense than at Princeton. Nestled in a then-rural stretch of New Jersey—versus the bustling cities of New Haven, New York, and Cambridge that housed its Ivy brethren—the institution existed in an airtight cultural bubble documented by F. Scott Fitzgerald in *This Side of Paradise*, the novel he wrote after dropping out of Princeton in 1917. "I want to go where people aren't barred because of the color of their neckties and the roll of their coats," complains the poet Tom D'Invilliers, decrying the minutiae that could seal a young man's social fate, placing him *in* or *out*. His friend Amory

Blaine offers no comfort. It's too late, he says: Tom has already internalized the code. "Wherever you go now you'll always unconsciously apply these standards of 'having it' or 'lacking it.'"[10]

Even as the rest of the country plunged into the Great Depression, the collegiate look—safe within the ivory tower, among a tribe largely untouched by the downturn—sailed into what writer and prep philosopher Christian Chensvold, founder and former publisher of the website *Ivy Style*, considers its golden period. Depression or no, a young man was still expected to show up at Harvard with a trunk full of battle armor. By evening, a tuxedo. By day, all the sportif accoutrements of the Palm Beach set. Call it the original athleisure: folded in with the same OCBDs and tweed jackets were the gold-crested navy blazers of English rowers; the sweaters of varsity lettermen; golf knickers; and tennis "whites," including navy-banded V-neck sweaters and elegant flannel trousers. In 1933, tennis champ Jean René "the Crocodile" Lacoste set out to market the shirt he made famous on the court. It was made of lightweight cotton pique, with a back shirttail elongated to stay neatly tucked in play, and a witty crocodile embroidered on the breast—said to be the first brand visibly displayed on the exterior of a garment.[11]

To finish the look off, campus men wore argyle socks (essential!) and either slip-on Weejuns—that cunning slot on the vamp just big enough to hold a shiny coin, hence the "penny loafer"—or white "bucks," named for the buffed texture of their soft nubuck. With apologies to M. Louboutin, bucks were the original red-soled status shoe. They walked straight off the tennis lawn and into the hallowed halls of "white shoe" law firms and Wall Street brokerages.

The sacred, secret ingredient to this recipe was one that a striver could easily miss. It wasn't enough to wear the right things—you had to wear them the right way. Even in 1933, looking like you tried too hard was a kiss of death. Pulling the look off required a studied negligence. What the Japanese call *wabi sabi*. What the Italian Baldassare Castiglione pegged as *sprezzatura* in the sixteenth century: "a certain nonchalance, so as to conceal all art and make whatever one does or says appear to be without effort and almost without any thought about it."[12]

Nothing identified an outsider like a too-crisp collar or a spit-shined brogue. Men who could not afford the best might have felt insecure, walking around in these unironed shirts, crushed hats, and frayed jackets. But young scions liked their clothes slouchy, roughed up.[13] Their patched elbows were both affectation and necessity. "Waste not, want not" was pure old money frugality; decades later, the *Preppy Handbook* would note that no item of the upper crust wardrobe was replaced until "all possibility of repair, restoration, or rehabilitation" had been exhausted. But it was more than that, too: A man who confidently strolled into class or an office in well-scuffed bucks didn't have to worry he'd be held back by some bourgeois triviality. He knew where he stood. So did everyone else.

When prep's pendulum swung back to egalitarianism in the 1950s, it was not because of some style whim, but because of a piece of legislation. Between 1945 and 1957, the G.I. Bill flooded American colleges with 2.2 million veterans. A generation of men from blue-collar backgrounds (who were almost exclusively white[14]) found themselves on the path to a newly burgeoning corporate America fueled by the postwar boom.* Like Brooks Brothers' nineteenth-century strivers, they needed clothes that were "correct." On campus, where jackets and ties were still required for class, the well-established "collegiate" look did the trick. Funny thing: this look perfected by the rich consisted of fairly straightforward, affordable building blocks that were built to last and never went out of style. Blue, white, and pale pink OCBDs. A tweed

* The G.I. Bill was supposed to be the great social leveler of the twentieth century. But like so many "democratizing" forces, it worked selectively, in ways that were only fully appreciated decades later. In the North, it sent a generation of working-class men to college. But across the country, and particularly in the South, its discriminatory implementation underpinned a wide variety of the race-based income inequalities that still plague America today.

jacket. A pair of Bass Weejuns. The G.I.s stirred their regulation chinos into the mix—sturdy, standard issue trousers, the inverse of everything "campus" had long implied—and made the look their own.

America's singularly advanced manufacturing industry—kick-started so long ago by Brooks Brothers' ready-made operation—was standing by, ready to churn out the campus look for the masses. (It would take Europe, recovering from back-to-back wars, decades to catch up to factory-made, off-the-rack garments that Americans had been ordering from the Sears catalogue since the '30s.) Sprinkle in rabid postwar consumerism, a booming economy, and the desire-stoking efforts of real-life Madison Avenue Mad Men, and you got a bona fide fashion trend: a clean-cut, optimistic wardrobe sold at the one-stop "college shops" that popped up in department stores across the country. Even people who had no intention of going to college could look like they did. Suddenly, "our clothes" seemed to be everybody's. The campus look was widely acknowledged to be the "American" look. Yet what did everybody call it, in the '50s? "Ivy style." The rarefied birthplace was baked into its appeal.

What that meant was that, among Ivy Leaguers, "authenticity" mattered more than ever. Details separated the insider from the arriviste, in his telltale shiny penny loafers. *Ivy Style* founder Christian Chensvold points to the memoir *Out of Place*, by Edward W. Said, a Christian Arab born in Jerusalem and raised in Cairo. When Said arrived at Princeton, class of '57, he looked around at the sea of identical white bucks, chinos, OCBDs, tweed jackets—and saw a look that struck him not as aspirational, but rather as hopelessly drab: If these boys could afford to wear anything they wanted, why were they wearing *this?* It was as if Said had just touched down on Mars. He watched "in astonishment" as students who "knew that by virtue of race, background, or manner, they could not make the club of their choice . . . set out to transform themselves into WASP paragons, usually with pathetic results." In years to come, fashion companies (including J.Crew) would employ high-tech wizardry to etch *wabi sabi* into brand-new clothes. But in 1957 the process was manual: "Two classmates in an adjoining suite applied sandpaper to a pair of new blue button-down shirts, trying in a matter of minutes to produce the effect of the worn-out aristocratic shirt that might get them into a better club."[15]

Yes, despite its mainstreaming, Ivy style's original DNA remained intact—its symbolism still redolent. This made it a powerful tool. In 1955, Miles Davis walked onstage at the Newport Jazz Festival in a boxy striped seersucker sport coat and bow tie purchased from tailor Charlie Davidson, whose Andover Shop sat right on Harvard Square in Cambridge.[16] At that moment, Davis was the coolest cat on the planet. He was also the son of a doctor, familiar with the uniform of the WASP establishment and its meaning. In 2021, the book *Black Ivy* captured Black leaders in the '50s and '60s from the worlds of literature (James Baldwin), film (Gordon Parks), and music (Thelonious Monk), in whose hands Ivy style looked inimitably chic—and politically forceful. These men weren't appropriating the style "out of a desire to be white, coming from a deep sense of inferiority," or as a "sign of conformity and compliance," writes author Jason Jules. "Black Ivy was a kind of battle-dress, a symbolic armor worn in the nonviolent pursuit of fundamental change."[17]

Indeed, both Martin Luther King Jr., the pacifist, and Malcolm X and Louis Farrakhan, the radicals so feared by white America—armed themselves in the quiet, unshakable dignity of Brooks Brothers. On these civil rights leaders, the uniform held as much sway, in its quiet way, as the black berets and leather jackets of the Black Panthers that were to come. Brooks Brothers had made the suit Abraham Lincoln wore when he was assassinated; it was the garb of American presidents. King's pacifist troops "were not fighting to escape the system; they were working to become fully integrated into it," wrote the *Washington Post* critic Robin Givhan in 2018. "Their style was conciliatory rather than confrontational. These were not clothes for a fight but clothes for a gentlemanly—or ladylike—negotiation." Their fashion said, "*We are just like you. . . . What is there to fear?*"[18]

But that came to a quick end. In 1965, Malcolm X was assassinated. In '67, one hundred thousand hippies in buckskin fringe and body paint converged on Haight Ashbury; Vietnam protestors took to the streets; the National Guard opened fire on race rioters in Detroit. When Bobby Kennedy and Martin Luther King Jr. were gunned down in 1968, the time for politely demanding change was past. An anticonsumerist, anti-establishment revolution was here. On campuses awash in tie-dyed tees and paramilitary jackets, dusty dining-hall dress codes were out the window—and, just like that, the clean-cut look sank like a lead balloon. "Once the Ivy League Look ceased to be fashionable on campus, it ceased to be fashionable period," Chensvold has noted. "One could argue that once guys at Princeton stopped wearing it, it was over."[19]

A LITTLE MORE THAN A DECADE LATER, LISA BIRNBACH WAS DEBATING whether to quit her job at the *Village Voice* to work on some silly stocking stuffer of a book. What she could not have known was that in 1981, America would inaugurate Ronald Reagan. Society, pulled left for two decades, was about to take a hard right. Despite its blue-jeaned populism, the '70s—the era of disco and quaaludes and suburban key parties—had been hard on Americans, who weathered a deep and sustained recession. Inflation soared; we lined up for gas. "I think I went to high school for a year in the dark," Birnbach quips. As that decade drew to a close, light was beginning to appear at the end of the recession's long tunnel. In a few years, the go-go '80s would be upon us. "Morning in America," Reagan's 1984 reelection ad called it: interest and inflation rates at rock bottom, businesses across the board riding high. After a decade of distrust of the rich, it would suddenly feel not so repugnant for a young person to be frank about the desire to earn money—and to have a look to match.

Not everyone was on board. In the fall of 1980, a group of Princetonians—offended to be lumped in with the prep revival—sold "Nuke the preppies" tees on campus. They featured the Lacoste croc detonating in a mushroom cloud.

But plenty of people seemed to have just been waiting in the wings, biding their time for the Ivy look to come out of hiding. Indeed, throughout the late '60s and early '70s, prep had been alive, if not exactly au courant, retreated into the spiritual bunker from whence it came: the cozy confines of private schools, golf greens, yacht clubs. It had become "our clothes," all over again.

In fact it was in 1967—the very year Christian Chensvold cites as the death of prep—that Ivy's ultimate arriviste founded his empire selling luxe, ultrawide ties. He was born Ralph Lifshitz, younger son of a Jewish émigré artist and painter from Pinsk, Belarus. Restyled as Ralph Lauren, he was savvily repackaging the fantasy he'd harbored as a kid in the Bronx, raised under the ever-present spell of Manhattan, memorizing the suave moves of Cary Grant (born Archibald Alexander Leach)[20] in the dark of the movie theater: the dream of upper-class belonging. The signature Ralph quote on the matter is now a meme: "People ask, how can a Jewish kid from the Bronx do preppy clothes? Does it have to do with class and money? It has to do with dreams."

By '69, even as Woodstock shook the universe and 250,000 Vietnam War protestors marched on Washington, Lauren was turning out buckle-back white linen trousers and anchor-print shirts, a look the *San Francisco Chronicle* said recalled F. Scott Fitzgerald's 1930s, revived in "all-American" red, white, and blue. Not everyone can be a revolutionary, after all. In the midst of cultural upheaval, Lauren made "instant heirlooms for the legacy deprived," wrote Michael Gross in *Genuine Authentic*, his unauthorized biography of the designer. And Lauren wasn't afraid to step on his forebears, either. In 1972, his Polo pony came galloping right for Rene Lacoste's sacrosanct crocodile. By that time, Lacoste was cutting its shirt in a synthetic blend fabric, in the name of progress: less fading, shrinking, and wrinkling. But Lauren saw that a shirt that never aged could never acquire the "real" preppie patina. So he made his polo in 100 percent cotton, introduced it in twenty-four colors—a marketing coup: that much choice, new at the time, looked rich in store displays and ads—and advertised it specifically for its ability to fade and age. (Soon he'd sell it pre-aged, leading the way for everyone from Gap to J.Crew to Abercrombie & Fitch.) *Voilà.* An easy-to-wear, relatively inexpensive staple that met the burgeoning preppy moment, worked on men, women, and children, and gave Macy's shoppers ownership of the same logo that the rich had begun to sport inside their designer suits. The polo was a single item that would fuel an empire.

For years, Lauren thrived by running counter to the counterculture. But the '80s fit him like a bespoke suit. Soon lavish Ralph Lauren ad campaigns shot by Bruce Weber would stretch across a dozen pages of the *New York Times Magazine*, inviting believers into more than a label, but an entire lifestyle—men's clothes, women's clothes, sheets, perfume, bedding, paint chips: a world.

But did Ralph Lauren make the cut for *The Original Preppy Handbook*? Nope. Plenty of old-liners were not so thrilled by the mass-marketing of their codes. Polo shirts pre-aged to look like they'd already spent a few years in rotation? That patina was supposed to be earned, not bought! And membership to their club could not be faked. "The only thing genuine about [Lauren's look] is the money required to swathe oneself in it," noted Jonathan Yardley in the *Washington Post*.[21]

HANDBOOK-ERA PREP MANAGED SOMETHING THAT NEITHER THE campus style of the 1920s and 1930s nor the Ivy look of the 1950s had bothered to do: It invited women to the party. The female of the species had been appropriating the look, to great effect, since the '30s, when Vassar girls perfectly scuffed their saddle shoes and wore their Brooks Brothers' camel hair "polo coats" (purchased in the boys' department) intentionally oversize and with the buttons on the mens' side as a badge of honor.[22] For decades, Ivy-adjacent women had been forced to borrow their menswear from their brothers or buy it under the counter from menswear purveyors. Brooks Brothers, by its own admission "pathologically reluctant" to cave to the demands of its female clientele, did not get with the program until 1949, when it begrudgingly launched a lone, pale-pink button-down for women—an event so significant it was covered in both *Life* and *Vogue*—and installed a women's customer service desk, "in a dark, unassuming corner"[23] of its wood-paneled New York flagship.

But in the '80s, women were acknowledged as full-fledged prep consumers. With women flooding the workplace, the timing could not have been better. Fashion scholar Patricia Mears, the deputy director of the Museum at the Fashion Institute of Technology—who in 2012 curated "Ivy Style," an exhibit examining the codes, as she puts it, of "these card-carrying antifashion people"—recalls her own arrival in Washington, D.C., in the early '80s. Armed with a freshly minted M.B.A., Mears saw almost no women on the corporate ladder ahead of her. In one job, she was sexually harassed, she says, "every single day. It was a sort of psychological warfare."

In prep, Mears saw not the power of looking like a "richie," but the safety of looking *correct*—like she belonged in a corporate world in which most women had hitherto appeared only as secretaries. Every move a woman made at work was critical to how she was perceived and promoted—not least how she dressed. The men Mears saw running law firms and Wall Street brokerages had come out of Ivy or pseudo-Ivy colleges and never parted with their trusty, banal Brooks Brothers basics. As Mears recalls it, fashion-conscious women at the time could have chosen a Diane von Furstenberg wrap dress—the curve-hugging style synonymous with the sexually liberated modern woman—or, by 1985, Donna Karan's fashionable "seven easy pieces," a feminized version of corporate dress for the rising alpha female. But either of these options would have made her stand out. That wasn't going to help her fit *in*.

Mears, like many of her sisters-in-arms, found safety in the female version of the gray flannel suit. She bought OCBDs at Brooks Brothers and tweed jackets at the preppy enclave Britches of Georgetowne. "There was a group of us who were not Ivy Leaguers, we were not people raised in that culture," says Mears. "We were looking for ways to assimilate and advance, and just not to be a target." Not only did the *Handbook* reset the style goals of popular kids at lunch tables across America—sending landlocked Midwesterners who'd never set foot on Nantucket to the mall in search of boat shoes—it also "gave a whole generation of young women coming into the workforce these guideposts," Mears says. "*Here, let me follow this.*"

Who was going to clothe these prep-hungry hordes? Ralph Lauren had an uncanny nose for the nuances of the upper crust, but if you weren't already anointed, most of his clothes would break your bank. Brooks Brothers, likewise, was expensive—and, at the dawn of the '80s, was enduring a rather ill-timed identity crisis. The old school preppy specialist J. Press and its ilk were niche operations, not in the business of catering to the masses (or to, say, women). And while L.L.Bean might have been the sleeper hit of the late '70s—in the prep awakening, it found itself on trend for the first time in its existence—at its core, it was a delightfully fusty outdoor outfitter. No one was capturing the elusive, seemingly effortless simplicity and broken-in cool that lay at the heart of prep, this "American" dress code. More to the point, from a boardroom perspective: no one was doing a cooler version of prep at a price that the nonelite could afford to buy into.

And almost nothing about Arthur Cinader—owner of a downmarket, family-run catalogue based in the fashion no-man's-land of Passaic, New Jersey—indicated he was the guy for this job. But as Lisa Birnbach skipped across the country introducing America to prep, she was opening a door that Arthur Cinader was about to walk through.

CHAPTER 2

Cognitive Dissonance

It all started in the least "J.Crew" place imaginable: the Botany Worsted Mills, a grim-looking complex of Victorian-era factory buildings sprawled across thirty-seven acres of Passaic. By the 1980s, the original mill was long kaput, leaving enough rental space to house dozens of companies. One of these was Arthur Cinader's Popular Club Plan.

When an ambitious young catalogue executive named Ted Pamperin parked his rental car in front of the Mills in October 1981, he had the same thought a lot of people had upon first laying eyes on this place: *This looks like a prison.*

Pamperin made his way through an alley webbed with steam pipes, up a flight of stairs set on oddly short risers—later, he'd learn these had been built to accommodate nineteenth-century child laborers—and into a cavernous office space. The Popular Club Plan HQ was "industrial" in a way that, a few decades hence, would be considered cool—the kind of place startup founders now furnish with Ping-Pong tables and matcha bars. Circa 1981, it was industrial in a purely Dickensian sense: creaky wooden floors, fifteen-foot ceilings, factory-style metal casement windows covered in sheets of plastic that failed to keep out the drafts. Workers sat in a hodgepodge of makeshift cubicles fashioned from the kind of wooden partitions Pamperin remembered from church-basement Sunday school. Trying not to let his face betray him, he told a receptionist, "I'm here to meet Mr. Cinader."

As he stood there waiting, Pamperin's mind flashed to the comfy, Frank Lloyd Wright–inspired office building he'd left back in Minneapolis. Hadn't he always said his one rule for a job was he'd never move to New York City? Now here he was, twenty miles from the Holland Tunnel, in an armpit that *wished* it was New York, about to interview with a man well-known in the catalogue business as eccentric, combustible, unpredictable. Arthur Cinader was said to be brilliant, but a bear to work with. When Pamperin had told colleagues whom he was flying east to meet, he'd been met with raised eyebrows: *That* guy? You sure?

But then a wiry, bespectacled man in his midfifties—balding but trim, energetic, and full of purpose—trotted into the waiting area, vigorously pumped Pamperin's hand, and introduced himself as Arthur. While most of America was recovering from the leisure-suit era, Pamperin included, Arthur dressed in scuffed white bucks and sport jackets that looked as if they'd once been expensive but now bore patches on the elbows, and not for the sake of fashion. If there was a whiff of preppy authenticity in this getup, it was thoroughly lost on the midwestern Pamperin. But he did like that Arthur put on no airs. To Pamperin's surprise, Arthur appeared perfectly charming, if rather immune to the shortcomings of his surroundings. "He was wonderful to meet," Pamperin says.

Arthur led Pamperin back to his own cubicle. What Pamperin would learn about the company he was walking through, he would mostly glean from others. Arthur Cinader was not one for small talk, and as Pamperin well knew, he had not brought him here to discuss Popular Club Plan. Pamperin was here because both he and Arthur Cinader wanted to build something new, something different—something ambitious.

Popular Club Plan was founded in 1947 by Arthur's father, Mitchell

Cinader, and a cousin, Saul Charles, a modest enterprise that started out selling candy by mail order. By the '80s the company sold a vast array of midtier goods—everything one might find today at, say, Target or Walmart: towel sets, sweatsuits, V.C.R.s, exercise bikes—all featured in a fat catalogue and sold via a model called "party plan selling." It was a bit like Avon or Tupperware: everything was sold through local sales reps known as "club secretaries," who often *were* secretaries, or secretary types, that worked at, say, a doctor's office and sold Popular Club steak knives and dinette sets on the side. What made the company tick, though, was the way its customers paid: in small weekly installments spread over months. If J. C. Penney wouldn't give you a line of credit, you could still get your kid an Easter dress at Popular Club Plan. "It was a store of last resort," says a former executive. The customer it attracted was "kryptonite to everyone else."

By the time Pamperin showed up, Popular Club had thousands of secretaries shilling $50 million worth of goods a year. It's safe to say this wildly exceeded the expectations of Saul Charles and Mitchell Cinader, back in 1947. But it did not satisfy Arthur. Popular Club still worked, but it was out of runway. Processing tens of thousands of individual checks a week—most for tiny sums—was an administrative horror. And the business model had only really taken off in tight-knit Irish, Italian, and Polish communities of the Northeast, where families knew their club secretaries from church or work. Arthur wanted a new offshoot, a business that could work on a national level and grow at double, triple, quadruple the rate Popular Club was capable of. He'd spent the late '70s casting the net wide: What kind of enterprise would have that kind of payoff? In the end he settled on one close to home: a catalogue.

Arthur's cubicle was no fancier than his employees', though slightly roomier. Pamperin took a seat at a cheap folding table, but almost before he could sit down, Arthur was pumping him for information: How do you build a mailing list? What would the back-end operation look like? What infrastructure was needed to take orders, to receive credit card payments, to accept returns? Questions to which Pamperin—who had started catalogue businesses for General Mills before moving to the Minneapolis-based mail-order family of Fingerhut—knew the answers. Questions that lots of entrepreneurs were asking circa 1981, with the catalogue industry on the brink of the single greatest boom in its history.

CATALOGUES HAD BEEN AN AMERICAN NECESSITY AND A PASTIME since 1872, when traveling salesman Aaron Montgomery Ward wrote up a one-page menu featuring 163 items, including hoop skirts, grain bags, and a "very stylish" writing desk that could be ordered through the mail and delivered to even the most far-flung rail station.[1] The prominence of the Montgomery Ward catalogue in the national psyche was matched only by that of Sears (established in 1888), which famously sold *everything* from build-it-yourself homes to serviceable undergarments. In the Cold War era, the Sears catalogue became required reading for spies in Eastern Europe and the Soviet Union: it was a head-to-toe guide on how to look, act, and think American.[2]

For more than a century we snatched these books from the family mailbox and dog-eared them with desire. But by the early 1970s, with malls mushrooming across the country, catalogues had largely lost their luster. Why drop a check in the mail and wait weeks for something to arrive when you could get instant gratification, and an Orange Julius to boot, at the mall?

But shortly before Ted Pamperin arrived in Passaic, a rush of infrastructural and societal change had changed the math on mail order.[3] The Wardses, Searses, and Penneys of the catalogue world had long made a fortune by selling at enormous scale; for most smaller companies, catalogues cost too much to produce and post to be a get-rich-quick scheme.

But now we had MasterCard! Credit cards had been a slow burn when they were introduced in the '50s, taking decades to catch on among the middle and lower classes—but by the early '80s, they would be almost ubiquitous: mail-order customers could pay instantly, over the phone—using an 800 number. Long-distance calls had long been a luxury, but the new 800 number meant customers could order for free. Plus, the United Parcel Service (UPS) was finally operating in all forty-eight contiguous states, giving the sluggish postal service some healthy competition. Even the humble zip code—first introduced in 1963—had a part to play: with zip codes, retailers could presort their catalogues in-house, dramatically cutting the cost of mailing.

On top of all this, the mini-skirted women's libber of the 1970s was giving way to the shoulder-padded career woman of the 1980s. According to the National Center for Education Statistics, college graduating classes had reached fifty-fifty gender parity.[4]

Women were starting to see work as a career, not a stopover between school and motherhood. In boardrooms across the country, companies were strategizing for the dawn of this modern woman. They could see that "having it all" would leave precious little time for browsing at Bloomies. But a *catalogue* . . . now that, a woman could peruse anytime, anywhere.

The early-'80s mail-order boom this all added up to was not so different from the revelation of online shopping that would dawn some fifteen years later: Suddenly, it was possible to shop from the comfort of your own couch, 24/7, for anything you could think of, that would arrive faster than ever.

That day in Passaic, in 1981, Ted Pamperin was as close as anybody got to being a smash hit with Arthur Cinader. The Popular Club Plan boss was always the smartest guy in the room—and he wanted you to know it—but in Pamperin, he'd made a rare find: someone who knew something he didn't. On that first day, as 5 P.M. approached, the two were already deep in sketching business plans and nowhere near finished. Pamperin's ticket back to Minneapolis was rescheduled, a hotel room booked: their work together had already begun.

Before he knew it, Pamperin had rented an apartment in New Jersey and lucked into one of the few real offices at Botany Mills—his had wall-to-wall orange shag. But even as he began to settle in, his new colleagues whispered, *Don't get too comfortable.* Arthur frequently soured on new recruits, and was quick to cut bait. Ted could be gone within the month. For Pamperin, this was a chance worth taking: he had a hunger to start a new company, and Arthur was giving him the leeway, and had the finances, to do just that. Still, for the time being, Pamperin's wife and three school-age daughters stayed put in Minneapolis. There was no telling how this experiment, whatever it turned out to be, was going to shake out.

COMPANY ORIGIN STORIES HAVE A WAY OF BECOMING STREAMlined and glossed over with time, and J.Crew's is no different. Lore has always held that Arthur Cinader envisioned a catalogue that sold upscale prep at an entry-level price. But in truth, when Arthur hired Pamperin, all he knew was that he wanted to make a catalogue. What *kind* of catalogue? Pamperin's first task was to answer that question.

Behind Door No. 1: computer gear. *Time* would soon shake up its annual "Man of the Year" issue to name the personal computer the "Machine of the Year"—the first nonhuman recipient since the award was founded in 1927 (much to the fury of Steve Jobs, who wanted to be celebrated as *the* man behind the machine). According to *Time*, by 1982

80 percent of Americans believed that "in the fairly near future, home computers will be as commonplace as television sets or dishwashers."[5] At the office, Pamperin and a colleague, Lawrence Lee, sketched up their new business plans on the tiny, square monitor of an Apple II, which looked as glamorous as a beige shoebox and was the first personal computer equipped with spreadsheet software. Even a year earlier, they'd have had to do this using pencils and graph paper. Big-box electronic stores did not exist. Techies were building DIY computers, ordering parts from ads in the back of *Byte* magazine. A catalogue that served this growing realm? A slam dunk.

Behind Door No. 2: prep. On the one hand, you had Ralph Lauren, making a mint mining the codes of prep—the very thing all the kids were suddenly talking about. On the other, you had L.L.Bean and Lands' End, both killing it in '81. Lands' End, in particular, was an early winner in the mail-order boom, selling middle America sturdy, inexpensive basics in a wide array of colors. Ralph was too pricey for the wannabes, and Lands' End was the *Prairie Home Companion* of catalogues, full of folksy articles and models who looked like your next-door neighbors—it had no reach, no romance. What about a catalogue that sold the dream, at a price that was in step with reality?

Pamperin presented Arthur with two choices: Computers? Or clothes? After much deliberation, Arthur went with Door No. 2. Pamperin recalls this as a decision based not on a passion for fashion, or for prep, but on straight business sense: Popular Club Plan knew how to source, photograph, and sell apparel. Preppy was a stretch, maybe, but not totally outside of its wheelhouse. They had a formula: take the best of Lands' End, and sell the look of Ralph Lauren.

Pamperin says the spectre of Ralph Lauren was palpably perched on the shoulder of every person involved in building the new brand. Indeed, it served as an excellent filter. The rule was, "If Ralph wouldn't do it, we won't do it," Pamperin says. The new brand's photographs would feel rich and layered; their fabrics and finishes would be excellent. After all, WWRD?

First, though, they needed a name. Arthur wanted to find a dusty-sounding surname with the ring of old-world lineage. "G.Frick" was an early contender, but the one he really loved was "Sir Edward Coke." The only problem was that nobody other than Arthur had the slightest idea who that was. "He's a famous English magistrate!" Arthur sputtered. "Doesn't everyone know this?" (Wiki it. Sir Edward Coke: greatest jurist of the Elizabethan and Jacobean eras.)

It was Emily, his eldest daughter, then earning a marketing degree at the University of Denver and weighing in from afar, who talked him down. *No way, Dad*, she told him, with a directness that few at the office would have attempted. Not only was capital-c Coke the most famous brand name in America, but lowercase-c coke was also a popular '80s commodity in its own right.

Who came up with J.Crew? Lots have taken credit. Everyone Arthur ever hired got the distinct impression it was the founder's own idea. A Harvard Business School study once stated that young Emily, sitting by a river one day—as every young prepster does—spotted a scull rowing past and thought: *That's it!*[6] (Never happened.) A respected art director who worked on the early catalogues once listed to a reporter all the reasons he had chosen the name—yet others say it had been chosen before he was ever hired. Lots of people believed Arthur's story, dreamed up well after the fact, that it was named after a chap called Josiah Crew. And Emily once heard from a friend who had been to a party where someone claimed to know the real "Jay Crew."

As Pamperin recalls, it went like this: "If Ralph owns polo, why don't we claim crew?" It's literally on Page 101 of the *Preppy Handbook*: Crew was "the sport of preps," largely because it is so "capital-intensive." According to Birnbach et al., circa 1980 an eight-man shell cost $10,000;

a one-seater, $5,000; and the only institutions well-endowed enough to support crew teams were prep schools and elite colleges. But that also made the sport feel specifically *collegiate*. Polo was a colonial sport played by princes. But crew conjured crisp fall days, term papers, canoodling in the stacks. It was a sport performed on a hazy, early-morning river to clear the head before a day spent pondering Chaucer. It was also a sport that no one at Popular Club knew the first thing about, and most could not have used in a sentence: Did you *do* crew? Go crewing?

This world of prep seemed totally foreign to the group of outsiders who were building a catalogue around it. But if any of them had paused to pay attention, they might have noticed that, all along, there had been bread crumbs—little hints that one among them, Arthur himself, knew the codes of prep better than he let on. It was Arthur, for instance, who knew from the get-go that their fledgling company needed a backstory, a plausible-sounding fiction they could anchor the idea to, something loftier than "Ralph, on the cheap." A true prep could spot a fake at fifty paces, after all. Arthur invented a history out of thin air: The company had started out as a men's haberdasher in Princeton, New Jersey, outfitting Ivy Leaguers; later, women caught on to the clothes, and began to shop there for themselves. And when *Crew* became the new brand's "surname," it was Arthur who chose the first initial, *J*. The going explanation was that the swoop of the J added design flair. But Arthur was well aware that it also borrowed rather brazenly from J. Press, the storied Ivy League clothier founded in New Haven in 1902. Though he never spoke of it, Arthur had once been a Yale man himself.

CHAPTER 3

Puzzle Pieces

Photographer Michael Belk has never forgotten his first meeting with Arthur Cinader and Ted Pamperin. Belk was a tall, natty Southerner who shot for the menswear brand Gant, whose salesmen "looked like they'd walked off the pages of GQ," he recalls. Now in walked two guys who say they're starting a preppy catalogue. It was clear why they had come to Belk: his photos were vivid, active, and shared enough of the glossy, inside-the-gates vibe of Ralph Lauren ads that Belk once received an irate letter from the agent of photographer Bruce Weber—the secret weapon behind Lauren's megabucks campaigns—demanding that he stop stepping on Weber's style. Less clear, however, was what *they* had to do with this project. Belk took in Pamperin's comb-over and Arthur's cracked belt, "all bonded leather with most of the bonding gone." Cinader looked "one step above a pauper" to the photographer. "*These guys* are starting a catalogue—what do they know about taste?"

Arthur, in particular, knew more than Belk would ever understand—and indeed, far more than he'd ever explicitly shared with Ted Pamperin. Arthur Cinader was a student of everything, a voracious reader and observer who loved, as one friend put it, "to roll around in ideas and concepts." He could make casual reference to the Federalist Papers; loved the writings of Winston Churchill, Boswell, Samuel Johnson; studied physics and philosophy for fun. Long before most of the rest of the world caught on, he was fascinated by the abstract ideas of computer science. And Arthur knew how to stoke consumer desire. He had found a way to give Popular Club shoppers—"kryptonite" to upscale retailers—a path to the ever-expanding list of domestic trappings that, by the '50s and '60s, had become a presumed rite of an American existence.

But when it came to his own personal life, the man was a closed book. He built J.Crew, a brand reeking of provenance and backstory—a fantasy of the good life for more than one generation of upwardly mobile Americans—but when it became a hit, and reporters wanted to ask him about it, he usually declined. "Let the clothes speak for themselves," he'd say. Most people whose wardrobes consist mostly of J.Crew have never heard of the man. One imagines that Cinader, who died in 2017 at the age of ninety, would be just fine with that.

Perhaps he just valued his privacy. Or perhaps he had an idea how a profile of Arthur Cinader—brilliant but also difficult, rife with peccadilloes—might read. Will Von Klemperer, a new C.F.O. hired soon after Pamperin, recalls that his first official undertaking in the Passaic offices was prosaic: heat. He took legal action to stop the landlord of the Botany Worsted Mills from shutting down the boiler on Friday nights—the place was an icebox till Tuesday afternoon. "I had accounting people wearing gloves with the fingers cut off just so they could hold their pencil," Von Klemperer recalls with a chuckle. A condition to which Arthur had been oddly impervious. "Arthur was unto himself," Von Klemperer says, insensitive to some things, hypersensitive to others. He'd been known to abruptly cut short a meeting because the paperwork was incorrectly stapled. And he hated noise. If an employee spoke too loudly on the phone, the C.E.O. himself was liable to peep over the side of their cubicle wall to shush them. A sign hung over the office well into the J.Crew era: "Popular Club Plan workers are quiet workers."

To those who worked with him tangentially, Arthur was a holdover from another era: reserved but usually courteous, and with occasional flashes of warmth. An odd duck, maybe, but then, so full of *information*. He knew about business, finance, consumers, computers, architecture—you name it. "Working with him could be an M.B.A.," says Lawrence Lee. Arthur knew how to manage a business, how to get the most out of people, how to minimize risk, how to consider a problem from every conceivable angle. "It was interesting to watch him work, and think."

But those who worked with him closely witnessed—or rather, suffered—behavior that would never fly in today's workplace. There was always a chance Arthur would go for the jugular. "Did you really go to college?" he might say, after some minor infraction, as a telltale flush of rage crept up from his collar. He sounded genuinely baffled in these moments, as if he truly believed no college-educated person could have done something so bone-headed. One woman told me that in a department Arthur later managed, not a day went by without someone ending up in the bathroom in tears after being berated by him. Several employees describe instances, rare but memorable, when Arthur got so worked up that he literally overheated: ripped off his shirt, threw it to the ground, and stood there quivering with anger in his undershirt. (Emily Scott denies that Arthur ever had a meltdown of this nature.)

There were the things Arthur did, and then there was a culture that surrounded the things Arthur did: For years, office urban legend held that Arthur once yelled at a woman at J.Crew to the point that she passed out. Did it really happen? Or was it an overembroidered myth? Most employees did not get close enough to find out. Whether you had experienced this behavior firsthand or had only heard the rumor; whether you were scared you'd get your head bitten off or—the more likely event—that you'd get stuck on the receiving end of one of

Arthur's lengthy over-your-head lectures, it was generally considered wise to give the boss a wide berth.

TED PAMPERIN AND THE TEAM SPENT MORE THAN A YEAR IN startup mode, building the guts of a new company: a new computer system, phone operators, a credit card operation, an order-fulfillment scheme. They found the right addresses to send their catalogue to: after all, no point sourcing and photographing *the* definitive rugby if your preppy catalogue is just going to get lost on the kitchen counters of ardent modernists. Catalogue mailing lists work in a curious way. Names and addresses are rented from mailing list brokers, who sell and trade lists between companies—sometimes even competitors. J.Crew bought many of its original names, or "prospects," from the lists of L.L.Bean and Talbots. Brokers would print these rented addresses on a magnetic tape that was sent straight to the catalogue's printer. The tape would only work for one printing, limiting access to those names to a single issue. Anybody who placed an order from that issue was added to an ongoing house list, and would become an MVP—someone who now received every J.Crew mailing. With each new issue, the company would rent a new batch of names. Eventually, other companies would begin to rent J.Crew's names, too, or to trade lists between them. (Which is why today, after you buy one pillowcase from West Elm, you may also unwittingly buy yourself five years of catalogues from, say, CB2 and Design Within Reach.) The process of pruning and growing the list is known as "name flow analysis": retailers closely monitor who's buying, and how frequently—who's actually an MVP versus who bought one OCBD and never came back—to decide how much money to invest in existing customers, versus how much to spend on acquiring new names. Even now this is the backbone of direct marketing.

What would the new J.Crew sell to the people who, so far, were just names on an expensive piece of tape? So many cultural factors were at work in that decision! *Annie Hall* had come out a few years earlier, and unisex dressing was big in the '80s—it was also baked into prep (remember those Radcliffe girls in their brothers' Brooks Brothers coats). Most of the clothes J.Crew sourced were identical for men and women. The early '80s was also the dawn of a hot new thing: exercise! Jane Fonda was bouncing around in belted, high-cut leotards; in movies like *Rocky II* and *The Goonies*, there were sweatbands in the hair and around the wrist, sweatshirts tied around the shoulders, running shorts layered *over* sweatpants. J.Crew courted the active weekender: rugby shirts, henley shirts, a boatload of what it called "fieldhouse sweats," and of course a polo shirt—cheaper than Ralph *and* Lacoste, but virtually identical, and described in the catalogue copy as "even better, perhaps, when worn and weathered." (Pamperin et al. toyed with the idea of a logo, too, but when they stitched their little man holding a crew paddle onto a shirt, the figure sowed nothing but confusion: What the heck was that stick pointing up over his head?) J.Crew had yet to hire a single designer—that expensive, time-consuming investment would come later, *if* they had staying power—so in the beginning, they sold private-label clothing: existing designs from various manufacturers, chosen in their J.Crew colors and slapped with a J.Crew label. Plus a few recognizable brands sprinkled in for authenticity, like Boston Traders button-downs, Sperry Top-Siders, Woolrich trousers.

Michael Belk, the photographer who was so skeptical of his new clients, had his work cut out for him. The clothing Pamperin and his team rounded up was . . . good. Totally in step with the moment. But in truth it wasn't all that different from the bright, colorful basics of Lands' End. Belk's job was to make it *feel* different. The preppy mystique that was supposed to make J.Crew different had to come from the photos. They had to feel cool, alive, like a party you wish you'd been invited to. They needed a sense of provenance—some proximity to the establishment the brand was trying to sidle into.

Provenance turned out to be the easy part. Pamperin called up the University of Pennsylvania and offered to make a donation to its crew club, in return for access to an Ivy League boathouse and even a few college rowers thrown in as background players. *Bingo.* In the fall of 1982, J.Crew drove right past the gatekeepers, literally—with Pamperin playing camp counselor, at the wheel of a camper van loaded with models, assistants, stylists, clothes, driving from Passaic to the boathouse of U Penn,* on the Schuylkill River. Of course, when they got there, Belk quickly realized he was clueless. He spent the first part of the day being lectured by a coach on Crew 101. How was this supposed to look? Who went where? How do you shoot a model on a moving boat so that you can still see his clothes . . . without falling in?

THE ONE PERSON ON THEIR TEAM WHO DID KNOW HOW THAT world worked was one who did not travel to photo shoots. Most of Arthur Cinader's bio appears, on the surface of things, about as "J.Crew" as the Botany Worsted Mills itself. He was born to a working-class Jewish family in the Bronx, that old New York of stickball games and elevated subway cars—a familiar tune in American fashion, shared by not just Ralph Lauren (born 1939), but also by Calvin Klein (1942), and Millard "Mickey" Drexler, the man who would helm the second chapter of Arthur's own company. (Mickey was born there in 1944, but let's not get ahead of ourselves.)

---

* J.Crew has long maintained that its first catalogue was shot at Harvard's Wald Boathouse, home of the men's crew team. But both photographer Michael Belk and Pamperin believe that while they did eventually shoot at Harvard, the first cover was shot at the University of Pennsylvania; the second at Dartmouth.

The Bronx is a major character in the mythology surrounding all three of these men, the embarkation point that put a hunger—for wealth, belonging, style, success—in each of their bellies, the humble beginning that illustrates how high they eventually rose. Arthur, too, was a striver, moving up in the world. But no mythology surrounds him. Colleagues who worked side by side with him for years never knew he was from the Bronx. Still, he *understood* what was necessary to belong, or at least look like you belong, among the upper crust—and that was a critical part of the pull of J.Crew.

He was born to Mitchell and Sadie Cinader in 1927, enrolled at age thirteen in the brand-new Bronx High School of Science—still one of the city's most elite public schools (Mickey Drexler would enroll there two decades later)—and, two years shy of high school graduation, skipped the goalposts to enroll at the University of Arizona at age sixteen. The family chalks up this move to World War II having somehow accelerated his schooling, and to Arthur's bad allergies. Whatever the reason, he left Arizona at eighteen—again, well shy of graduation.

That's when life took a decidedly J.Crew turn. It's a little mysterious: How does a man with neither a high school nor a college diploma enroll in medical school at Yale? Maybe it had something to do with the fact that Yale had been rocked first by war and then by the G.I. Bill. For much of WWII, the school served as a de facto military camp, training some twenty thousand cadets. In 1945, it began a process it called reconversion,[1] retrieving rare books and manuscripts from bomb shelters, returning stately portraits to mahogany-paneled walls, and educating a backlog of Yalies—including George Herbert Walker Bush, '48, whose father, and father's father, had also been Yale men—plus an influx of a whole new kind of undergrad. (This new diversity was mostly financial; Yale remained mostly white, and was male-only until 1969.) Enrollment nearly doubled. Students overflowed from dorms into faculty houses and a former army barracks. Hundreds camped on cots in the gym.

Even in this tumult, the Ivy League should have been Arthur's promised land. This was a man devoted to history, theory, who studied physics for fun! But Arthur knew that back home, a new family business had bloomed. After three years, he left Yale, capping his lifetime graduation at 0 for 3—ironic, to say the least, for a man who berated employees for not living up to their college bona fides—and headed to Popular Club Plan.

In all the months Ted Pamperin was cold-calling Ivy League crew clubs, even going so far as to bring in an on-set expert to weigh in on the shoots' authenticity—the "consultant" was really just a friend of a staffer, who was raising a pack of her own genuine preps in Connecticut—Arthur never said, "Well, when I was at Yale . . ." or "On our family vacations on Nantucket . . ." or "At my daughters' prep school . . ."

Yet at the end of the day, Arthur did not drive home to some suburban New Jersey house. He returned to 1185 Park Avenue, one of the most distinguished addresses in Carnegie Hill. He loved English-style horseback riding. He collected art; by 1956, he had already loaned his Jackson Pollock for the artist's one-man show at the Galleria Nazionale d'Arte Moderna in Rome. He conducted what he called "ski-lift research" on Christmas vacations in Vail. His middle daughter Maud had attended the Spence School, a pipeline for Harvard and Hollywood, where students accessorized their regulation plaid kilts with Tretorn sneakers, Fair Isle sweaters, and "alligator shirts." Long before Ted Pamperin's preppy brain wave, Arthur was living with the target demo: Maud and her younger sister, Abigail, were at home, feverishly poring over the L.L.Bean catalogue.

"Arthur was very, very careful with the outward appearances of wealth," says Popular Club employee Lawrence Lee. "He did not want to be identified with the people he saw on the Upper East Side." Men like Ralph Lauren and, indeed, Mickey Drexler dreamed of escaping the Bronx to live like kings. To Arthur, a not-rich Jewish kid who had entered grade school in the Great Depression and made it all the way to Yale, the cracked belt he still wore—the one Michael Belk recalled, forty years later—was a point of pride; he'd been wearing it since college. Soon, when his daughter Emily started working at J.Crew and needed a way to get to New Jersey every day, Arthur would be so conflicted about buying his daughter a car using company funds—a perk not offered to the executives he employed—he'd purchase Lee's serviceable Volkswagen Scirocco, hardly a car that screamed, "boss's daughter." Will Von Klemperer says, "This is not some guy who sits at his country club and is embarrassed to tell his investment banker friends that he sells cheap dishes." Popular Club Plan might have been downmarket, but it was Arthur's life's work; on some level, those "kryptonite" shoppers had once been *his* people. Says Von Klemperer, "He had the humility to get down there and work and sweat."

Arthur was, like Lisa Birnbach—like Calvin Klein, like Ralph Lauren, like Mickey Drexler—an insider-outsider. But his family life, one that relatively few from J.Crew ever got a close look at, appeared uncannily like what would later come to embody J.Crew. In adulthood, his middle daughter Maud Bryt, an artist and photographer (who spent several years as J.Crew's photo editor and shot some memorable catalogue covers) would do a series of paintings based on old photos from childhood summers in a rental house on Nantucket. In one painting, based on 8 mm film shot by Arthur in August 1965, a pretty young woman swims laps in the bay in a white swimsuit, a few blond curls escaping the edge of her swim cap. The painting's description tells us she's a mother; two-month-old Maud is likely napping in a bassinet nearby, "under the watchful eye of a nanny on the beach." Another one, *Picnic at Brandt Point*, is based on a photo Arthur shot: A scrum of kids scramble over the rocks at the foot of a lighthouse. The children wear plain navy and white swimsuits, crisp against the sand; the adults' pale pink shirts blow in the breeze; the sky is a sheet of flat, pale blue. The focal point is the same blond, sunlight glinting off her bright hair and the curve of her shoulder. She wears black sunglasses and a modest, dead-simple black maillot—the kind of suit you could find in a J.Crew spring catalogue anytime from 1989 to 2019.

It's all here: the fresh air, the relaxed athleticism, the multigenerational clan—clearly well-off, but not rich in any obvious way, dressed in pragmatic Yankee simplicity with a hint of Scandi minimalism. The carefree ease of the T-shirt-and-swimsuit life.

Did the real Cinader family—large, athletic, attractive, and conversant in the canon—serve as literal source material for the fictional catalogue clans of J.Crew? When I put this question to Will Von Klemperer, he told me not to take the bait, comparing the creation of J.Crew to the work of the movie director who torments everybody on set but manages to produce a film of heartbreaking beauty. The world of J.Crew, he said, was Arthur Cinader's invention, his business—not some souped-up family photo album. "They weren't telling their life story," he said. "It's their work." This, by the way, was not a criticism: it didn't have to be autobiographical to be good.

Everything Von Klemperer said made sense. And yet, I can't resist the parallels between the real Cinader world and the catalogue world they created. Maybe it's self-indulgent fantasy, but the more I learned about the Cinaders, the more every blond in every early J.Crew catalogue hearkened back to *the* blond in Maud Bryt's paintings: Johanna Cinader, love of Arthur's life.

They met on a ski trip in 1958, when Arthur was a thirty-one-year-old bachelor on holiday in Davos, Switzerland. Some say he was on a wife-shopping expedition, but his children describe it as a romantic fluke: their dad went to a dance one night and met a willowy Dutch nurse, Johanna van Riel, who was there on a monthlong surgical residency. With ice-blue eyes and champagne curls, Joke (pronounced "Yoke-uh," as she is still known to friends today) was the intriguing

Euro counterweight to the button-nosed American blond. She had survived childhood tuberculosis and the German occupation of Holland, and loved to swim. Working as a nurse, she sent money to her family back home. She was athletic, outdoorsy. She wore no makeup. She was so . . . J.Crew.

After Davos, Arthur and Joke corresponded by letter. Within a year, they were on a honeymoon fit for landed gentry: fox-hunting in Ireland. Back in the United States, they set about building a large and boisterous family—Emily came along in 1961, followed by Martha, Maud, Abigail, and finally, in 1969, Arthur Jr.

By all accounts, Joke Cinader had a singular effect on her husband. Arthur could be midtirade at work, about to blow a gasket, but when a call came in from his wife, he was transformed. "One second he'd be saying, 'Why don't you just take your latest paycheck and turn it in to HR, because you're obviously a fraud!'" says a former Popular Club Plan employee. "And the next it's, 'Oh honey, how are you?'" When Arthur, who dug in his heels at every turn, acquiesced relatively easily to the name J.Crew, some wondered whether it was really because the initials J.C. matched those of Johanna Cinader.

Like the J.Crew catalogue itself, Maud Bryt's series of paintings depict an idealized world in which the sky is always cloudless blue. Everything is clean and calm, harmonious, healthy-looking. In a canvas titled simply *The 5 of Us*, a clutch of happy children pose loosely on a sun-bleached wooden deck. Green hills line the background, and a baby boy—presumably Arthur Jr.—perches in a lobster pot.

What *The 5 of Us* doesn't reveal is that a sixth was poignantly missing. The Cinaders held a deeply private, painful truth that most people who worked for them never knew about. Arthur and Johanna's first child was a son. As a close ally of Emily tells it, as a small child, the son stepped off a curb in New York City, and was struck by a car and killed. According to this person, both Arthur and young Emily were present when the accident occurred. (Emily Scott and the Cinader family chose not to discuss the matter.)

What damage did this do to the Cinaders, as a family and as individuals? Impossible to know. But perhaps since the Cinaders dropped so few clues about who they really were—Emily's interior life, when she came to rule J.Crew, was just as off-limits as her father's—the few who did know about it couldn't help reading into the tragedy. It offered a possible explanation, really the *only* explanation anyone could see, for the dissonance between who the Cinaders were and what they created at J.Crew. Those who knew about the tragedy couldn't help but wonder: Was this what made Arthur so closed off? Was this why he and Emily kept their private world—seemingly so relevant to the fictional one they created every day—so impenetrable? The story gave those who knew it a deeper empathy for the Cinaders, a loyalty to them, and to their privacy. And it put a different lens on Arthur's rages. "The level of hurt he was experiencing, the frustration—in today's language you would say he was catastrophizing," says a staffer who worked closely with him on catalogue layouts in the '90s. "Nobody gets *that* upset over a comma or a headline, you know?"

NOBODY HAD TIME TO OVERTHINK ARTHUR'S BEHAVIOR IN 1982, though. The tiny team behind the nascent J.Crew was working too hard to deeply ponder what went on behind the Cinader curtain. With the infrastructure of the new company mostly established, it was time to make the sausage. Here, Michael Belk was a full-service operation: He not only shot the lifestyle photography but also brought in an art director to design the pages. The '80s fever for color made shooting still lifes especially tricky: eighteen shades of pleated trousers (with contrasting belts!) had to be meticulously folded and laid out by hand. The full array was so big, a photographer with an 8 × 10 camera had to climb a ladder all the way to the ceiling to get everything in one frame.

So much of what they were doing could now be done on a computer in a matter of seconds. Especially the text: every headline and caption was written and edited on a typewriter, then sent off to a typesetting house to be reconfigured in the desired font, point size, and shape for the layout.

Finally, every piece of this puzzle—model photos, still lifes, words—was cut out with X-Acto knives and stuck onto a board with rubber cement. The boards were photographed, and the resulting picture was the proof of a finished page. That proof was marked up with corrections, and the whole thing was redone, as many times as it took to get it right, before it went to the printer.

Arthur had been hands-off in the creation of the images, and only marginally involved in the selection of the items. He would become far more involved as the company took off, but in truth Ted Pamperin, whose name has since been erased from the annals of J.Crew history, laid most of that initial groundwork. But there was one part of that first issue that Arthur dug into. He toiled for weeks on the copy. He could spend an hour discussing the height of the capital letter at the start of a paragraph. "You'd be ready to shoot yourself," Belk says, laughing. It was a sign of things to come.

Just as they were set to launch, there was a flurry of activity. Popular Services, Inc., moved, abandoning the Botany Mills for a new HQ in Garfield, New Jersey. It was only a few miles away, but a world apart. No one had to wear their gloves inside anymore. The new building was clean, well lit, and had actual cubicle walls—no more church basement partitions—and an intriguing new recruit. Emily Cinader walked in the door in January 1983, a month after collecting her diploma, and just as the first issue was on its way out.

Ted Pamperin recalls standing by the press as the issue printed, to be sure the colors came out right. On the cover, a man and woman—each holding a curiously elongated oar—are bathed in golden sunlight against a backdrop of rippling water. They are as perfectly matched, yet utterly sexless, as a set of glossy golden retrievers, from their steadfast expressions—she gazes at him, he stares off into the middle distance—to their clothes, which are nearly identical and elaborately layered: navy-ringed white henleys (hers atop a butter-yellow turtleneck), *tucked into* wide-leg gray sweats. *Quality for the long pull*, read Arthur's labored-over copy. *The heritage of J.Crew weekend clothes is 100 years of outfitting rugby, lacrosse, and crew. Whence their long-wearing construction. And authoritative style.*

"Whence": a classic Arthurism. Who'd have guessed this thing had been dreamed up in Jersey, at a company that had in fact never outfitted a single player of rugby—or of any other sport, for that matter—by a creative team that didn't know a coxswain from a gunwale?

"It felt like a race right up to that moment," Pamperin says. After a year and a half of fevered gestation, J.Crew was out the door. Within days, ten thousand American preppies, wannabes, and never-would-bes would open their mailboxes to find *J.Crew Outfitters*. There was nothing to do but head back to the office and wait for the phones to ring. "We were reasonably confident we didn't have a complete dud," Pamperin says. "But we weren't so sure we had a success."

CHAPTER 4

Girl, Boss

If J.Crew had just fallen on its face, it wouldn't take long to find out. When a new catalogue clicks with customers, the orders come in fast, arriving a day or two after it lands in mailboxes. When it doesn't, a tepid response says it all. You can usually tell if you've got a success on your hands within seventy-two hours. By the end of J.Crew's first week, its new bank of telephone operators were inundated.

The response was "astounding," recalls Will Von Klemperer. Too good, in fact. There was no way they could keep up with all these orders. In a panic, they phoned Michael Belk: Could his office design a gift certificate for the customers whose orders they were unable to fulfill?

In his first meeting with Arthur Cinader, Ted Pamperin had spelled out the early financial picture for a brand-new catalogue from a company no one had ever heard of: two and a half years in the red. That's how long it takes, on average, to prospect a mailing list large enough to generate enough sales to cover the cost of putting out the catalogue. J.Crew beat that by a year, breaking even within roughly eighteen months. Pamperin recalls, "Out of the box, you could see this was going to be a hit."

But after shooting the first few catalogues almost entirely—and, as far as he could see, successfully—Michael Belk was shocked to get a call one day informing him he'd been cut loose: catalogue production was being taken in-house. Change was afoot at J.Crew. In 1984, Arthur hired a new merchant, Carrie Stone. She recalls that in her first interview, the C.E.O. "made it clear that it was my job to train his daughter to be president of the company eventually."

"There was no 'daddy's little girl' about Emily," Stone says. When Stone arrived, Emily was twenty-three. She didn't flounce around the office with a sense of ownership, but she was no mere assistant, either. As yet, J.Crew had no real "departments" for a newbie to work her way up through: it was all hands on deck. Arthur and Ted Pamperin had all they could do, racing to keep up with a startup that was now galloping ahead. What Emily had by way of know-how was her marketing degree, plus a hot second of modeling experience. Most women would have been unable to resist blabbing about having been scouted to compete in superagent Eileen Ford's famed "Face of the '80s" contest. Emily, true to her parentage, was tight-lipped. Ford's offer had come shortly after Emily arrived at J.Crew in '83, so after a few months at work, Emily set off for Italy: why not give it a shot? She walked a handful of runways, posed for a few brands, and came home. Within months she was back in unglamorous Garfield, ready to work. Perhaps, like her father at Yale, she couldn't ignore the lure of the family business. Perhaps she just wasn't the sort of woman who enjoys being a blank canvas for someone else's vision. Emily was built to be the one in the driver's seat.

She might have been young, but she was already discerning; Stone recalls her innate eye for style and quality, her instinct for what "was" and "wasn't" J.Crew—and her willingness to speak her mind. Not everyone describes this quality as appreciatively as Stone does. Young Emily was either very smart, with every reason to be as confident as she appeared, or she was boldly entitled, with no one there to stand in her way. "She presumed herself a leader of rank," recalls an early executive, "and she took it, was good at it, and it was never challenged."

But Emily possessed something most others at the J.Crew table sorely lacked: firsthand knowledge of the young, outdoorsy, preppy life.

To everyone else at Popular Club, Inc., the J.Crew customer was a demo, a promising target market. To Emily, this wasn't a focus-grouped lifestyle, but her own generation. To a degree, her world.

Pamperin's J.Crew 1.0 struck a small tendril of nerve fiber in the culture, and established a crucial genetic code: clean-cut, sporty, up-tempo prep. But it was leagues away from the catalogue that would become a cultural phenomenon, even an identity—"so J.Crew." In 1.0, the couples were as wistful as romance-novel cover art; the playful group shots had a whiff of *fromage*. Just by hitting the right preppy notes, it had found initial success. But it was a long way from cool.

Emily knew that to be cool, J.Crew needed people who were cool: young, talented creatives, not from other catalogue businesses but from the realm of fashion. People who could see as clearly as she did that, while hitting the market as a watered-down Ralph had served its purpose, to move forward—to *matter*—the company needed a look and a vibe of its own. It wasn't long before Emily had assumed responsibility for the look and feel of J.Crew, selecting models, bringing in new photographers, choosing shoot locations, and—despite her total lack of design experience—taking the lead on hiring J.Crew's first in-house design team. She wanted to make J.Crew great. To do that—though she almost certainly never saw it this way—she would slowly but inexorably remake J.Crew in her own image. The J.Crew that fans from the '80s and '90s still harbor such nostalgia for today? That was 2.0: Emily's J.Crew.

THE FIRST NIGHT TIERNEY GIFFORD HORNE MET EMILY CINADER, it wasn't Emily's clothes that she noticed. In the glitzy, shoulder-padded Manhattan of 1984, Emily's wardrobe was serious, strict. Over the years, some would see it as boring and uninspired; others as chicly understated—the mixed reviews not so different from ones J.Crew itself would later receive, in fact—but her style was almost beside the point: the first thing anybody saw when they met Emily was classic American beauty in the vein of Ali MacGraw. She was tall, slim, and athletic-looking, with ramrod-straight posture, espresso-dark hair cut in a sleek chin-length bob—even at the height of the White Rain era—and skin that appeared perpetually fresh-scrubbed, with a light scattering of freckles. Like her mother before her, Emily was the kind of woman who looks stunning in a plain men's button-down shirt. She *was* the look that would later be "so J.Crew."

"Oh, Emily was super beautiful," recalls Horne matter-of-factly. Considering that Horne was an assistant editor at *Vogue* at the time, dressing supermodels for a living, that was saying something. The two women met on a double date at a Manhattan hotspot that was, at the time, "the coolest place in town." Today, Horne can't say for sure which one—possibly Indochine, unofficial clubhouse of everyone from Iman to Warhol—but she does recall, with the photographic memory of a born fashion person, her own outfit that night: a silk charmeuse wrap skirt by Zoran, the designer *Vogue* had recently dubbed "the wizard of ease."[1] Zoran was all about languid, slinky minimalism—basically the opposite of everything J.Crew stood for in 1984. All other details, including the identities of both of their dates, have faded into the background in Horne's memory. What remains is an instant, magnetic curiosity about Emily Cinader.

Horne was twenty to Emily's twenty-three. Somehow the age difference felt like a quantum leap. Emily seemed so *adult*. She was still practically a girl, but she operated at a totally different frequency than other women their age. There was a stillness to Emily, a formality, and a complete lack of feminine affectation. She did not go out of her way to make Horne feel at ease in the tractor beam of her attention. Nor did she turn on the charm. If Emily didn't feel like smiling, she didn't smile. It was hard to imagine something as silly as a giggle escaping her lips.

But her ability to zero in had a powerful effect on Horne, who was the opposite, a creative flibbertigibbet—fun, full of ideas, all over the place.

Arthur's daughter shared her father's impatience with small talk and his ability to turn a chance meeting into a fact-finding mission. That night, she wanted to know everything about Horne's job at *Vogue*. How did the shoots work? How was the styling put together?

In fashion, the lowest spot on the totem pole sometimes affords the best view. At the dawn of the supermodel, Tierney Horne had been on beach shoots with Cindy Crawford, assisted on Christy Turlington's first *Vogue* sitting with the legendary Irving Penn. And though barely out of her teens, she had also assisted at Ralph Lauren, mapping little intarsia designs for his twee "teddy bear" sweaters; shopping Army-Navy stores to inspire his collections. She'd done a brief stint styling the windows of Lauren's new Bond Street store in London. She told Emily about all of it that night.

"Emily locked in on me," recalls Horne. "She saw something in me that I did not see in myself." (This would prove to be one of Emily's superpowers.) Her questions weren't aggressive, but they weren't casual, either. Inside her cool, composed exterior, the wheels were obviously turning. Still, Horne never expected what came next.

Bright and early the next morning, Emily called the front desk of *Vogue* and asked to speak to Horne: Would she come work for J.Crew?

Poaching from *Vogue*? That took chutzpah. By then, J.Crew may have been a $2 million company but it was a dust mote in the kingdom of fashion, where high and low did not mix—and catalogue brands were strictly steerage class. J.*Who?* When Tierney Horne told her magazine colleagues about the job offer, most had never heard of J.Crew. They practically put out an APB. Photographers and editors united to talk sense into her: You don't leave *Vogue* for a startup . . . catalogue . . . in New Jersey. Was she nuts?

But Horne was intrigued by the wide, blank slate of J.Crew. She asked her father what to do. "Tell them you'll come if they quadruple your salary," he said (her editorial salary was meager at the time, she emphasizes today). Emily agreed. And before she knew it, Horne was walking into the Popular Services, Inc., HQ in Garfield.

Which, OK, wasn't super glam. The fact that Popular Club Plan's new headquarters was a major step up in the world was utterly lost on young Tierney Horne. The building formerly housed a Two Guys appliance store. Imagine a low-rent Sears—a low, flat, beige box mired in acres of black parking lot. Inside lay a fluorescent-lit space, as wide as a bowling alley. In the front, row after row of women in polyester slacks received payments and orders for Popular Club Plan. In a back corner sat the tiny operation that was J.Crew. Horne, fresh from the see-and-be-seen offices of Condé Nast, took in her new workplace much the way Ted Pamperin had once absorbed the scene at the Botany Mills. The warnings of the *Vogue*-ettes sang in her head. Seriously, *was* she nuts?

It wasn't just the building: Horne wasn't sure what she'd been brought here to *do*. Emily had a gift for spotting talent and was aggressive in pursuing it, but she wasn't a big one for spelling out the mission. Lots of people would come to work at J.Crew for the very reason Tierney Horne just had—because there was something about *Emily*. They found her not warm or funny or friendly exactly, but something more elusive: compelling, inspiring; they marveled at her youth, her beauty—some found her low-key uniform chic, and assumed that meant J.Crew could become chic, too—and after meeting her they just trusted that she had a vision. *What did she tell you she wanted you to do, exactly?* I asked over and over; most couldn't quite say. Emily did not do stirring speeches about a grand plan. She had a sixth sense for people who got *it* and brought them in, and somehow they figured out the vision and got on board . . . by osmosis? By slowly grasping what it took to please her? Or because, as she sensed, they just had the right taste and gut instinct. It seemed to be some combination thereof.

What Emily wanted was to make a catalogue that didn't feel like a catalogue, with images as good as the ones in fashion magazines, that made everyday basics—clothes that people like Horne and Emily herself would want to wear—look incredibly appealing. But even Horne doesn't know how Emily had divined, over a double date, that this Zoran-clad fashionista would bring to the table an internal slideshow of her own childhood summers in the Long Island beach town of Amagansett. There, Horne recalls, her parents would wake up the children at 5 A.M. some mornings, grab fishing poles and a frying pan, and head to the beach to catch fresh snapper. They'd fry it up on the spot, with eggs, and breakfast in their swimsuits.

When Horne first told me this, the scene sounded so cinematic I figured it had to be partially manufactured, or at the very least gilded. But the next day she emailed a scan of a white-edged family photo with "1966" scrawled on one corner in Sharpie: a family of five, perched on a rock outcropping before an expanse of deep-blue water, a crisp white sail jutting up in the background. Two slim parents, three kids, all in shades of madras—silver frying pan glinting in the sun on the portable barbeque at their feet.

Like Maud Cinader's Nantucket paintings, this photo presaged the Americana that would soon underpin J.Crew, images that wafted happiness and freedom but also—gently, and without spritzing anybody straight in the face with it—privilege. Photos in which cozy rollneck sweaters and sandy-kneed chinos are part of the tableau but, like the costumes in a play that is really about this place, this time, these people, never feel like the point of it. The clothes are essential, but no more so than, say, the dog lazing at your feet, the vintage convertible overlooking the dunes, the smiling boyfriend with the floppy *Dead Poets Society* haircut.

J.Crew was not the first to pioneer what we would soon call "lifestyle photography"—far from it. If you had to pinpoint the birth of that invention, the summer of 1977 would be as good a time as any. That's when the up-and-coming Bruce Weber booked the model Jane Gill to play a preppy girl in a group of all-American college guys. Weber was planning a test shoot that he hoped would hook a big fish—Ralph Lauren. Gill, twenty-three, was a freckled champagne blond who had grown up on Long Island, hitchhiking to Montauk to surf. She didn't have the screaming '70s sex appeal of, say, Jerry Hall, but in her aquamarine eyes and ruffled blond curls Weber saw a timeless blue blood.

Gill was the only professional model Weber cast that day; her costars were locals he discovered on location. Weber liked working with amateurs. Real models, especially men, had a habit of staring directly into the lens. They were too canned for the look Weber wanted to capture: the gorgeous youth of the guy who serves you a gin and tonic at the club. The approach worked just fine for Gill. "I'll never forget it," she recalls with a laugh, "there were so many handsome boys."

Weber dressed this group not in Ralph Lauren—he didn't have the job yet—but in the staples of prep school boys: Brooks Brothers button-downs, Paul Stuart cashmere sweaters, tweed jackets. Their pant legs were rolled up, their feet bare, shirts untucked. Together, they spent the weekend fishing, cavorting by the water's edge, the hems of their pants damp with seawater.

Since the dawn of fashion photography, an army of stylists had toiled behind the scenes, pinning every sleeve and steaming out every wrinkle. Weber, a prep-school boy himself, aimed for the opposite—an unposed, seemingly natural tableau of people so at ease in their preppy clothes, they looked born that way.

Back in New York, Weber took the images to Lauren, who according to Gill was instantly on board: *This is what I want to do!* Weber had captured the patina of authenticity that Ralph had always sought. The ads they went on to make together portrayed a heightened reality never before seen in magazines. Today, in the wake of #MeToo allegations levied by more than fifteen former male models against Weber (which Weber has denied), that legacy has been tarnished.[2] But at the time, he had invented a new kind of fashion mythmaking. And people fell for it, to an almost eerie degree. For years, everywhere Gill went, people asked about her husband and children from the Ralph Lauren ads.

At the dawn of J.Crew, Ralph Lauren ads were a *thing*. Dorm room walls were wallpapered in them. People memorized the models' names. Even Hollywood knew what Ralph Lauren models meant. Kristin Holby—the model known to the fashion world as "Clotilde"—who was frequently cast in Lauren's ads as the brunette counterpart to Gill's patrician blond, played ur-WASP Penelope Witherspoon in *Trading Places*.

But once the newness of the Ralph look began to rub off, you had to admit, his models *did* look a little morose. They were forever playing tennis, but never broke a sweat. They wore Amelia Earhart–style goggles behind the wheel of a vintage Rolls, but the car was always in park. These people had it made—why weren't they having any fun? An advertising critic once noted—in a critique that, to be sure, reads differently today—that the woman in them always looked pained, as if the man had just confessed he was gay.[3] Ralph riffed on cowpoke Americana and Greenwich prep, but through a Vaseline-smeared Hollywood lens. The result was vaguely costume-y, a little camp. At his Upper East Side mansion-turned-store, the Rhinelander Mansion, shop assistants dressed like *Great Gatsby* extras peered down their noses at wayward looky-loos. In his Manhattan offices, it was not unusual to see a woman show up for work in jodhpurs. Nothing wrong with a rich fantasy life, clearly: customers ate it up. Ralph was king! But there was room in the game for something different. While Ralph was obsessed with the *idea* of authenticity, the worlds he created were always a little heightened—preppier than prep itself. This made for an ideal jumping-off point. There was space for a brand that was not just more affordable than Ralph, but more fun, more welcoming, more *real.*

J.CREW LEAPT INTO 1985, THEN 1986, THEN 1987, WITH A SENSE of unbridled potential. Every year, the V.P. of marketing, Charlie Silver, started out with the same question for Arthur: "Okay, how much do you want to grow this year?" The growth was nothing less than "magic," Silver says, and the only constraints were functional: did they have sufficient warehouse space, a strong-enough supply chain, a big-enough telemarketing staff to keep up with the demand that would inevitably come from sending out more catalogues? The question was not *How much J.Crew will people buy?* but rather, *How much J.Crew could they give people?*

The shoestring-budget days of loading a camper van and driving a couple of models to a college boathouse were over. Emily OK'd shoots in San Francisco, Newport, Harbor Island. In 1986, when the Western photographer Kurt Markus released *After Barbed Wire: Cowboys of our Time*, a book of black-and-white pictures of cowpokes in Nevada and Texas, Horne simply brought it to Emily: *We have to do this.* Done. Arthur did not second-guess the necessity of spending money to hone the image of J.Crew, and he did not appear to second-guess Emily.

That's not to say they were jetting in zebras and baby lion cubs for *Out of Africa*–themed extravaganzas. This wasn't Ralph. Budget mattered, as did efficiency. J.Crew didn't shoot single ad campaigns, but rather books of one hundred–plus pages, fourteen times a year, showcasing hundreds of items each time. To pull this off, they had to pioneer a new way of shooting.

On most catalogue shoots, one day might yield a total of eight, maybe ten shots if you were moving at a fast clip. To eke out more, Horne began styling a whole group of models in layers, so they could peel clothes off as the day went on. "I'd put on a T-shirt, then a polo shirt, then a chambray, then a jacket," she says. "I'd layer the shit out of everybody, and then we'd give them a task: Okay, make pancakes over an open fire. So there you've got your jacket photo." The heavily layered J.Crew look that became both revered and, eventually, an inside joke among followers—on nonwaifs, four shirts was not the most *flattering* look—started out as a practicality: it meant they didn't have to break for outfit changes between every shot. Throw off the jacket, on to the next. Taking a cue from Bruce Weber (and from generations of Princetonians) they made the clothes look lived-in. Soon enough, J.Crew would manufacture them this way, prewashing chinos until they were as soft as the pair you wore every day of college. Until then, though, fresh-pressed samples were tossed in the washer and dryer—sometimes repeatedly—until they looked properly aged. Belts were dunked in water, boots were stomped in puddles and twisted until the leather was broken in. Horne scoured prop houses and rental companies for the perfectly aged station wagon, a gross of surfboards, a litter of puppies. All the flotsam and jetsam of the "having it" life: dainty tea sets, Adirondack chairs, backgammon boards, stacks of Western blankets. She borrowed vintage luggage from T. Anthony, antique watches from Upper East Side jewelers. Shooting things that weren't for sale? This was how magazines worked—not catalogues.

Their other secret: J.Crew was always in *motion*. For every shoot, there was a destination, and for every destination there were activities: Ice-skating in the Adirondacks. Beach picnicking in the Hamptons. Skiing in Deer Valley. J.Crew models were forever shimmying up the mast of a sailboat, strapping a Christmas tree to the roof of the family Wagoneer, racing along a train platform, bags in hand, en route to someplace even better. All that activity kept models from looking like "catalogue people," those cardboard cutouts who existed solely to sell you things. If a model looks stiff, throw her on a bike. Hand her a picnic basket. Assign her a boyfriend with whom to play an endlessly thrilling game of tag. Give the boyfriend some shaving cream and a razor. This guy is shaving . . . on the beach? In his swim trunks? Just go with it.

"They had this incredible technique, which I absolutely loved," says photographer Tierney Gearon. Her first J.Crew shoot, when she was just starting out in the late '80s, was in St. Barts with Tierney Horne and Maud Cinader, then J.Crew's photo editor. The crew brought as many as ten or fifteen models with them, and split them into two teams—dispatching both teams to different activities in different locations. Gearon prefers to work like a film director: "I create a lot of chaos, so the models aren't really paying attention to the camera," she says, and to her amazement, "that's just how J.Crew was working . . . huge crews, big productions, like a film scene. And it was all about feeling good."

These photos ran "full-bleed"—that is, stretched across a whole page, sometimes two, as opposed to cropped small and jammed into the busy layout of a traditional catalogue. That gave them the impact of magazine photos, and helped weave romance and richness around what were, really, very simple clothes—good clothes, sure, but clothes that could easily have looked like nothing special in a business-as-usual catalogue.

Back at the office, for years to come, the litmus test of a great J.Crew picture was: Does it feel *real*? Could it pass for a snapshot?

Emily was learning as she went in the '80s, following her gut. But by the '90s this basic rule—no fakery—would be both ingrained in J.Crew and also honed to a fine art. A '90s catalogue editor recalls the process of reviewing new art that came as one of the best parts of the job. The staff would gather in a dark, tiny photo-editing room, sitting on the floor or balancing on the Formica countertop, as the photo editor clicked through a slideshow (art was still shot on film, and reviewed as slides). "We'd all call out: *Fake smile! Too model-y!*" he says. Or the damning, "*Tee hee!*" That meant the model was giving a cliché, hand-over-mouth giggle: J.Crew girls didn't *tee-hee*. They really laughed. "You quickly understood what made a picture look like a real snapshot, and how that was different from a catalogue," he says. "You could immediately identify the one or two or four things that are wrong in that picture: None of the food's been touched. Nobody's looking at each other. Everybody's talking at the same time—all the things that made it fake."

This didn't just make for better photos. It also defined a perceptible difference between what everybody else was selling and what J.Crew was about: it gave J.Crew its own look, its own vibe—a lifestyle that was enviable, but also relatable.

It felt unstudied, as if these clothes had just fallen together. But that, of course, was another sleight of hand. The space on a catalogue page is roughly equivalent to the square footage of a brick-and-mortar store: every inch equals money. Emily went into a new season knowing how many pages she had to fill, and how much of each page would be devoted to each item. When samples arrived at the office, usually about six months before a new season began, they were laid out on the floor on giant white foam core boards, exactly as they would later appear on the page. Before any item ever left the office on a shoot, its fate had already been decided. If a season's big "hero" was the pocket tee, they knew it would need to be shot on a man and on a woman, as a still life, in a stack of colors: the customer could not miss it.

From start to finish, this was grueling work. Fashion shoots are always surprisingly arduous jobs—behind every perfectly composed scene lies months of planning and an army of physical laborers hauling trunks of clothes and accessories and photography equipment from Paris to Timbuktu. But herding whole teams of "friends" and dozens of body bags stuffed with clothing up the side of a mountain in frigid predawn darkness, pitching tents in the snow, all so you're ready to begin shooting at first light—that's next-level effort. That serene ice-skating shot didn't just require a picturesque little pond; it required hiring locals to shovel two feet of snow off the pond before the sun came up. "Other catalogues might drag a sailboat onto the beach so everybody could pose in front of it," says Eve Combemale, a stylist in the late '80s. "J.Crew would take three boats out on the water and really be sailing."

All along, as Emily was hiring people to improve J.Crew's photos, she was simultaneously fixing the clothes those photos featured. Rewind back to 1984. In her early days, Emily elevated the product range as best she could—mostly by bringing in things to copy, sometimes as an outright knockoff, more often to lift a single detail: the manufacturers J.Crew worked with could replicate the shape of a sweater, or match its color, or mimic a great button detail. Emily's finds would be shipped off to a faraway factory and returned as J.Crew product. But the copycat game—one played by every fashion company, high and low, to some degree—can get dicey. One early designer recalls that Emily was eventually banned from Ralph Lauren's Manhattan store: They figured out exactly what she was up to there. (Emily denies this.)

Another early staffer recalls filling her arms with several thousand dollars' worth of men's zillion-ply cashmere sweaters during an inspiration-shopping spree at Barneys. She carried them up to the register and handed over her corporate card. The company name on it read, Popular Services, Inc.

The salesperson did a double take. Looking from the card back to the fresh-faced woman wielding it, she asked, suspicious, "What is *Popular Services?*"

This J.Crew staffer was fast on her feet. "Oh, it's an escort service," she blurted. "I'm doing the Christmas shopping."

They'd always planned on hiring their own design team. Maybe now it was time?

In 1985, Emily hired designer Linda Snyder, installed her in an office right next to her own, and tasked her with setting up the company's first sample room, ordering sewing machines, steamers, pattern tables, dress forms. Eager to show her young boss how this investment would pay off, one Saturday morning before these supplies even arrived, Snyder came into work with her assistant from her former job, toting her own sewing machine, a pair of sawhorses borrowed from her dad, and a drill. The two women unscrewed the hinges on a stockroom door and set it up on the sawhorses to make a cutting table, and started draping a pattern. By the end of the day, she says, "we had made J.Crew's first proprietary sample."

Little by little a real design team began to take root. Tierney Horne spotted a dapper young Southerner named Sid Mashburn* at a cocktail party. He was twenty-four, married to Ann Mashburn, a chic friend from Horne's *Vogue* days, and, in Horne's estimation, he possessed immaculate men's style: J.Press Oxford-cloth shirts, sharp khakis. "My filter was always, would my dad wear it? Or would I date a guy who would wear it?" she says. "It had to fit into one of those. Sid got it."

Soon, designer Claire McDougald was hired to develop knits. Lisa Anastasi made the leap from Ralph Lauren to oversee sweaters. This little team commuted to Garfield every morning the way city kids get to summer camp: a company van would pick them up on a corner in Manhattan, cross the George Washington Bridge, and deposit them in New Jersey. This arrangement, though deeply unstylish, had its upsides: No late nights. If you missed the bus when it came back at the end of the day, you were screwed. McDougald still recalls Mashburn, always last to leave, yelling, *Hang on! Just one more thing!*

Not one of them was over the age of twenty-seven, and most had

---

* Today, Mashburn is beloved as a hip elder statesman of Southern-inflected prep. Together with his wife, Ann—Horne's one-time *Vogue* pal—he helms a thriving chain of chic, eponymous boutiques and his-and-hers clothing lines that often play on the same strains of classic American style Mashburn once imparted to J.Crew.

only a few years' experience—some barely any at all. "Emily and Arthur were hiring for talent—future talent—work ethic, energy, and attitude," Mashburn says. "They were scrappy, and they were coming from behind. They were building something out of nothing."

This core team churned out a handful of designs that, for a certain generation of believers, still define J.Crew. The thinking behind these garments was not grand or conceptual, but deeply pragmatic: these were things the designers longed for in their own closets. One by one, they zeroed in on specific essentials they wanted to perfect: flat-front khakis at exactly the right length and feel; T-shirts with a pocket, in the perfect weight of cotton, with the stitching just so; chambray shirts that felt like they'd already weathered years. "The kind of items that you go out shopping and expect to find, but never can," recalls Horne. "They don't quite exist."

You never knew how you were going to stumble on that one perfect thing. Horne remembers walking into the office one day, when Emily stopped her in her tracks. "Let me feel your pants," she commanded. They were a holdover from Horne's *Vogue* days, made by Chevignon, a French brand that made spot-on remakes of classic U.S. military-issue staples. Army-Navy pants, but better. It had taken Horne years to properly break them in to a texture that, to Emily, was the holy grail. "*This* is what we have to do," Emily said. As Horne tells it, she handed over her favorite pants. Without missing a beat, Emily took out a big pair of shears and sliced off a piece of the fabric; it would be sent to a factory that would replicate the wash. Horne stood there, mouth hanging open. But what was she going to do, tell Emily *no*? That did not happen. Plus, she knew Emily was right. "It was for the greater good, you know?" she says, laughing.

In case you're wondering, no—no one paused to ponder the irony of "all-American" J.Crew copying a shmancy French copy of an all-American (OG preppy) military staple. The practice of riffing on "borrowed" ideas, or appropriating, or abject stealing, depending on how you look at it, *is* fashion: designers take the best of one thing, combine it with the best of another, and make something new. Er, newish. The Greeks had it right: nothing comes from nothing.

Some of J.Crew's greatest hits were relatively subtle improvements on existing items from the canon. Carhartt had its classic Engineers Chore Coat; Horne emailed me a photo of her father duck-hunting in the '60s in L.L.Bean's version, the Barn Coat. Both bore a strong resemblance to J.Crew's Barn Jacket. Mashburn inspected an armful of vintage hunting and field jackets and devised a drop-shoulder shape that was appropriately '80s-boxy, added a plaid flannel lining, and sourced a canvas that was a bit more forgiving than the stiff stuff real hunting jackets were made of. Some thirty-five years later, he recalls every inch: from the faux-tortoiseshell buttons, to the "half-banana" shape of the collar stand, to the specific 11-wale corduroy the collar was made of. The end product looked like something that had been hanging in a family cabin for decades.

Other designs, like the beloved J.Crew anorak, were similarly nostalgic. Emily brought in one of Arthur's old sailing jackets, a pullover she remembered him wearing when she was a kid. Mashburn tweaked the fit, modernized the fabrics, and chose new colors. People still reminisce about the old J.Crew anorak.

The J.Crew rollneck sweater—a multimillion-dollar item and, to my mind at least, the brand's most iconic—was also Emily's idea. It was inspired by an old woolen sweater her ex-boyfriend had inherited from his grandfather, so well-worn it was unraveling at the neck. "There aren't a lot of ways to reinvent the sweater," says knitwear designer Lisa Anastasi, but the rollneck did, if quietly. It was made without the ribbed trim that usually finishes the hem and neck of a sweater, allowing the edges to roll up naturally. The rollneck was initially a men's sweater, but as the popular girls at my own school would soon discover, it was alluringly oversize, just right for pulling over one's hands on a chilly day.

THE FIRST TIME EMILY WAS CERTAIN J.CREW WAS A BONA FIDE hit, it was because of a photo of Jane Gill—yes, star of the Ralph Lauren campaigns. Preppy archetypes, it seems, are a niche market. Gill recalls Emily as unique among the bosses of her day: young and female in an industry run almost entirely by men, which gave her a unique perspective. On shoots with male designers and creative directors, no one asked, *How do you feel in that, do you like it? Does it feel right to you?* Emily was a stickler for texture, she cared how clothes *felt* almost as much as how they looked. Plus J.Crew had perfected a way of wearing clothes, a host of little throwaway styling tips that made them cool. "They could put a shirt and a pair of jeans together with some fabulous old vintage belt or a pair of old sneakers," Gill says, "without anything looking too done."

In that fateful photo of Gill, she's wearing nothing more elaborate than a pale pink T-shirt. Her smile is partially shaded by a wide Stetson, and—of course—there's a tiny Jack Russell nestled in her arms. It's a pretty picture, but no more so than a thousand other J.Crew pictures, so maybe Ralph was right, and something about Jane Gill really did make people want whatever she had. Or maybe Emily was right, and the formula they'd been tinkering with—aspirational, relatable, comfortable, *American*—had finally struck gold. Whatever the reason, that photo had an effect that today would be called "breaking the internet." Emily had gone into it thinking the T-shirt would be a success, so she ordered what was for J.Crew a large amount, five thousand. But then eighty thousand orders poured in. This time around, they didn't send out a gift certificate: *Oops, sorry!* J.Crew went into overdrive; someone was dispatched on a plane to a factory: More, *now*!

Through it all, Emily worked as hard as anyone. To her young team, she appeared undaunted, tireless. So sure of herself, and her decisions. While the other twentysomethings—her peers—went home at a reasonable hour on the van, Emily and Tierney Horne often left the office at 11 P.M., driving back to the city in Emily's little Scirocco. Like her father, she was never too high and mighty to roll up her sleeves and sweat. But like her father, she could also be condescending, brusque, a taskmaster in pursuit of perfection. It's hard to imagine the pressure she was under in those early years. But sometimes when Emily was on set and the models took a break, you could almost hear her mentally calculating the dollars and cents of every lost minute—*ch-ching, ch-ching*—waiting for them to get back to work. That wasn't particularly conducive to the happy-go-lucky "realness" J.Crew demanded from its photographers. On one occasion, an elaborate shoot was planned at a ranch in Jackson Hole. But when the team of models, photographer, stylists, and assistants was en route, their connecting flight never arrived. They had to rent a U-Haul, load in clothes, props, lighting and photography equipment, and drive the rest of the way. They didn't get to the ranch til 8 A.M. the following day, bleary-eyed and desperate for sleep. But when they phoned New York to check in, Emily's orders were unequivocal, and merciless: Get to work. No day could go to waste.

CHAPTER 5

Hooked on a Feeling

When a brand catches fire, even the people who lit it can never be sure *exactly* what caused the conflagration: There's good timing and solid design and great photos, but then people's love for a brand starts to take on a life of its own. That's alchemical—it exceeds the sum of its parts. By the late '80s, J.Crew was a *thing*. Smaller, maybe, than the "thing" Ralph Lauren had first become a decade earlier, but no less ardently felt among its believers. Customers loved the outfits so much, they began to order every item on a model's body: not just her snowflake sweater, but her turtleneck, chinos, sunglasses, and that cunning pom-pommed ski hat, too. Tierney Horne laughs: "It got to the point that if we showed a model holding a teacup, people would call up wanting the teacup."

In 1989, Kelly Hill was a coed on the grassy, redbricked campus of Virginia's James Madison University. Among her cohort, the arrival of a new J.Crew catalogue was an event. Back in their dorm, Hill's roommates enacted a ritual that had nothing to do with shopping: reading the J.Crew catalogue like a bodice ripper from the supermarket checkout.

"Oh. My. God," the girls would shriek in mock outrage, poring over each glossy page, beers in hand. "Mary Ann left Mark for Bob?"

This wasn't something you did with Lands' End or L.L.Bean. You didn't do it with *Glamour* or *Vogue*, either. In Jersey, Arthur had recruited a team of marketing talent with freshly minted Ivy League degrees—Charlie Silver called them his "whiz kids"—who divined new ways to target J.Crew's emerging sweet spot, college and prep school kids. Just as Brooks Brothers had done in the 1920s, dispatching its army of salesmen to campuses all over the Northeast, now J.Crew claimed the (upwardly mobile) youth vote, pelting campuses with issues, tracking student addresses, and dropping great lashed-together bundles on campus mailrooms, to be grabbed at will.

For the coeds of James Madison, J.Crew was always around—it arrived more frequently than any magazine, for free, and everybody read it. And it spoke their language, beckoning to an early adulthood that was just out of reach but could conceivably be theirs soon. The people in its pages had become familiar, reappearing month after month. They looked like the most attractive people from their own campus parties, having the time of their lives. Over several years of careful study and intense yearning, Hill and her friends had come to know J.Crew, to *own* J.Crew. These were *their* clothes, their beachhouses. Their square-jawed "J.Crew guy" and their freckled, laughing "J.Crew girl." Were these people named Mary Ann or Mark or Bob? Who cared?

For the clean-cut, white-toothed paragons of WASP virtue in these pages, the college girls conjured byzantine backstories littered with love triangles and infidelity. It made for a fun drinking game. In the J.Crew universe, a hot night was one spent playing board games in matching union suits—which made their whipped-up narratives all the more hilarious. When "J.Crew guy" hauled wood to the fire, his woolly sweater dusted with snow, they speculated: whose heirloom quilt would *he* be climbing underneath tonight?

The catalogues' familial, intergenerational configurations of attractive people gave them plenty to work with. What was up with Mark and Bob, who seemed to gallivant off with a different girl in every issue? How come no one ever wore a wedding ring? Was the silver fox in this month's issue Mary Ann's boyfriend . . . or her dad? Sometimes random kids popped up: Who did *they* belong to? To these girls, J.Crew was no mere catalogue.

"J.Crew was a movement," says a staffer from that era, who had just graduated from a Seven Sisters school with lofty journalistic aspirations when Emily offered her a job. "If she'd asked me to come work at Lands' End? No."

Even people who would not be caught dead in a Barn Jacket could not ignore the J.Crew *thing*. "I remember a specific moment in the late '80s when some of my more fashion-y colleagues started shrieking about the J.Crew catalogue," says Simon Doonan, then the creative genius behind the quirky windows of Barneys New York. "They would have their boxes of plain-looking pants and shirts shipped to our office." This was a real head-scratcher for Doonan. "We all had our fabulous Barneys discount cart, but instead of Jean Paul Gaultier or Commes des Garçons, they were choosing to buy bland preppy duds from some mail order catalogue." And not even a nice, tawdry catalogue like Frederick's of Hollywood or International Male, "which, at least, sold something cheeky and sizzling!"

In some cases, the people toiling inside of J.Crew were the last to know their thing was now *a* thing. For Tierney Horne, the lightbulb clicked on in 1989, at a shoot in Oxford, Mississippi, in a town so tiny that, as she recalls it, their crew's arrival made the front page of the paper, and the mayor was enlisted as a production assistant. The shoot had all the J.Crew hallmarks—hay bales, bucket o' puppies—and of course the J.Crew guy, a cute, curly-haired twentysomething who was a recurring character in its pages for years. His name was not Mark or Bob. It was Matthew Barney.* He was an art student at Yale who modeled on the side.

* In a few years, the irony of this moment would deepen as Barney emerged from the chrysalis of J.Crew apple-picker-in-chief to become creator of the Cremaster Cycle, one of the most influential—and among the more disturbing—artists of his generation, who would go on to have a child with the delightfully odd Icelandic pop star Björk. Barney's secret past as Mr. J.Crew resurfaces from time to time, to the delight of the internet. Ole Miss, this guy was not.

They were shooting Barney on the campus of Ole Miss when word got out that the "J.Crew guy" was in town. A gaggle of coeds appeared out of nowhere and chased Barney all over campus. Horne was flabbergasted. Wait, was J.Crew . . . famous?

To people on the outside, J.Crew had a magic you couldn't quite put your finger on. To the people on the inside, this mysterious quality was specific to the odd but effective pairing of two people most J.Crew fans had never heard of: Emily and Arthur. "You would never on paper put these two people together to create a fashion brand," says Paul Raffin, an industry vet who has run John Varvatos and the boot company Frye, and who spent part of the '90s as president of J.Crew's retail operation. "Emily was the right-brained creative side, overseeing the images, the casting, the photography, and the product itself." She was the one the creative team lived to serve. But Arthur, "this meticulous, Mensa-quality mind, wrapped in a completely socially inept package," running the business side, was the other half, no less vital.

Investor Matt Rubel, a C.E.O. of Popular Club Plan in the '90s who worked closely with Arthur and developed a real affection for him, says that in order to appreciate Arthur, you had to understand that his brain operated with a rigid but beautiful sense of order, "almost like a computer works with a hierarchy of knowledge." This system dictated many of the things Arthur was so bewilderingly obsessive about: the way a spreadsheet of numbers should be arranged, or a business report should be labeled. It governed the way Arthur thought a conversation ought to proceed. And it applied to the way the information should flow—left to right, words to image—across a catalogue spread. Arthur knew *exactly* how he wanted it done.

This precision extended from the way the J.Crew business was run, to the hyperspecific language in its catalogue. "That was really his genius," Raffin says.

In 1987, Ralph Lauren was the king of American fashion, mugging in white cable-knit on the cover of *Time*, and playing a sexy cowboy in his own ads, posed with a beer in a white tee and Stetson. Designer Scott Formby was working at Polo Ralph Lauren when he got a call from a headhunter about J.Crew—from his vantage point, still a two-bit catalogue, biting Ralph's style and selling it at half or a third the price. Why would you leave the original for the knockoff? Still, Formby was intrigued enough to take a meeting with Arthur.

Arthur sometimes saved Manhattanites the schlep to Jersey by holding meetings at home on Ninety-Third and Park. As he must have been aware, the location made an impression. Walking in, "I was a little skeptical," Formby says. "Who was this guy?" But Formby found Arthur to be something of a revelation. For one thing, if Arthur's peers weren't knocked out by his rumpled jackets and scuffed shoes, younger creatives like Formby saw in them a "college professor" vibe and a certain old-school cool. In Arthur's home, nicely furnished with Joke's Scandinavian simplicity but absent the polished chintzes and elaborate silks of the '80s Upper East Side decorator, Formby saw a library filled with books that were not mere set design. When they sat down to talk, Arthur seemed surprised to learn that the designer—who'd majored in international relations at Brown before studying fashion—was more than able to keep up. They covered books, politics. Everything but design. Arthur never asked to see Formby's portfolio.

"Holy shit," Formby found himself thinking. "This guy's the real deal." To the young designer, Cinader, with his patched-up jackets and esoteric notions, "was realer than Ralph."

Emily and Arthur ruled separate spheres and kept their dealings mostly behind closed doors. "I don't ever remember them talking in a normal tone of voice to each other, or even acknowledging each other in a normal way," recalls a former catalogue editor. "It was very to-the-side, quiet, sort of clandestine." Emily might walk over to where Arthur was working, communicate something "in a subhuman whisper," and float away.

Arthur's sphere was the business side, but he was intimately involved in the catalogue. Emily developed the clothes and oversaw the imagery; he controlled the language that framed J.Crew. Back when the photographer Michael Belk was banging his head against the wall, waiting for Arthur to sign off on the copy for the first catalogue, it was not immediately clear that what the boss was doing was going to matter. But the spell Arthur was weaving would last a lot longer than those first pictures. From the first issue, a J.Crew polo shirt wasn't blue, it was *copen blue*. Corduroys came in *palamino, cedar,* and *nutmeg.* It's hard to imagine today, with our walls painted "sea salt" and our sea salts subspecified into Brittany Grey versus Hawaiian Onyx, but this small thing—evocative, pretentious color names—was new to mass-market fashion. A J.Crew sweater did not come in some podunk, run-of-the-mill green, it was *grass.* The Barn Jacket was not brown, it was *ochre.*

In the late '80s, Arthur pressed a copy of *Living Well Is the Best Revenge* into the hands of a young catalogue editor. This was Calvin Tomkins's famous biography of Gerald and Sara Murphy, the magnetic American expats who served as the inspiration for Fitzgerald's *Tender Is the Night.* When writer Louis Auchincloss—whose private-school novel, *The Rector of Justin*, is a prep classic—reviewed *Living Well* in the *New York Times* in 1971, he wrote that while the Murphys believed "there was a place for style in everything: how you talked, how you entertained, how you dressed," they were not slavish to style. Trappings were important, but never too important. "One could be too well dressed as well as too badly. Style was being just right."[1] This was the very essence of J.Crew. Arthur was putting as much distance as he could between his company and "Ralph at half the price."

Of course, he made the journey fairly miserable. He hired excellent copywriters—again dispatching recruiters to the Ivy League: no degree too exalted for a future bottom-rung J.Crew caption writer! But he policed their words until, in the end, he might as well have written every syllable himself. This is not something a C.E.O. typically spends a great portion of his workdays doing. But as J.Crew grew, Arthur invested even *more* time in the minutia of wordsmithing, spending hours a day in the design department, riding the haunch of whatever unlucky sod happened to be holding the computer mouse—*move that left, no right, no up, no make it bigger*—until every letter was placed to his satisfaction.

As J.Crew grew into itself, Arthur became more of an essentialist in regards to the copy. He wanted the smallest number of words, edited for the maximum amount of impact. He favored sharp, staccato pacing. A woman's oversize blazer: "the unmatched suit, from dawn through dusk." "Man's sweater. On woman." He loved a slight, unorthodox twist of language. "Two get away with one bag," read the cover of a resort wear issue. *Huh?* "One of the only phrases I ever wrote that he liked was 'taking it eased,'" recalls one-time copywriter Nathan Lump (now editor in chief of *National Geographic*). "That was my gold star moment." It wasn't *quite* grammatically correct, and also wasn't a pun. It was almost nonsensical, yet you knew what it meant. A 1989 cover, bearing a photo of a dreamy waterfront house, its shingles weathered gray, featured Arthur's favorite coverline. "Campobello to Cape May." Four words defining J.Crew country, from the southernmost tip of the Canadian shore to the beaches of New Jersey. There was a cadence to this that Arthur—and only Arthur—knew in his bones.

Nathan Lump was, ostensibly, Arthur's kind of guy: he'd graduated summa cum laude from Harvard with a degree in folklore and mythology. But Lump never quite gelled. Once, after he handed in a riff on Valentine's Day pajamas, Arthur made a low murmuring sound as he read. Had the impossible happened, Lump thought—was the man *pleased*? Arthur picked up a pencil and began to cross out words, line by line. Halfway through, the pencil broke. He stopped, sharpened it, and resumed editing. When he had crossed out every word, he turned the page sideways, jotted three sentences in the margin, and handed it back. "See?" he said. "Just off the cuff." To Lump, this wasn't editing, it was "ritual abuse."

But Arthur's way with language did have a kind of magic. He once described a set of patterned fall sweaters as having "great strains of crumhorn, hautbois, and sackbut." The line echoed his insistence on the name Sir Edward Coke years earlier: Nobody besides Arthur had the first clue what a *hautbois* was. These were obscure Rennaissance-era instruments, of course! "We all thought it the funniest thing we had ever read. Like, tears were running down our faces," says a catalogue editor from that time, with affection. "But for him it was real." And Arthur did not take corrections well. When one copywriter challenged him on an unorthodox word usage, she walked away dejected. "Oh well, *it's only Webster's*," she muttered under her breath. The line became an office joke.

When the J. Peterman catalogue came along in 1987, it took highfallutin' copywriting to a comical nth degree. J. Peterman had no photos; customers were expected to purchase pricey mackintoshes and safari jackets based only on loose sketches and captions that read like creative writing assignments. John Peterman inspired Elaine's hilariously eccentric boss on *Seinfeld*—a grandiose, Hemingway-esque catalogue magnate who scours the globe in search of arcane merchandise. (*Seinfeld*'s Peterman: "Then in the distance, I heard the bulls. I began running as fast as I could. Fortunately, I was wearing my Italian Cap Toe Oxfords.")

But before there was a J. Peterman, there was an A. Cinader. And while the Peterman catalogue always seemed to be trying to evoke an invented persona, Arthur was just being himself—esoteric, academic, exacting—assuming that the right people would understand where he was going with this, and get on board.

Scott Formby, the designer so unexpectedly won over by Arthur, turned out to be an even better fit for Emily. By the time Formby arrived at J.Crew, Ted Pamperin was long gone. By 1986, Pamperin had seen the writing on the wall: no matter how astounding the launch of J.Crew had been, Arthur was never going to give him an ownership stake. After Pamperin, Emily was named president of J.Crew. She was twenty-six at the time.

Formby was slight, dark-haired, and quietly good-looking, with a sly sense of humor that occasionally flashed on. In Emily, he saw not the cold fish that many recall, but rather a fellow introvert. He liked her, and more than that, he *got* her. Even at a time when large swaths of the catalogue still hadn't shaken their early-'80s hangover—there were still corduroy dirndl skirts and prim ruffled blouses that needed to be put out of their misery—Formby could see Emily was trying to do something new with J.Crew.

By 1988, Emily had achieved J.Crew 2.0: the company had its own aesthetic, and sold a handful of wear-forever pieces that people loved. But she wanted more—more than college kids, more than chinos and sweaters, more than weekends. Formby would help her tackle 3.0. In their first conversation, "we talked a lot about our favorite companies," Formby recalls. In this conversation, Ralph Lauren never came up. To Formby's surprise, and his great pleasure, Emily shared his love for small, cool European companies like A.P.C. and agnès b. that were selling elevated, simple clothes—"basics, the way we liked to dress," Formby says—that felt newly of the moment. "We held those as goals," he says. "Could we do something as important as that: not over-designed, and still relevant, but more for an American market?" Emily had, from the beginning, been working on refining those perfect, basic items one by one. Now, from their first meeting, she and Formby were assembling a mental mood board of the J.Crew that would take shape in the 1990s—a quietly elegant, high-quality, total-lifestyle brand at reasonable prices, in which every item was as quietly refined as those first ones—a brand that, eventually, would have very little to do with cliche '80s prep.

Indeed, one word Emily and Formby did not use, ever? *Preppy.* It may come as a surprise to learn that the people who built this kingdom of prep—the company referred to in practically every article ever written about it as "America's preppy retailer"—didn't think J.Crew *was* preppy. Asked about it, most offer some version of Tierney Horne's response: "Funny, I never thought of the look as preppy," she told me, as if surprised (and a little disappointed) that I would ask such a thing. As if I had just revealed that I really didn't get J.Crew at all. "We were *cool.* Preppy wasn't cool."

In part, this was a sign of the times: As the '80s aged out, *preppy* was slinking back into the closet, alongside its equally problematic cousin, *yuppie.* Oblivious displays of class and wealth seemed uncouth all over again. In pop culture, prep survived as a four-letter-word for windbags and bullies. (See: Ted McGinley's smug frat boy in *Revenge of the Nerds.*) By 1987, the villain in *Dirty Dancing* was not Johnny, the swivel-hipped rebel from the wrong side of the tracks, but Robbie, the arrogant richie in bow tie and madras, who abandons his summer fling in her moment of need.

To people who'd been wearing penny loafers and Shetland sweaters long before the *Preppy Handbook* slapped a label on it, the omnipresent stereotype of '80s prep cast a pall over what had once been simple, durable good taste. "Preppy" gave the look a bad name, implying that those who wore it suffered from a certain constitutional brattiness, not to mention an exceedingly narrow worldview. Who wants to be associated with that?

No daughter of Arthur Cinader, that's for sure. Stylistically, Emily associated the P-word with all of the cutesy stuff that came along *after* Miles Davis–era cool, mostly in the technicolor '60s: the eye-popping Lilly Pulitzer shifts; the "critter pants" crawling with embroidered crustaceans and anchors; the prissy piped Pappagallo flats. Emily was not a playful person. She did not do *cute*. Under her auspices, anything deemed "too Connecticut" was axed.

Emily had spent her early adolescence not in the preppy Northeast but in the high desert city of Albuquerque, NM, thanks to a professional swerve Arthur pulled in 1969, when she was just eight years old. Arthur had a knack for finance—he'd built the thriving credit operation at Popular Club Plan, after all—and wanted to diversify, so he bought a bank. This was not a slam dunk. By the late '70s, the family had moved back east—not to New Jersey, where they had previously lived, but to Park Avenue. The detour meant Maud Cinader and the other younger Cinaders came of age among the Georgian mansions of the Upper East Side. But Emily, the eldest, had been marked by a jeans-and-T-shirts, outdoorsy New Mexico childhood. She was a tomboy who dressed in boys' chinos and would forever love a mens' button-down. By the time her family moved to New York, she was at Cranbrook, a bohemian-leaning boarding school in Michigan, and would soon head to college, far from Ivy territory, at the University of Denver.

Though she had been imprinted by the Nantucket summers and Vail ski trips, just like her siblings, Emily did not have the social currency of an Upper East Sider. She was no blue-blooded WASP (after all, she was half Jewish). And never once had she considered herself preppy.

In her mind and in those of her designers, J.Crew aimed to be "stylists for America": a route to being "well dressed"—not victim-y—in practical, trend-proof, good-looking clothes. The company may have started selling the Ralph look at a price, but in Emily's view they were beyond that now. The goal wasn't to sell entry-level elitism; indeed, they envisioned J.Crew as an alternative to that kind of thinking. They saw no gates on the world they had created: a catalogue, fundamentally, is open to everyone. You didn't have to walk into some intimidating boutique to buy J.Crew. You just called the sweet Southern-accented salesladies at the new, giant fulfillment center in Virginia. (Current address: Three Ivy Crescent.)

How could J.Crew be preppy? It was based in *New Jersey*, for god's sake. Their models weren't strolling the manicured grounds of country estates. The word Emily used to define them wasn't *rich*. Arthur might have gone out of his way to hire rarefied graduates, but Emily did not; she never said, or even thought, *Ivy League*. The word they most often used to describe the look was "American." Emily had banished logos; she loathed all that status-conscious boasting. "One of our basic beliefs," she once noted, "is not having our name on our clothing." Indeed, J.Crew was maybe the first company to do away with labels altogether on its T-shirts, printing the necessary info inside the shirt itself—making it less scratchy *and* less braggadocious. In two senses, more comfortable. And anyway, as one designer after another reminded me, J.Crew was affordable.

Is there a word more subjective than *affordable*? To Emily, who could afford Rhinelander Mansion Ralph Lauren—not just the stuff at Macy's—J.Crew was a bargain. The designers she was poaching from Calvin and Ralph felt the same. In their previous jobs, they could barely afford to outfit themselves for work, even with their corporate discounts. Now they wore J.Crew all day, every day, at prices that seemed almost throwaway. Plus, the company itself was still a Little Engine That Could, looked down upon by fashion snobs. Viewed from this perspective, J.Crew was a force for good, bringing timeless good taste to the masses.

But most Americans weren't buying Ralph Lauren in the first place. Emily might have seen J.Crew as a club anyone could belong to, but to teenagers begging their parents for each new color combo of the now-cult-beloved J.Crew rugby—a shirt with the power to help them pass muster at the popular kids' table at school—J.Crew was in every sense aspirational. And J.Crew sold the uniform of a comfortable, unhurried existence. One that, by the way, checked almost every box of the original Ivy style code. All that apple-picking and picnicking in the catalogue—the brand's "tyranny" of ease, as the writer Matthew DeBord put it in a 1997 academic screed?[2] That was deeply preppy. The Yankee durability of an oxford cloth shirt, its cuff perfectly frayed, like you'd worn it forever—even when it was straight out of the box? As preppy as Princeton undergrads, sandpapering the collar of a brand-new Brooks Brothers in 1957. The tomboy cool of styling that same shirt on a no-makeup girl, over her bikini and cutoffs? You get the drift.

Indeed, DeBord argues that the logo-less-ness of J.Crew, which Emily saw as so egalitarian, was maybe J.Crew's preppiest act of all. They were solving the very thing that dyed-in-the-wool preps resented about the ubiquitous Ralph Lauren polo: "Many people liked the idea of what he was up to—abhorred synthetics, adored 100 percent cotton, disliked the extremes of fashion, lionized comfort, and wanted their clothes to outlast the millennium," DeBord wrote, "but hated the stupid little pony he insisted on sticking on seemingly everything he manufactured."

Maybe it makes sense that Emily was a preppy denier. One seemingly reliable litmus test of a true prep: Does she say she's not? Lilly Pulitzer, of course, was revered for decades as prep's white-haired, perpetually upbeat queen mother—the aesthetic's very embodiment. But when she penned the foreword to the 2012 coffee table book *Preppy: Cultivating Ivy Style*, even Pulitzer revealed her ambivalence about the term. "For a long time now, my clothes have officially been classified as preppy. I admit that a lot of my friends probably went to some prep school along the way, but I never thought of them, or my clothes, as preppy."[3] If Lilly Pulitzer wasn't a prep, was anybody?

CHAPTER 6

625 Sixth

At Emily's J.Crew there was such no thing as "all right, pencils down." There was no good enough. There was the right way, and however many tries it took to get there. According to one designer, Emily once sent an assistant back to the mat for some sixteen days until she found a name Emily was willing to approve for a single shade of green. Eventually the whole design team got in on the effort. By the time someone came up with *mallard,* they were ready to stage a walkout.

Picture the scene: Emily, in the office, eyeballing a man's neck. Specifically, the collar of a shirt, worn by a fit model. In menswear, change often comes in millimeters: ties, collars, lapels, pant legs—they expand and contract, usually minutely, to move with the times. This time, the collar needed to be just a skosh narrower—an eighth of an inch, a quarter at most. The kind of detail shoppers never detect until it's done wrong, in which case they never buy that shirt again. Emily stepped up to the model, put her fingers around his collar, and pinched just so. There, *that* was the shape she wanted. But when she let go, it fell. "It's all wrong," Emily snapped, her frustration growing. "This isn't *it.*"

Two J.Crew emissaries were about to fly overseas to visit the factory that would make thousands of this shirt. How could Emily be sure they would communicate the *exact* shape she wanted? Then, according to a merchant who was in the room at the time, Emily got an idea: "Put the shirt on," she said to an employee who was going on the trip. Then—not pausing to ask permission—she grabbed a black Sharpie, pinched the collar just right, and drew a dot on his throat, right where she wanted the collar to sit. *There.* The guy would now take that dot around the globe.

He walked out of her office fuming. "What the fuck was that? She put a *dot* on me?" Then he got on the plane and did exactly as he'd been told.

It was Emily who had insisted J.Crew move, at last, to New York City. If they were going to compete for talent, stake a place in the industry firmament, they couldn't do it from New Jersey. In 1988, J.Crew left its slightly embarrassing older stepsister, Popular Club, behind and took over two floors in 625 Sixth Avenue, on the corner of Nineteenth Street in Chelsea. The open-plan, loft-style building had creaky pine floors and bright white walls and housed an operation that, to members of the original team, had grown to be almost unrecognizable. Their little J.Crew had morphed into a sprawling company. It had separate departments for styling, design, marketing, and production; there were teams for men's catalogue and women's catalogue, all staffed by people wearing J.Crew clothes, with a recognizable New York cool. *Whoa.* When had they become a real fashion company?

The move felt significant, electric. It hadn't been easy to hold their heads high in the world of New York fashion when they were taking a school bus—OK, a van—to work every day. The vibe inside of 625 was fertile, scrappy, alive. Designers literally ran from one department to the next, slowing down just outside of Emily's and Arthur's offices, before picking up speed again. There was no more leaving at a decent hour; they worked feverishly, stayed late, came in on weekends—whatever it took. They became tight-knit, shared beach house rentals in the summer, ate takeout lunches together; the women sunbathed on the roof of the building during lunch break. Working there was *fun*. "There was a belief in what we were doing, and the work ethic was insane," recalls designer Scott Formby. "People jived on it. It felt like a mission that was easy to sign up for."

And Emily, now twenty-eight, was their absolute center of gravity, working thirteen-hour days, employees perpetually lined up seven deep outside her office. Arthur was still running the business, but most people who walked in the doors of 625 every morning were conscious of the desire to please one person: Emily.

She felt symbolic of something bigger, too, at what seemed to be a turning point for the working woman. The career woman archetype, in her heels and shoulder-padded suits, attaché case in hand, was everywhere you looked in the '80s and '90s. From *Working Girl* to *9 to 5*, bold, brassy gals were staging takeovers. The year J.Crew moved to New York, Candice Bergen begat Murphy Brown, the hardened journalist who had clawed out a place for herself in the media firmament and had no designs on marriage. In the movies at least, the career woman often outshone her man: Remember Teri Garr, leaving the lunch boxes and the laundry to Michael Keaton in *Mr. Mom*?

But while Hollywood was taken with this new model, she was still an exceedingly rare species in the real world. The fashion industry long escaped the label of sexism by virtue of optics: it catered to women, was powered—from the cutting room to the sales floor, at least—by legions of female employees. Fashion did not have the "ambition gap" that plagued other fields, like the sciences or law: women felt no barrier to entry. And powerful women seemed to be everywhere in fashion: In 1985, Donna Karan had launched her "seven easy pieces," specifically to dress the archetype in question. Liz Tilberis was running *Harper's Bazaar;* Anna Wintour was appointed to the helm of *Vogue* in 1988. The top fashion critics at the *New York Times* were women. With women as its most powerful arbiters *and* its consumers, how *could* fashion have a woman problem? Of course this was a little like saying, How *could* J.Crew be preppy? Somewhere along the route from middle management to the C-suite, the vast majority of fashion's female workforce hit a wall. This wasn't something most people were talking about back in 1988, so let's use more current data: in 2015, one survey found that only 14 percent of major brands were run by a female executive.[1]

Emily, running J.Crew nearly thirty years before that survey, while still in her twenties, was a virtual anomaly. Looking around the industry, it was hard to spot any young woman in a comparable position.

I asked dozens of people what Emily was really like. One told me point-blank: *You will never truly understand her.* Even back then, working with her every day for years, nobody did: "She's an apparition, I swear to god." In an office full of hip twentysomethings—her peers—who lunched together and partied after hours, she remained aloof, untouchable. Whether this was a self-protective mechanism, an effort to retain control, given her age, or just a function of her own internal wiring, was unclear. What they did know was that a twenty-foot privet hedge surrounded Emily, and few colleagues ever truly scaled it. "She hired me at twenty-two years old and gave me all this responsibility," marvels a former staffer. "And yet in all the time I worked there, I don't ever recall having a how-are-you moment."

One long-timer recalls visiting a friend's apartment in the '90s. He was shocked to spot a photo of Emily Cinader—*their* Emily!—at sixteen, lithe and happy, leaning against a convertible on Nantucket. The following Monday, as he and Emily reviewed layouts on the floor, he asked about the photo. "Emily looked at me like I was asking when she lost her virginity," he says. "As if it was a personal violation." He found himself in an awkward pas de deux; either Emily genuinely had no clue who he was talking about, or she was pretending not to. "What was I thinking?" he says. "Why would I think I could go there?"

Emily's office lacked all physical evidence of a startup on steroids.

Her desk was almost sterile, not a paper clip out of place. She was exquisitely disciplined, rigorously efficient. Long before the gym became a fixture of modern life, she worked out with a trainer and practiced yoga. She shared Arthur's hypersensitivity to noise. Women took off their bracelets before walking into her office; she couldn't stand the clattering. There was no pencil-tapping, no click-y pens, no crinkly candy wrappers. Women wore minimal makeup; men wore undershirts—was this a stated rule, or simply the J.Crew way? Either way, everyone did it. Memos circulated about what employees could keep on their desks, including, once, height restrictions for potted plants. That got a laugh: What happened if the plant . . . grew?

She was well aware of how weird this all sounded, but also utterly unapologetic; Emily had zero shame about demanding the conditions she needed to operate. "I have a reputation of, 'Don't chew on ice, don't click your watch on the table consistently during meetings,'" Emily would tell the *New York Observer* in 1997.[2] "I'm distracted by noises. I know this is my problem, but it makes it hard for me to think at the pace I have to think here . . . Everyone knows not to come to meetings chewing gum."

She could also be cutting, condescending. A former designer recalls the time Emily walked into the ladies' room and spotted a staffer whose black bra was visible through her white shirt. Emily pointed it out in the mirror, as if she was helpfully pointing out a piece of spinach in the woman's teeth. "See how that doesn't look good?"

Scanning the landscape for someone to compare Emily to, many latch on to *Vogue* editrix Anna Wintour, whose combination of exquisite power and self-contained demeanor has obsessed the global fashion world for decades. (I should mention I worked for Wintour in the early days of my career.) Within the J.Crew snow globe, Emily was their Anna. Indeed, once people started pointing this out I could see the similarities immediately: Emily ran J.Crew like an imperious editor in chief, taking her big spring and fall issues just as seriously as Wintour takes her annual September issue. Like Wintour, perpetually hidden from public view behind her black sunglasses—her remoteness attracting endless speculation—Emily's froideur brought out different things in different people: Some saw her as "a fucking ice queen," one woman told me in no uncertain terms. Others saw it as a mask for some hidden vulnerability. Scott Formby, for instance, has always felt Emily was misunderstood: where others saw coldness, he saw shyness. But many fell under the spell of that hard-to-reach persona. She was the reigning enigma in their midst: she kept you at arm's length, yet no detail passed by without her approval. Inaccessibility is a kind of power unto itself. What made Emily tick? Everybody had an opinion.

Indeed, in 2022, when the writer Amy Odell published *Anna*, a semi-authorized biography of Wintour, I was struck by a line in the *New York Times*' review of the book: "Odell doesn't seem to have her mind made up about Wintour," Willy Staley complained. "Is she a cold apparatchik of this harsh industry, or an exacting, driven and visionary boss who is subject to sexist double standards?"[3] To be sure, I am left with the same indecision about Emily. And so are a lot of the people who once worked for her.

Like Wintour, Emily wasn't about to change to try to please anybody. At J.Crew, it was her way or the highway. To those who stuck around, her quirks were completely worth it. People didn't just *like* working at J.Crew—decades later, they recall it as their greatest job ever. At a more established company, the young pups Emily hired would have spent years running errands, picking up pins off the design studio floor. Under Emily, they helmed departments, launched divisions, traveled to far-flung shoots and suppliers and factories. She let them run with ideas that might have died a slow death in a more top-heavy organization. In this, they saw a real kindness, and loyalty—not obvious affection, perhaps, but something even more real. To be clear, the people who offered up many of these anecdotes—the unceremonious Sharpie dot to the throat; the *mallard* mishegoss; Tierney Horne and the slashed Chevignon chinos—saw them as evidence of Emily's toughness, sure, but also of her brilliance. Of the unyielding perfectionism that drove the whole endeavor that was J.Crew.

Emily wasn't the kind of creative director who throws hissy fits and hurls scissors across the atelier—and fashion had plenty of those. She was just highly *specific*. Many believe that, in a company that specialized in basics, Emily's precision—personally inspecting every contact sheet from every photo shoot, magnifying loupe and grease pencil in hand; signing off on not just the colors but the *order of the colors* of every stack of T-shirts they photographed—was the secret sauce. In the world of button-downs and turtleneck sweaters, the collar that's an eighth of an inch slimmer or the sweater that is not just green but rather *mallard* can be the difference between blah and vivid, defined. Memorable.

In truth, most people at J.Crew were a little in awe of Emily. Long before the era of the "unicorn" or the "girl boss," they served a young, female leader who had natural beauty—in an image-based business, great bone structure goes a long way—decisive instincts, and a rare position of creative control, and who was building what was beginning to feel like a true powerhouse. People who worked with Emily in the '80s and '90s now look back through the lens of the 2020s and wonder: Would a man in her job have been expected to be warm, friendly, intimate? Would he have been "mean" just because he pointed out something you'd done wrong, or told it to you straight when an idea was shit, or didn't especially care how your weekend was?

The rules made J.Crew a little like Catholic school. When their stern mother superior walked out of the room, full-grown staffers immediately regressed: they threw on their bangle bracelets, clicked their pens, chomped their gum. "Bad kids" got a little thrill smoking in the back stairwell at 625, or sneaking out of the company Christmas party to do shots at the bar across the street. Every workplace has its thing. Emily and Arthur were theirs.

BY THE CLOSE OF THE '80S, THE FIRST WAVE OF CUSTOMERS WHO had fallen for J.Crew in high school and college were getting jobs, buying homes, having kids. Going to work. J.Crew already owned their weekends. Emily wanted to get her hands on their nine-to-five lives.

She envisioned the company as a one-stop-shop for a creature of the fast-approaching '90s: upscale, career-minded, polished—but still J.Crew, still simple. A creature like Emily herself. She would target this woman with Classics, a new range of tailored jackets, trousers, office sheaths. If Classics went over well, Emily had an even more luxurious and unabashedly pricey range in the pipeline. That one she called Collection.

How to convince people to buy silk blouses and $350 jackets from the catalogue that made their favorite $15 tee? Soon after moving into 625, Emily hired a new photo director, Therese Ryan Mahar, to level up the shoots: hire more prestigious photographers, book models who looked like models, not college coeds. Soon, J.Crew shoots would not by definition include puppies and hay bales; they would be staged on city streets, in photo studios, at train stations, and sidewalk cafés. J.Crew had "arrived" in the city in more ways than one. This was no small transformation. "Emily told me to go for it," says Mahar, who had come from Ford Models. She had an extra phone line installed at her desk for jockeying between model and photo agents, and piled up photographers' portfolios from all over the world. The pace of the shoots seemed to quadruple overnight. By the dawn of the '90s, J.Crew would pound out 124-page editions that were mailed to 3 million households, fourteen times a year. They churned through eight thousand rolls of film *per catalogue.*[4] "It was like going from first gear to fifth, in a Ferrari," Mahar says.

Mahar's first big assignment: find a model for the cover of the Fall 1989 catalogue, which would debut the new Classics range. Aim big—that was Emily's directive. Still, when Mahar told the boss who she had in mind, Emily gave a bemused smile: *Oh, really?*

With her mile-long neck and jutting brows, Linda Evangelista was already a favorite of Chanel's Karl Lagerfeld and Italian *Vogue* snapper Steven Meisel. By 1989, she'd starred in Versace ads. Been photographed by Richard Avedon for Revlon. Even within the exalted ranks of the supermodel, Linda had a special magic. "She was the enigma," says Mahar—a chameleon who shape-shifted so dramatically from one shoot to the next, she couldn't be nailed down. J.Crew might have been leveling up, but Linda? Get real. She was laughably out of their league.

Lands' End and Eddie Bauer probably weren't trying to land Linda Evangelista. Nor were Ann Taylor, Banana Republic, the Limited—all of whom were exponentially bigger and richer and yet, in the retail landscape, the closest thing Emily and Arthur had to direct competitors. The sight of a model who walked the runways of Valentino and Prada on the cover of J.Crew would deliver a wake-up call to the industry: this little catalogue company has more gas in the tank than anybody suspects. If they could get her.

For six months, Mahar pestered Evangelista's agent at Elite, with no luck. Eventually, with the catalogue deadline looming, she bypassed the handler and tracked down Evangelista herself. When Mahar got her on the line, the model was on a yacht off the coast of Ibiza, vacationing with her boyfriend. Of course. After some long-distance pestering, Evangelista gave in, with palpable reluctance. "Probably just to get me off the phone," Mahar recalls with a laugh.

Mahar took that yes to the studio of *Vogue* photographer Arthur Elgort—as big a get for J.Crew as Evangelista herself. Models and photographers tend to present a chicken-and-egg conundrum for brands: top-shelf photographers won't take a job without a big-name model. Big-name models won't sign on without a top-shelf photographer. If Mahar had Linda, she had Elgort.

Indeed, when I reached out to the eighty-one-year-old Elgort at his Hamptons home, the legendary photographer did not hesitate: "Linda is the best model of all."

But *did* J.Crew have Evangelista? A hasty yes from a model on a yacht does not a signed contract make.

Weeks ticked by, as Mahar pestered Elite for that contract, chasing and following up, generally making a nuisance of herself, while also bluffing Elgort's people: *Of course Linda's booked!* J.Crew was just waiting to confirm her exact dates. After a while, bluffing got dicey. Reputations were at stake. Finally, Emily stepped in. She told Mahar to call off the dogs. "It's not going to happen," she said. "Let it go." No way was Mahar letting it go at this point.

At the eleventh hour, word arrived from Elite: the contract was being drawn up. Mahar grabbed a colleague and charged over to collect it in person. On the way, they rehearsed what they'd say if the agent tried to back out last-minute. When they arrived at Elite, a celebration was under way, champagne was flowing, and no one seemed especially interested in contract signing. Mahar cornered the agent: I have a whole team on hold. Let's do this. *Now.*

When the paperwork was finally signed, the two women walked back to J.Crew, skipping and screaming like they'd just won the lottery. Mahar burst into a meeting in Emily's office, something you did not do. "We have Evangelista," she announced. "Signed, locked, and loaded."

In her own hypercontained way, Emily was thrilled. A smile spread across her face. The rest of the team erupted in hoots and high fives. But that smile from Emily: that was the reward.

On the cover of the Fall 1989 issue, Linda Evangelista looks as clean-cut as a prep school boy. Wearing a soft, pale chambray shirt and not a speck of makeup—none visible to the naked eye, at least—she gives a winning J.Crew smile. Everything about this photograph could have been shot in the 2020s; there is not a woman on Earth who would not want that shirt, those cheekbones, that neat, puckish haircut. (Evangelista had just chopped it on set with the legendary Peter Lindbergh. It would soon be iconic as "the Linda.")

How many permutations of this woman had fashion lovers already seen? But this one, somehow, felt like the "real" Linda. Super *and* human. Across the bottom of the cover ran a perfect Arthur-ism: "Now, J.Crew the week round."

For a small player, this was a big flex. "It was confusing to certain people," says Scott Formby. "To take that kind of model and put her in clothing that was not a European fashion house or a Fifth Avenue label? I mean, we felt it." Fashion people are visual learners, and the Linda cover packed exactly the punch J.Crew had hoped for: It made people sit up and take notice of J.Crew's transformation from preppy weekender to legit outfitter of the well-dressed workforce. That cover opened doors that were previously locked: J.Crew would go on to shoot with Christy Turlington, Amber Valetta, Famke Janssen, Elaine Irwin, Inés Sastre. Steven Klein would photograph taunting-eyed blond Tatjana Patitz. And Arthur Elgort would return again and again, photographing his own wife, the model Grethe Barrett Holby, and their kids—including what is, in my estimation, J.Crew's greatest cover ever: a black-and-white photo of their white-blond, bare-bottomed toddler, Warren, on a shaker-shingled beach house, in front of a screen door. That photo is a perfect encapsulation of family, beach, and summer; and it is nothing like a "catalogue" picture. For years, Elgort would shoot the American icon Lauren Hutton for J.Crew. And it all started with Linda: she took them to higher ground.

As for Evangelista, this mythic creature who could have, and wear, anything she wanted—the girl who, the following year, would utter her career-defining line, "We don't wake up for less than $10,000 a day." What did she request at the end of her shoot? The clothes. She kept them all.

CHAPTER 7

Malls of America

By 1989, when Linda Evangelista's $10 million smile forced fashion fans to reconsider the entire value proposition of J.Crew, Arthur and Emily Cinader had taken their "little catalogue that could" from sales of $3 million in 1983 to a reported $160 million. They had a brand with instant name recognition, an aesthetic anyone could spot. But there was no time to pat themselves on the back. With the '90s ushering in a new, hypercompetitive mall culture, J.Crew's exhilarating upward climb was in danger of sputtering out.

In a rare *New York Times* interview, Arthur acknowledged that after six years of "explosive" growth of 25 to 30 percent a year, J.Crew's mail-order business was expected to grow by just 15 percent in 1990.[1] Still the kind of uptick most entrepreneurs would kill for. But not quite *explosive*.

Partly, deceleration was inevitable: By now the initial target market was well and truly tapped. Arthur reckoned every "J.Crew person" in the continental U.S. already got the catalogue: "Wives of investment bankers talk about the latest J.Crew catalogue the way they talk about shopping at Bergdorf's," he boasted. According to the mailman of his own Park Avenue abode, of the 130 families in residence, thirty were already J.Crew customers. "How much more market penetration can you get?"[2]

The impending slowdown was way bigger than J.Crew. Throughout the mid-'80s, the mail-order industry had grown 12 percent or more a year, outpacing any other form of retail three to one. But by '88 it had plateaued, growing by less than 1 percent. That year, Americans received 12.5 billion catalogues—fifty for every man, woman, and child. The shiny booklets that once seemed so exciting had begun to pile up like junk mail. There was more competition for everybody, even overachieving J.Crew: Tweeds, a popular new rival that melded prep with a velvet-leggings Euro vibe, had been founded by none other than Ted Pamperin, with the help of a crew poached largely from J.Crew. And the industry faced new challenges. Just as, a decade earlier, infrastructural progress had aligned to give mail order a major boost, now the opposite was happening: paper costs were up, postal rates had been hiked by almost 30 percent, and some states had tacked new sales taxes onto these thriving mail-order businesses.[3]

When J.Crew launched, catalogues had been *the* thing. But anybody who's ever watched an '80s movie knows that in the ensuing decade, American life revolved around a new playground: the mall. We were living in a material world.

This love affair with the mall was not new, exactly. The indoor shopping mall was born in the '50s, as a radical proposition by architect Victor Gruen, an avant-garde Viennese socialist who envisioned a two-story, interior-facing, climate-controlled space with wings radiating outward from gurgling fountains, and sunlight flooding in from overhead skylights.[4] Gruen's intentions were idealistic; he saw the mall as a solution to the cultural wasteland of suburban sprawl, those eyesore swaths, he once lamented, of "billboards, motels, gas stations, shanties, car lots."[5] He aimed to lure disconnected suburbanites out of their beloved automobiles and into communal gathering places, like the archway-covered shopping arcades of Europe. (In later years, faced with the consumerist revolution he had unwittingly wrought, Gruen would disavow his invention.) Writing for *Esquire* in 1975, Joan Didion marveled at "all those Plazas and Malls and Esplanades. All those Squares and Fairs. All those Towns and Dales, all those Villages, all those Forests and Parks and Lands . . . Toy garden cities in which no one lives but everyone consumes." Malls, she wrote, were "profound equalizers, the perfect fusion of the profit motive and the egalitarian ideal."[6] But by the mid-'70s they had become old-fashioned, dated, she said—like suburbia itself. Surely the mall was on the way out.

Didion must have been shocked, then, when the opposite occurred. In the '80s, the mall went into overdrive, fueled by another "perfect fusion": that of Reagan-era money and the MTV-era notion that you are what you wear. If you've made it this far in our story, you're well aware that clothes had always reflected income level and social ambitions. But in the '80s, clothing became increasingly tribal, a public declaration of your taste in music, your side of the aisle, your place in the crowd. Were you the kind of person who subscribed to *Sassy*—or *Thrasher*? Did you read *The Bonfire of the Vanities*? Or *The Prince of Tides*? What you wore likely offered some indication. It made a new kind of detail matter in a new way. Whether jeans were ripped, pegged, or acid-washed; whether an earring glinted in your left lobe, or your right—it all took on a new significance, especially among teenagers. Youth culture really was a little like a John Hughes movie, subdivided into punks, nerds, and sportos. To say nothing of hip-hop fans, goths, metalheads, ravers, and all of those *new*'s: the New Agers, New Romantics, the nouveau riche. Preps were pervasive in the '80s, but they were also one subculture among many. All of that sorting and classification—assembling the look that aligned you with your chosen people, or at least didn't get you summarily rejected by them—took a lot of shopping.

By the mid-'80s, Americans made seven billion trips a year to shopping centers—some twenty-six thousand of them, mushroomed across the nation. Full of neon signs, teal accent walls, and crowded food courts, these were hubs, hangouts: the place to get your ears pierced, go roller-skating. High schoolers got their first jobs slinging Froyo at the mall. Dads took the kids to see *Indiana Jones and the Last Crusade* at the mall. Perhaps Victor Gruen's original vision was realized, in a way: "Like it or not, the mall offered access to a broader world than flyover country could easily access," author Ian Bogost wrote in the *Atlantic*, in a defense of the now much-maligned institution. "And unlike the Sears catalogue, it did so directly and immediately, live and in person."[7]

To compete in this climate, J.Crew needed stores. *Lots* of stores. For decades, department stores had been the mall's main attraction, the anchor that brought foot traffic to the smaller boutiques. But in the '80s, the department store had already begun its long, slow decline. The name of the game was "specialty-apparel retail" (soon just "specialty retail"), i.e., Gap, Aéropostale, Banana Republic, the Limited, and Benetton. Each had morphed from a modest chain of mostly urban stores into a mall-dominating behemoth, leapfrogging into every medium-size town in America, hawking clothes that were well-made, wearable, and did not cost middle-class shoppers an arm and a leg.

Specialty retail was arguably a child of the '60s, born in Columbus, Ohio. That was where Leslie "Lex" Wexner first envisioned a chain of smart-looking shops that sold a single label—as opposed to the "house of labels" of a department store or other small boutiques—via an operation that was as standardized as fast food. "I looked at all those McDonald's . . . ," Wexner once told a reporter. "I was amazed at their consistency. I thought, 'You can do that in retailing. It doesn't have to be a free-for-all out there.'"[8] He named the Limited for its focus on "separates"—nifty blouses and skirts, rather than dresses. In recent years, Wexner's legacy took a hit after his disastrous association with Jeffrey Epstein was outed, and sexual misconduct accusations within Victoria's Secret came to light. But for decades, he had an enormous influence on how Americans consume: starting in the '70s, he pumped

Limited stores into the malls popping up across the nation, erecting a "vertically integrated" network of manufacturing, design, and sales to cut out the middleman from start to finish. This increased his slice of the profits, but it also gave him exquisite control, for the first time, over both the quality of the product and every beat of his shopper's experience, down to the moment she trotted out the door, Limited bag in hand. Those bags—and the logo they trumpeted—mattered. The very *uniformity* of the Limited created something new to retail and alluring: a chain that was a recognizable, reliable brand. A covetable identity. Millions happily bought into it.

J.Crew, too, had a brand. Arguably a great one. But it was seriously late to the specialty retail party. And while Arthur and Emily were catalogue savants, neither had a whit of experience in stores. At the end of the '80s, J.Crew was still relatively tiny—they were just proud to have escaped New Jersey and landed on two creaky floors in Chelsea. It was family owned, with no major source of outside funding—a flea on the flank of Gap (which had bought Banana Republic and launched Gap Kids) and Limited Brands (by the '80s, parent company of Express, Victoria's Secret, and more). Both were publicly traded corporations with huge workforces, deep executive ranks, and seemingly bottomless funds.

Would J.Crew, the store, even *work*? Just because shoppers like a catalogue doesn't mean they will follow it into stores; one expert I spoke with estimated the odds on a mail-order company successfully transitioning to brick and mortar at fifty-fifty. This feat seemed especially risky for J.Crew. Absent the carefully constructed context of its photos—the touch-football games, the bobbing sailboats—and viewed for the first time under dressing room fluorescents, on the lumpen bods of regular folk, would these chinos and tank tops suffer a sort of Emperor's New Clothes effect: Would people see they weren't so magical after all? "We didn't have the sunny sky, the beach, the ocean," says a former store merchant. "We were the reality."

Arthur was ready to take that risk. The way he explained his rational was very . . . Arthur. "A general is at war," he told a group of employees around this time: He has a cannon, but he isn't sure exactly where his enemy lies, and cannonballs are precious. Does he conserve his resources, knowing he can't be sure he'll hit the target? Or does he fire away, knowing that wherever the cannonball lands, it will eventually bring him closer to his goal?

For once, his point was succinct: Shoot the damn cannon. If you don't, you'll never get anywhere.

For this battle, he needed a new lieutenant. Arnie Cohen was a charismatic young gun, palpably brimming with ambition, plus a little something extra—a kind of eager, wheeler-dealer energy that felt foreign to the understated types who tended to populate J.Crew Land. In this tastefully cool, carefully executed company, Cohen saw a cult brand, idling on the launchpad, ready for liftoff. He was dying to get his hands on it.

In a poetic prep twist, the site Cohen zeroed in on for J.Crew's first store was located mere blocks from the first outpost Brooks Brothers established in 1818. South Street Seaport, a once-grimy wharf on New York's Lower East Side, had just been revamped as a shiny tourist destination. Of course, no self-respecting "real" New Yorker would be caught dead there; the Seaport was basically a middle-American mall clinging like a barnacle to the edge of Manhattan, a long way from anything that could be considered fashion. But it had two things going for it. After work, a surge of suits from nearby Wall Street swept over the area like a human wave. "All these kids coming out of college, going to Wall Street—those were our kids," Cohen says. "We knew we had them." And the Seaport developers were a little desperate. Once again, J.Crew was coming from behind; other mall developers had turned up their noses at the catalogue company that wanted to open stores. The

Seaport was hoping preppy, proud J.Crew would reel in an upscale shopper their renovation had so far failed to impress.

What *was* a J.Crew store? They could have gone literal—parked a Land Rover in the middle of the floor, tacked some shingles to the walls, filled the windows with photos of frolicking youth. Instead they conceived a "library of product": old-money, collegiate, clubby. A little Ralph-esque, if we're being honest. Arthur was not pinching pennies here. The walls were lined with wood paneling, floorboards were pricey quarter-sawn oak, hardware was solid brass. When you turned the knob on a fitting room door, "it had to feel solid, sturdy. Cold to the hand," Cohen says. "As you would expect from J.Crew." He quizzed prospective store managers about their taste in movies and music. There was no right answer, but they had to have *an* answer: He wanted sophisticated, "J.Crew people." New hires were handed a catalogue and told to brush up; they had to be able to talk the talk: *grass*, *moss*, *bottle*. There was a reason for this. Gap was pumping out white-box stores stuffed with logoed sweats at an alarming rate. J.Crew couldn't be bigger. It had to be *better*.

Cohen's bet on the young cubs of Wall Street paid off. On opening day in 1989, the Seaport store was so packed, the fire marshal threatened to shut them down. As Cohen tells it, police brought in stanchions to hold back the crowd. Notably, there was no ceiling on what customers were willing to spend. If a $100 sweater sold out, they'd replace it with a $150 sweater. That sold out, too. They had worried J.Crew's je ne sais quoi would be lost in translation, but they found the opposite was true. The store offered something the catalogue could not: instant gratification. Emily had put so much emphasis on tactility, the "hand" of the clothes, from the beat-up wash of the chinos to the label-free comfort of a T-shirt. In a store, "you could touch it, try it on, see how it fits," says Carol Sharpe, a longtime merchant who joined J.Crew at the opening of its third store. And "you didn't have to wait for it to come to you." Waiting lists sprung up. If one customer happened to return a wool Melton blazer, someone behind her in line would snap it up before it ever made it back to the rack. Sharpe had spent her whole career in stores: "I'd never seen anything like it."

Arthur told reporters that some fifty more J.Crew stores would be coming soon.[9] By the time the Seaport opened, outposts in San Francisco and Costa Mesa, California, were already underway. J.Crew would never have Gap-level billions to fuel expansion. But at least now they had a track record, evidence that J.Crew stores *did* work. By the time Cohen was negotiating for a location in Chestnut Hill, a tony area outside of Boston, he was having very different conversations with mall developers. He had the stats from the Seaport. And, thanks to the catalogue, he knew exactly how many J.Crew customers lived within a ten-mile radius of Chestnut Hill, how many times a year they purchased, how much they spent on average. He could say with certainty that the Chestnut Hill mall was sitting on a J.Crew goldmine: it was minutes from Wellesley, Boston College, Babson College, Pine Manor College, Boston University, Harvard, and MIT—absolutely clogged with expensively educated youth.

Back in Manhattan, Emily's design team did not operate with the Ivy League on the brain. They considered cliché, textbook prep gauche, outdated. Increasingly, their energies were turned to timeless houndstooth miniskirts, silk blouses, well-cut trousers, slouchy linen sweaters. Clothes that didn't scream "preppy." Clothes that didn't scream, period. The Classics range was gradually shifting J.Crew's identity, as intended, and its demo: within a few years, the median age of their customers would rise to thirty-six—older, at that time, than Emily herself. People were as likely to buy a caramel-colored wool overcoat or a perfect pair of pinstripe trousers as a cozy sweater dotted with snowflakes.

Yet even as Emily was steering away from the look (and implications) of pure prep, Arnie Cohen was planting her fine-tuned brand in well-to-do enclaves around the country, and the words *Ivy League* and *preppy* were the bull's-eye of his sales pitch. As Cohen saw it, the collegiate and the to-the-manor-born were their sweet spot, and everybody else—the aspirants, the strivers—radiated out in concentric circles.

CHAPTER 8

California Girls

Less had always been more in Emily's universe. And now, as fashion rounded the corner from the over-the-top '80s into the minimalist '90s, it was as if she had bent the style gods to her will—something her staff would not have put past her. Under her strict orders, J.Crew had waited out fashion's "loud" years as a conscientious objector, refusing to bend to trends, even when her own designers went nuts for them. Every time big, glaring logos or, say, neon swimwear swung back in on the trend merry-go-round, and one of the designers or merchants had the temerity to ask why J.Crew wasn't doing their version, too—why not cash in?—she replied, "But what about the people who *don't* want that?" J.Crew people didn't do sweatshirts that spelled out *J.CREW* in absurd twelve-inch letters, or tennis-ball-green bikinis, thanks. J.Crew people relied on them to provide the tasteful alternative to that nonsense. But at the dawn of a new era, what had been the tasteful alternative *was* the new big thing. More and more women were dressing like Emily Cinader. "Just the way she showed up every day was an object lesson in itself," says a former designer. "I can still see her in my head, the white shirt, the gray trousers, the slightly clunky loafer."

Less seemed to be more everywhere. After a decade of lavish Lacroix bubble skirts and Versace prints, the names on everyone's lips were Helmut Lang, Jil Sander, Martin Margiela—designers who considered black, white, and nude a full color palette, and whose aesthetic had been forged not in the arrondissements of Paris, but in the whitewashed studios of Antwerp.

By the time J.Crew debuted a new outpost in Dallas in 1992, the company had pivoted hard from the clubby "library of product" look of the Seaport store to an aesthetic that had Emily's fingerprints all over it. *Texas Monthly* writer Mimi Swartz described the spare store as solemn, reverent, as if "designed by a Shaker splinter group." It was a world apart from the feel-good warmth of the catalogue, she said: "A chapel of worship for the fashions of the nineties."[1]

Swartz wasn't talking about Helmut Lang here. Nineties minimalism was more than a fashion pivot: recession had struck in the summer of 1990—sparked when Iraq invaded Kuwait, sending oil prices sky high. The dip technically lasted less than a year, but recovery was sluggish. Among other things, this had a cooling effect on J.Crew's heady retail expansion, which would come much more slowly than Arthur initially anticipated.

But it would also have an effect on how people shopped. The fashion of the '90s that Swartz had in mind was the uniform du jour of the middle and upper middle classes: bland khakis and blue buttondowns, the "Brooks Brothers meets L.L.Bean" look peddled in one form or another by everybody from Gap to Banana Republic to J.Crew. It was a uniform fueled by the rise of "Casual Friday"—the slippery slope that ultimately left us where we are today, with all workplace standards of dress lying in a mangled heap—which was itself a side effect of the recession: Casual Friday originated as a way to boost employee morale without spending any money.[2] (Can't afford that cost-of-living bump? Let 'em wear khakis!) Swartz witheringly described the look in question as "survivor wear for diminished expectations and a tightened economy." But the case she made for its timeliness in 1992 was not so different from the reasons Ivy style had been so useful to G.I. Bill strivers of 1950: Clean-cut preppy basics didn't cost a ton, lasted from one year to the next, and as Swartz pointed out, they will forever "evoke good breeding and good taste." Prep had been through ups and downs, but its face value remained intact.

Emily would hardly have considered J.Crew "survivor wear." With Classics in full swing, J.Crew sourced yarns from Loro Piana and Zegna Baruffa, mills Calvin Klein and Ralph Lauren also used. J.Crew manufactured its loafers and smart city boots in the same Italian factories that made designer accessories. Indeed, longtime J.Crew accessories designer John Ascher, who has also logged years at both Calvin and Ralph, asserts that J.Crew's quality in the '90s "was equally good, if not better" than designer.

If Belgian austerity was one side of '90s minimalism, and office-drone khakis were the other—well, J.Crew found itself in a sweet spot between the two. Whether it was economics or simply an evolving notion of what constituted "modernity," even capital-F Fashion creatures found it newly cool to wear a dress that cost 150 bucks, or to pair their Prada skirts with $25 cotton tees. A new, unsentimental concept, "uniform dressing," had emerged; it made sense to minimalists, but also to a new class of time-crunched professionals. Like, say, Emily Cinader. "You had your black jeans, you had your white jeans. Your six T-shirts. The idea was paring down aesthetically," recalls Holly Brubach, a fashion editor at the *New York Times Magazine* in the '90s. Baked into this mentality was a certain pragmatism about price, too. "There was some notion that if you were buying your T-shirt at the Gap as opposed to from Helmut Lang, you were getting the essence of something. It was a reverse snobbery about basics—this idea that you're not a sucker, right?"

Economic woes aside, the zeitgeist had palpably turned in J.Crew's direction. It positioned them to succeed at something that fells many retailers: J.Crew had embodied one era ('80s prep) and would soon embody another ('90s minimalism)—all without a dip in relevance.

THE IRONY OF THIS MOMENT—IN SO MANY WAYS, *EMILY'S* MOMENT—is that right when it dawned, Emily was spending most of her time 3,000 miles away from 625 Sixth Avenue.

Many expected that if Emily ever settled down, it would be with some clean-cut, all-American scion with a very nice sailboat. Someone who looked like the J.Crew guy. Cary Woods, then, presented a real head-scratcher. He was a kid from the Bronx—sound familiar?—who'd made it big in Hollywood, first as an agent at William Morris, then as an executive at Columbia Entertainment. But where Emily was all Ivory-soap looks and rigorous discipline, Woods seemed a little rough around the edges, not conventionally handsome, *not* WASP-y. He dressed in all black. While Emily was circumspect, difficult to read, Woods came across as a smart but freewheeling party guy. "Emily certainly did not marry her father," is how one former colleague outs it, with a chuckle. "Maybe her deep-down psychological rationale was that somebody so different, so wildly outside the mold, would send a message."

Emily had never seemed the "head over heels" type. But soon she was managing a bicoastal life, racing nonstop between J.Crew—and the job that had consumed her since she was twenty-one—and a new existence opening up in Los Angeles. In 1991, she and Woods exchanged vows before a small handful of guests, barefoot on a Caribbean beach at sunset—the bride in a short, silk-crepe tank dress, the groom in a navy linen suit, all by J.Crew, of course. "I'd be happy living *anywhere* with Cary," she said, sounding disconcertingly gushy. "I spend every available second with him."[3]

The team at 625 Sixth recalls an existence ruled by FedEx deadlines. From three time zones away, Emily ceded no control. In the technological Dark Ages, when email was still a novelty and cell phones were the size of bricks, long-distance business was conducted by fax and phone. There was a constant, mad rush to ship Emily Polaroids and fabrics. New stripe designs for the rugbies, still painted by hand, got sliced down the middle—half for Emily, half for their reference in New York. The most terrifying moment of the day came when Emily phoned in and had to be transferred from one department to the next. "If you lost the connection, you were a failure," laughs Sharpe.

For some, this was more than inconvenient. It was dispiriting. Emily had trained them to take every cue from her; her stamp was on everything they did. Her employees dressed like her—hell, a lot of them eerily *looked* like her (some noted an odd preponderance of makeup-free all-American brunettes wafting around the office). As far as they were concerned, Emily *was* J.Crew. Without her, they felt untethered.

In 1990, Emily was in Los Angeles when she got a call from the head of HR, who had just met with a young designer, fresh out of Parsons. Emily was not going to want to miss this one.

The HR director was right: this girl was bright, charismatic, and—at six feet, reed-thin, with long brown hair—striking. Plus, she had just done something rather unorthodox. At twenty-one, with no money to speak of, and no great prospects ahead of her, Jenna Lyons had just turned down a job in high fashion—the kind of job most designers in her position would kill for. She wanted to make relatable clothes for "real" people.

In 1990, there was no more coveted spot for an ambitious young Parsons student than the Seventh Avenue offices of Donna Karan, the personification of female power in fashion. By '92, Karan would be dressing First Lady Hillary Clinton—speaking of personifications of female power!—in her trademark "cold shoulder" gowns for state dinners.

Jenna had spent eight months of her senior year interning for Karan, nestled right in fashion's inner sanctum, standing by while Donna herself (legendarily comfortable in her own skin) stripped down to try on her latest zillion-ply cashmere sample.[4]

But when the company offered Jenna an entry-level job, she declined. She *loved* high fashion, excellent craftsmanship, fine materials—oh, how Jenna Lyons loved these things—but she had learned something about herself: making beautiful things did not, in and of itself, light up the reward circuitry in her brain. She'd grown up on the fringes of wealth, in the not-fancy part of a fancy neighborhood in Palos Verdes, California—in one of the most expensive zip codes in America—supported by a single mother who made her living as a piano teacher. At Rolling Hills High, Jenna knew twin sisters who got matching Maseratis for their Sweet Sixteens. But she had never forgotten a trip to the grocery store in middle school, when she picked up a can of tuna and her mother shook her head: "It's a little expensive, let's not get it this week."[5]

Designing $2,500 Donna Karan jackets "felt very disconnected for me," Jenna told me. "I wanted to work somewhere where I wanted to buy the clothes, my friends wanted to buy the clothes, and even my mom wanted to buy the clothes. That felt exciting to me." (A part of the story that is less often repeated: Jenna once noted that the salary she'd been offered at Donna would have been "like working for free.")

So she walked away from a dream job, collected her diploma, and flew home to her mother in Palos Verdes, jobless, to waitress and figure it out. At the end of the summer, when she'd begun to worry that she'd made a terrible mistake, she got a call from J.Crew.

Plenty of idealistic young designers eager to make their mark on Fashion would have looked down their noses at a catalogue company that sold everyday basics. But Jenna exhibited Emily's favorite quality:

she instinctively got the promise of J.Crew. Indeed, Jenna was living proof of the Linda Evangelista effect on J.Crew's image: in a simple photo of a supermodel in a chambray shirt, Jenna saw the brand's big ambition—but she also saw true *style*: Why shouldn't an everyday T-shirt be sexy and gorgeous?

"They were trying to make something beautiful for people who didn't have millions of dollars. That's why I went to work at J.Crew," she told a crowd, speaking on a panel in Brooklyn in 2018. "Because I wanted to make anyone feel that they were beautiful, and not just people who had lots of money and were stick-skinny."[6]

Emily hired Jenna on the spot. She was to report back to New York posthaste, for the only job they had available: a bottom-rung position designing men's rugbies.

Jenna floated out of the meeting. On the street, she ran to the nearest pay phone and scrounged around for a dime to call her mom. "I got it!" she squealed. "What's the salary?" her mother asked. She had no idea. She'd been too excited to ask.

IT WAS BRUCE WILLIS WHO TALKED EMILY INTO MAKING BOXER-briefs. Chris O'Donnell told her J.Crew ought to make a tuxedo. When Dechen Thurman modeled for the catalogue—barefoot, in a red union suit, on a snowy dock floating on an ice-cold lake—a car was standing by, ready to whisk him off to the Academy Awards so that he wouldn't miss the big moment of his Oscar-nominated sister, Uma—another friend of Emily's, and therefore of J.Crew. When Emily was back in New York, Julia Roberts dropped by to say hi. (She happened to show up on the day there was a fire drill.)

What the heck was going on here? As J.Crew settled into its '90s sweet spot, it was becoming something it had never quite been before—

oddly hip. Yes, they were nailing the look of the time. But this also had to do with Emily, who was now half of a Hollywood/Fashion power couple.

Her new husband was making some of the edgiest, most zeitgeist-y fare of the decade: Woods took a gamble on filmmaker Harmony Korine and Larry Clark's raw NYC skate-rat flick, *Kids*, making stars of Chloë Sevigny and Rosario Dawson; teamed up with Harvey Weinstein—whose epic fall from grace was still a long way off—on the horror spoof *Scream*; fast-forwarded the careers of Vince Vaughn and Jon Favreau with *Swingers*. The Woodses lived in a cool, starkly decorated house in Benedict Canyon, "the only New York loft in Los Angeles,"[7] she called it, with Emily's prized Porsche—painted a custom shade of navy, naturally—parked in the drive. Emily, who had never seemed to find her tribe in New York, was hanging behind the scenes in a new milieu.

J.Crew gone Hollywood? There was no denying that Emily's new proximity to fame sprinkled valuable fairy dust on the brand. And Woods's projects opened a rare portal into the boss's life: Emily talked about his movies more freely than she had ever talked about herself. When he produced the 1993 football classic *Rudy*, the staff got *Rudy* baseball caps and a private screening (Emily, meanwhile, went to the screening of the film at the Clinton White House). But occasionally, she let slip—in a way that didn't always seem inadvertent—that she'd been at Brad Pitt's pool that weekend. Coming from a woman who dropped so few hints about her interior life, it felt odd to be tossed these strange morsels from the lifestyles of the rich and famous. "She would let you know it," recalls a staffer. "It would be dropped: *We were at Julia's*." That was awkward. Bragging seemed so off brand, so . . . *un-Emily*.

According to a high-ranking exec, at some point questions began to arise about whether Emily's head—always screwed on so tight—

had been turned. Was her new scene impairing her judgment about J.Crew?*

Such questions tended to focus on J.Crew Collection. As planned, after Classics hit the bull's-eye, Emily quietly launched a small, pricey women's range that many recall as very much her baby. Collection was made in small quantities and rarely featured in the catalogue, lest its high price point alarm the average customer. It appeared mostly in a handful of stores in moneyed markets. It was helmed by a young designer named Lena Youm, who had been poached from Calvin Klein, and the Calvin imprint was palpable. Collection was trend-proof, luxurious, with a vaguely Katharine Hepburn slant—cuffed flannel trousers, well-cut camel coats. It included pants reportedly cut from the same cloth as Hermès riding breeches.[8] But it was also, in essence, totally in keeping with the ethos of those early, perfected chinos and T-shirts: a piece-by-piece distillation of the ideal wardrobe. Old-school J.Crew employees still get a little misty talking about Collection. The clothes were just *that good,* they say. When I spoke to the writer Holly Brubach, she walked to her closet, phone in hand, and plucked out a leather-trimmed black wool peacoat from the '90s, still perfectly in step today, and checked the label. Yep, J.Crew Collection.

Collection was Emily's day-to-day uniform, worn in her usual subdued way, with clunky loafers and no embellishment other than the discreet flash of a diamond tennis bracelet.

Could J.Crew's little stab at luxury be a modest but influential hit? The idea was not totally out of the question. By the mid-'90s, fashion was no longer the preserve of the .01 percent. Designer names and brands and logos were woven into pop culture as never before, name-checked in movies and TV, documented in a slew of celeb-focused fashion magazines. Regular Joes knew their Marc Jacobs from

---

* In a case of history repeating itself, this criticism would be echoed, times a thousand, when Jenna Lyons revived the high-priced "Collection" range during her reign.

their Tom Ford; ogled Cindy Crawford on *House of Style*; tuned in to watch Kate Moss work it on the *VH1 Fashion Awards*—the "Oscars of fashion," or so it was marketed. With so many hungry new eyeballs tuned in, the fashion business was dividing and replicating like cells in a petri dish, trying to find new entry points to offer a fashion-literate mass consumer. Sub–designer labels like BCBG staged runway shows at New York Fashion Week, just like Calvin and Donna. (Was nothing sacred? In *New York*, one designer waved off these arrivistes as "Kmart Collections."[9]) In response, Oscar de la Renta had a new baby, "Oscar." Isaac Mizrahi birthed "Isaac." Michael Kors launched "Kors." If designer fashion was "bridging" its way to the middle class, why couldn't bourgeois little J.Crew punch its way up?

Or so the thinking went. But if J.Crew creatives were reverent about the sheer beauty of Collection, some on the business side were significantly less devout. As far as they were concerned, the number one priority was growth: J.Crew had a big, bright future as a fast-growing chain of stores, but reaching it would require marshaling all their resources. A quarter of their sales were still to college kids. Viewed from this angle, Collection looked like a distraction. Who was paying $800 for a strapless black evening dress from J.Crew? "I think Collection was Emily's dream. Something she wanted," says a former executive, his effort at diplomacy palpable. Did it make business sense? *Well* . . . "It was questionable, how it really fit in."

Some saw a direct connection between the ambition of Collection and Emily's new social position. Was *she* now the striver, trying hard to fit in with the cool kids—and losing sight of her base? "She wants her friends to buy J.Crew," an employee would later tell the *New York Observer*. "It's impaired her judgment on a few things . . . and has a huge impact on the way she edits the line."[10]

What of Emily's long-held vision of an approachable J.Crew, the club that anyone could join? It was hard to see where that vision fit in with

Collection. A senior exec recalls Emily once musing about a new pair of Collection trousers. "Oh, I have to have Uma try these!" It was one thing to photograph their clothes on a star, another thing entirely to design them *for* a star. In the era of the "influencer" this is hard to imagine, but back then, it wasn't entirely clear why a brand like J.Crew should care if a woman like Uma Thurman—Oscar nominee, magazine cover star, A-lister—liked their pants. Was Emily getting a bit big for her, uh, britches?

CHAPTER 9

Go Big or Go Home

Nineteen ninety-six. A group of architects creep through the basement of a boarded-up, graffiti-splashed building on the corner of Prince and Mercer Streets, smack in the middle of SoHo, a neighborhood still in the process of transitioning—for better or worse—from artists' lofts and galleries to $9 coffee shops and Prada It bags. 99 Prince was a historic building, on a great corner, in a cool neighborhood, and this group was anxiously scanning the walls for anything that said "money pit." Prince Street was a big swing—and J.Crew needed one.

Back in '89, Arthur and Arnie Cohen had proclaimed that J.Crew would have fifty stores by 1994. Two years past that deadline, Cohen was long gone. They had thirty-six stores, but in the specialty retail era, that was small potatoes, mom-and-pop stuff. J.Crew's growth as a brick-and-mortar player had been nothing like its growth as a newbie catalogue. The stores performed well, but had done little to shift perception. J.Crew was still a "catalogue company" that happened to have a handful of stores, including, as the business pub *Crain's* noted, "a nondescript site in Manhattan's sleepy South Street Seaport." Ouch.

J.Crew had never quite reached the longed-for tipping point at which one store begat the next, when growth would begin to self-fund. Instead, each new location took a boatload of cash, and a major commitment: three- to five-year leases in a mall, ten years for a store on the street. And each new store took at least a year to turn a profit.

The early '90s recession was part of the problem. But the trademark Cinader perfectionism did not help. It had taken three and a half years for Arnie Cohen to find the right spot for a store in the preppy haven of Westport, Connecticut. When he finally did, the space needed a frame-up restoration. One day, well into the project, Arthur dropped by to check on their progress. He fixated on a single column that was sixteen inches off-center. Refabricating the steel beam would cost thousands and delay construction by weeks. "Arthur, I'm bringing this project in on time, on plan," Cohen protested. But Arthur stood firm. Customers might not *see* that the column was off, but they would feel it, and it would be wrong. "We don't do wrong," he said. Period.

Nearly thirty years later, Cohen offered up this anecdote fondly, an illustration of the fastidiousness Arthur instilled in him. "I loved the guy," he says. But colleagues say Cohen was often stymied by the Cinaders. Emily refused to cut any corner, or to produce a single item that didn't live up to her standards, even if it would have sold like hotcakes. And Arthur had been known to treat his own retail division—the supposed engine of his company's growth—as an ugly stepchild. He fretted about what he called the "parasitism" of the stores stealing business from the mail-order side. Cohen "had to fight that tooth and nail," says his colleague Carol Sharpe. "It's not an encouraging mentality."

Exhausted and, perhaps, fallen out of favor, Cohen had left the company in 1993, and over the next few years the necessity of retail growth only became more critical. A spike in paper costs by as much as 40 percent sliced deep into catalogue profits. And competition was fiercer than ever: at Gap Inc., the new kid, Old Navy, had become a billion-dollar brand overnight, pumping out new stores by the day. Banana Republic was pushing a new citified street-casual look that, to the menswear department of J.Crew, hit a little too close to home. Over at

Limited Brands, Les Wexner had hired Mike Jeffries to execute a ballsy redo of his latest acquisition, Abercrombie & Fitch (founded in 1892, and purchased by Wexner out of bankruptcy almost exactly a century later, in 1988). Now Jeffries, too, served up a version of prep, his aimed laser-sharp at frat boys and sorority girls and their younger siblings. He cranked the store music and covered the windows so passersby couldn't peer in, creating a clublike ambience, posting shirtless, young (almost exclusively white) hunks—their logoed boxers peeking out from low-slung jeans—as sentries at the door. It was the touch-football life, with a strong undercurrent of underage sex, all photographed in black-and-white pinup shots by none other than Bruce Weber. Jeffries once infamously detailed his target market in *Salon*: "In every school there are the cool and popular kids, and then there are the not-so-cool kids," he said. "Candidly, we go after the cool kids. We go after the attractive all-American kid with a great attitude and a lot of friends. A lot of people don't belong [in our clothes], and they can't belong. Are we exclusionary? Absolutely."[1] This philosophy—and countless other missteps—would come back to bite him, a situation dissected in *White Hot: The Rise & Fall of Abercrombie & Fitch*, the 2022 documentary about its downfall. But in the mid- to late '90s Abercrombie ruled the mall, hitting J.Crew menswear hard, just as some classics—now relegated to the status of old standards—were starting to "down-trend," as it is euphemistically put. Generation Abercrombie was not swayed by crisp J.Crew anoraks. They wanted logoed sweatshirts, not cozy rollnecks. J.Crew had been early to pre-age T-shirts and chinos. But now Abercrombie—and its many followers—were distressing every item in their wardrobe.

If Abercrombie was going low, catering to horny teens and the adults who still longed to look like them, Emily was determined to go high. "We're building a mini-Barneys, Dave," she liked to remind Dave DeMattei, the president of retail she hired in 1995—the guy who, by the following year, was creeping around the basement of a building on

Prince Street. In what seemed like a meaningful shift, DeMattei reported directly to Emily, not her father. Emily was the one setting their lofty goals: she wanted DeMattei to open fifteen new stores a year, for a total of one hundred by the year 2000. The most important of these was Prince Street, a real New York flagship. A store with the potential to do for J.Crew retail what the Evangelista cover had done for the catalogue, seven years earlier: make the gatekeepers of style, trotting up and down the streets of SoHo, sit up and take notice.

SoHo wasn't the only frontier J.Crew was attempting to conquer. In '96, a twenty-year-old college dropout named Brian Sugar got the bright idea that the brave new world of online shopping was especially well suited to mail-order companies, which already had everything they needed to thrive on it: the photography, the merch, the order-fulfillment infrastructure. As Sugar saw it, for a company like J.Crew, going online was simply the logical next step.

Sugar was just a kid. He had no fashion experience or industry contacts, but he *had* sold an early web browser he had designed with some buddies. In his free time, he started mocking up sites for Lands' End, L.L.Bean, and J.Crew. He saved them to CD-ROMs marked with his name and phone number, and mailed them off to the companies. A few months later, having heard nothing back, Sugar was idly wondering if it might be time to reenroll in college when he got a call from someone named Arthur Cinader Jr., from the headquarters of J.Crew in New York: the company had just fired its C.I.O., and in the guy's desk drawer, they found Brian Sugar's CD-ROM. It held "exactly the vision we're looking for at J.Crew.com."

Arthur Cinader Jr. first popped up around the offices of J.Crew a few years earlier, fresh out of college. He was smart, a little geeky, and trim like his father, with a prep-school-kid look offset by prematurely balding hair. He did not make a splash. His eldest sister's tastes had been shaping J.Crew since before she even worked there. But Arthur Jr. arrived at a well-established company. Those who bothered to give the youngest Cinader any thought—and many did not—considered him a classic case of the boss's son. He seemed a bit lost. "In this dynamic family of very strong personalities, he was trying to find his way," says a former colleague. "He was young and in a really tough spot."

What most people didn't realize, or appreciate at the time, was that the youngest Cinader *did* have a sense of purpose. It just happened to be on a side of the business that fashion people tended to think very little about: tech.

In 1994, *Money* magazine explained how to shop this wild new thing, the "computer store." All you had to do was "click on a box next to the desired gift, type in payment information and the shipping address and then hit a 'Submit Order' button."[2]

By then, one in three American adults considered their personal computer "indispensable."[3] We relied on email, but whatever lay outside the familiar confines of "you've got mail" was still alien and, for many, alienating. *Cyberspace* was a shadowy zone riddled with legitimate risks, not least of which was sex, said to be whizzing around the information superhighway unchecked. "Cyberporn" was a hot topic among parents and on the floor of the U.S. Senate.[4]

"The new news," wrote the fledgling novelist MacKenzie Scott (then Bezos) to her mentor, Toni Morrison, in 1995, was that MacKenzie and her husband, Jeff, had moved to Seattle and started a business selling books on the internet. "Our customers can browse an electronic catalogue of 1.4 million titles by author, title, subject, and keywords and place orders via computer."[5] They shipped Amazon's first order out of their converted garage that year, reportedly for a book called *Fluid Concepts and Creative Analogies*. Which tells you what kind of person shopped "the net" in 1995.

Lawrence Lee, the onetime Popular Club Plan marketing exec who worked for Arthur in the '80s, was by then managing direct mail for Barnes & Noble, which was in a pitched battle with Borders (RIP) for superstore dominance. Back then *those* stores were the ones ganging up on independent bookshops across the country. Lee still remembers the day the C.E.O. of Barnes & Noble asked him, "What do you think of this guy out in Seattle, creating an online bookstore?" Lee's response: How could any new bit player catch up with the mighty Barnes & Noble? Plus, how could you sell *books* online? Bookstores had to hire employees who had deep knowledge—people who had known a lot about books, for a long time. "I said, *meh*," Lee recalls now, with a rueful chuckle. "Let's focus on the superstore expansion."

There was a similar attitude in the ranks of J.Crew: Why would anyone buy *clothes* online? Fashion companies were still an analog world. At J.Crew, catalogue pagination and store planning were still worked out on oversize white foam core boards, pinned with dozens of tiny hand-inked technical drawings, like little paper dolls. Jenna Lyons remembers spending her days like the rest of them, doing deeply unglamorous busywork: phone calls with button vendors, lengthy handwritten faxes to far-flung factories. Sketching on paper. Not until the mid-'90s did everyone have a computer on their desks. And nobody said: *This is ridiculous! There's got to be a better way.* This was just how it was done.

Most could not imagine their customer going online, punching in her credit card number—what if some hacker stole it?!—and pressing "Submit Order." And then, what, crossing her fingers that the request had actually landed somewhere and she'd get what she ordered . . . someday?

By the time Brian Sugar arrived, Arthur Jr. and an intern had put up a starter site—really just a landing page. Customers could request a catalogue, or type an item code into a little box to place an order. It had limited ability to search, or to filter items by category. And it shut down for ten to twelve hours a night. But it was a start.

With Sugar building 2.0, there were existential questions to answer. This was not unlike the challenge Arnie Cohen and Arthur Sr. had grappled with years earlier, opening the first stores: How did you bring the aspirational J.Crew vibe into a new dimension—in this case, one distinctly lacking charm and warmth? What *was* J.Crew.com? A store? Or a version of the catalogue—that is, a linear read, with pages that flipped from beginning to end—that somehow lived online? And what did you even call the thing: www.jcrew.com, or just jcrew.com? (They went with the latter, following the lead of the *Wall Street Journal*, which had just put up its first site.)

For eight months, Sugar spent every waking hour on the site. He was racing the competition. L.L.Bean was one of the few catalogues that already had an "internet page." But Sugar had learned that at Gap's San Francisco HQ a woman named Aileen Lee—now the Silicon Valley rock star behind V.C. firm Cowboy Ventures—was leading the charge to launch gap.com. "Aileen Lee was my nemesis," he jokes.

In the hallways of J.Crew, this endeavor was viewed as either a wacky science project or a territorial threat. There was already internal jousting between stores and catalogue. If a website did take off, whose business would it eat into? "I remember the conversation," says merchant Carol Sharpe. "What are they gonna do—are they gonna type? Are they gonna call? Are they gonna walk? Or was the same person doing all three?"

MEANWHILE, ON PRINCE STREET, DAVE DEMATTEI WAS ROMANCING André Balazs, the insider's insider who owned the storied Hollywood hangout Chateau Marmont. For years, Balazs had been making noises about turning 99 Prince into SoHo's first boutique hotel, a newish concept at the time. He needed a retailer for the ground floor, both to shore up financing and to help lure the "right" people to a part of town that was not yet their natural habitat. Did J.Crew fit the bill? Balazs was skeptical.

It wasn't a matter of recognition. By now everybody knew J.Crew, and what it implied. On nascent online dating sites, potential mates were described as "very J.Crew."[6] David Letterman referenced the company's color names on one of his legendary Top 10 lists. Years of describing a no-frills canvas jacket as equally suited to "fly casting in waders" and "placing a bid at Christie's," and proclaiming that a pair of low boots could take you from "Park Ave. to Patagonia," was paying cultural dividends: In the *New Yorker*, to Arthur's delight, cartoonist Roz Chast riffed on T. S. Eliot's stream-of-consciousness poem *The Love Song of J. Alfred Prufrock.* "The Love Song of J. Alfred Crew" featured a pair of middle-aged schlubs conversing in angsty J.Crew-ese. "I grow old . . . I grow old . . . I shall wear the bottoms of my relaxed-fit, button-fly, size-38, in Wheat, trousers rolled." (This was one of at least three *New Yorker* cartoons riffing on the company that ran in the '90s.)

In 1995, there were two different ambitious J.Crew spoofs. One was a full-size glossy mag generated by students at Middlebury College—J.Crew territory if ever there was one. Title: *J.Crewd.* It zeroed in the signature heavily layered styling with a "nine-in-one" layered look, from an anorak down to T-shirt: "Are you fat? Try on a three piece. Like to sweat? Then go for the bulk."[7]

Then, from the dark wizards of *Spy*, came "Crew," a multipage parody that gave the J.Crew treatment to the gold chains and boxy flannels of what it called the "gangsta" look—for instance: $24 "bad-boy crewnecks" in shades of Bloods, asphalt, crack, and Dorito. *The Crew Flak Jacket. Practical? Oh, yes. It can fend off winter winds or hot 9mm slugs.*[8] Culturally insensitive? Deeply. But today, what jumps out about both renditions is J.Crew's language—visual and verbal. Both spoofs copy it to a T: the products arrayed on clean white backgrounds, the stacks of multicolored merch, the arch copy. Even taken wildly out of context, that look and tone could only refer to one company, J.Crew. It wasn't just that the zeitgeist had spun in the direction of J.Crew—the company was part of the zeitgeist.

With that prominence came new scrutiny. "If you dropped dead tonight and were reborn in a mail order catalogue, you'd say, 'Please Lord, let it be J.Crew,' " wrote *Village Voice* cultural critic Lisa Jones in an essay titled, "1-800-WASP."[9] The J.Crew aesthetic was "not as strait-laced Yankee as L.L. Bean, but urbanely WASP (more a state of dress, a wallet size, than a rigid racial criterion)," said Jones. "Even Afrocentric iconoclast-bohéme-girl writers hunger for some version of it." As Jones saw it, what J.Crew sold was nearly universally appealing: the company had an opportunity to sell to everyone. But it "oozes Anglo out of every 100 percent cotton pore"—and was doing little to counteract that fact. Yes, there were Black models in the catalogue, more than many of the catalogues of the day, but still not a lot: four, in the issue Jones happened to analyze. The bigger problem was that J.Crew operated in a world of assumed whiteness. Of course, it was hardly alone in this. Jones cited a study of "minorities" in magazine ads and mail-order catalogues from New York's Department of Consumer Affairs; of 157 catalogues reviewed, less than 5 percent of the 22,685 models featured were Black, "despite the fact that Blacks buy from catalogues at nearly the same rate as whites."

Working on this book right around the height of the Black Lives Matter protests of 2020, I happened to interview a J.Crew stylist from the '90s on Zoom. The woman visibly cringed, remembering that "so J.Crew" was a joking way to describe someone who was not just white but, like, *super*white. Which is, of course, what spoofs like *Spy*'s "Crew" were jabbing at, too. It would be unfair to hold a brand of the '80s and '90s to the cultural standards of the 2020s. But like many of us, this stylist had spent a lot of 2020 rethinking old assumptions, and regretting the fact that while nobody at J.Crew had *liked* this fact about their image—to be clear, superwhite was never something they wanted to be, and in the '90s, Emily's ideas of beauty were arguably more progressive than most of her competitors'—it did not occur to them to actively change it, either. In those days, brands did not "get political," or choose sides; the safest place was out of the fray. "We don't do race-oriented marketing," a J.Crew operative lamely told Jones. "We try to make the product available to everyone." Sadly, Jones's essay did not appear to deliver a wakeup call. J.Crew stayed J.Crew: quietly, cautiously on the sidelines, safe within the slice of the cultural pie that it did serve.

At the time, their bigger concern: Was that slice chic enough to woo *the* André Balazs? Emily and DeMattei invited him to the office to see a mockup of their "mini-Barneys," conceived as a small department store with separate areas for men's, women's, weekend, workwear, and a discreet entrance for the "Collection" room—or rather, *chamber*: a few spare rods displaying clothes as self-seriously as any minimalist temple on Madison Avenue. Balazs was sold. It wasn't surprising: what he was really witnessing was the most aspirational version of J.Crew, Emily Woods herself. If her customer was anything like her, Balazs's location would be all set.

How is it that glossy magazines were not crawling all over Emily, thirty-five years old and already vice chairman of the J.Crew Group? In the heyday of the working woman, she checked all the boxes, both superficial (young, gorgeous, connected, married to a big-time Hollywood producer) and substantial (powerful, talented, female). Emily was the lodestar within the walls of J.Crew, but outside of it—save a handful of interviews here and there over the years—she remained virtually unknown. In 1996, with 99 Prince set to open and a proper website about to launch, J.Crew was on the verge of being what everyone in the business was suddenly talking about, a multichannel "omniretailer," with stores, mail order, and the web. It was time for J.Crew to really sell itself. Or rather, *herself*. Not just in the catalogue, but in the press. What ambitious American woman would not buy into Emily Woods?

There was one problem: Emily fundamentally did not believe that J.Crew should have a "face." To her, that was an advantage it had over a Ralph Lauren or even a Calvin Klein. It wasn't about one person's fabulous life. And anyway Emily hated press. Like her father, she wasn't built to be a public-facing person. Journalists tended to pick up on her chilliness. According to an early catalogue staffer, Emily had hated a 1988 story in *Manhattan, inc.* so much, all copies of the issue had been hidden from view in the office. Even a glowing 1991 puff piece in *Mirabella* had acknowledged her reputation for being "difficult" and "demanding."[10]

But by 1996, either because duty called, or because she had spent enough time in the cocktail shaker of Hollywood to acclimate to the idea of self-promotion, Emily was ready to submit to what was, by her standards, a barrage of press. Which is not to say she stopped scrutinizing offers with her usual zeal. When *Esquire* offered to send the respected photographer Michel Comte to photograph her for the magazine's annual "Women of the Year" issue, she put J.Crew's model booker, Gayle Spannaus, on reconnaissance. Spannaus got Comte's studio manager on the phone. Someone at the magazine had read that Emily loved Katharine Hepburn, who loved to garden. Ergo, they were thinking: Emily in a garden, wearing overalls and a big hat, maybe holding some gardening shears? Spannaus almost laughed out loud. "Okay, absolutely not," she said. "That will never happen." Here's the deal, she told them: Emily will wear what Emily wants to wear. Probably a white shirt or a cashmere sweater, hair straight, no makeup.

Much to the surprise of everybody at J.Crew, what *Esquire* got was a hell of a lot better than a woman weeding her vegetable patch. Emily, after all, had once been a model herself, and it showed.[11] In the layout—opposite a photo of Kristin Scott Thomas, Oscar contender for that year's *The English Patient,* Emily was positively scorching: hair mussed, dark shirt open to the navel, one leg pretzeled into a yogi position. GQ credited her with "redesigning the American uniform," and quoted her pal Brad Pitt: "I love Em . . . she's great to hang out with, great style, very laid back." (Back at the office they weren't sure what was more surreal: the bra-free sensuality of the photo, the use of the term *laid back*, or the diminutive. *Em?!*)

But it was *Harper's Bazaar* that gave Emily her due. Art director Fabien Baron and editor Liz Tilberis—a dream team, even by Emily's standards—agreed to photograph several pages of models wearing J.Crew Collection. For Emily's portrait, they dispatched Patrick Demarchelier himself. In his black-and-white shot, taken at her apartment, Emily is a quiet paragon of a late-'90s female power, someone Sandra Bullock might play in a movie, her dark hair tucked casually behind one ear, her black ribbed sweater and wool pants chicly nondescript. The whole outfit cost less than $350. "Who do I wear besides J.Crew?" Emily told writer Alix Browne. "Nothing." She made a compelling case.[12]

Bazaar also caught the message J.Crew wanted to impart. Emily wasn't the "daughter of"; she was the one running the show. The torch was being passed. "The real story of J.Crew," wrote Browne, "is the story of Emily Woods."

CHAPTER 10

Five . . . Four . . . Three . . . Two . . . ONE

In the summer of 1997, Arthur, Emily, and a SWAT team of J.Crew execs zigzagged on flights across the country, taking a series of meetings that most people back at the office had no idea about—and that would forever alter the fate of J.Crew. Everything they had worked to achieve for fourteen years, and especially over the previous eighteen months—the opening of a head-turning New York flagship, the launch of an ahead-of-its-game website, the burst of media drawing a spotlight on Emily—had come to this: finding the highest bidder for a majority stake in J.Crew.

Annual sales were up to $808 million. J.Crew produced seventeen catalogues a year, going to 4 million homes, generating fifty thousand orders annually.[1] In the predawn of the internet era, they were, in business-page parlance, a "multi-channel brand-centric retailer"—the coin of the realm. And J.Crew had pulled off a feat that was critical to retail analyst types: it had leapt from '80s prep to '90s minimalism without missing a beat or alienating its customer. Its DNA was malleable enough to stay relevant, no matter what cultural curveball came next.

Arthur and Emily had made it this far—no mean feat—the old-fashioned way. That is, with blood, sweat, and (ahem) family money. Today we'd describe J.Crew as admirably bootstrapped. But while its early growth had been magical—and its place in the culture was secure—J.Crew had spent the better part of the '90s burnishing the brand, yet never quite managing to jump into the fast lane. In 1997, they had forty-eight stores. Banana Republic—a small chain when it was taken over by Gap in 1983, the same year J.Crew launched—had zoomed up to 226. Eddie Bauer and Victoria's Secret had 385 and 737, respectively. To compete, J.Crew would have to open ten, twenty, thirty stores a year. That would take the kind of financial firepower that a bootstrapped company with modest profits doesn't have. And, perhaps, a style of aggressive real estate wheeling and dealing that a pair of founders whose hearts lie in catalogue pages don't possess, either.

Plus, with Arthur approaching seventy, he needed a succession plan. His original shareholders—mostly family members, also in their golden years—were ready for their long-awaited windfall. Emily was the obvious choice to take the throne, but she didn't have the kind of cash it would take to buy out her father and his investors. The only way she could take over, and Arthur could exit, was by selling a chunk of J.Crew to the right buyer. "Right" meaning one was willing to pay up, but also to preserve their vision for J.Crew's glorious future—with Emily firmly at its helm.

That summer's investor meetings were like speed dates: at each stop, the J.Crew delegation would buy breakfast for a group of suits and proceed to sell them, point by point, on the world of J.Crew. Its cult status, its legions of adoring fans, its business model and earnings. Finance bros were less interested in the gestalt than in the potential payout. Could J.Crew scale—could it grow large enough to be taken public in an I.P.O. that would pay back their investment many times over? The number one question at every stop: *How big can J.Crew get?*

There was the rub. The Cinaders believed J.Crew had the potential to join the ranks of major players, right up there with Nike, Calvin Klein, Gap. But any investor scrutinizing the balance sheet could see at a glance J.Crew's dirty secret: On some level, the company had never quite been what it seemed. It *appeared* to be a major hit of the '90s, a golden brand that radiated prosperity. But as one retail veteran put it to me with a shrug, "Yeah, but they didn't make any money."

Sales of $808 million was nothing to sneeze at. But that money largely went back into the company. New "mini-Barneys," as sleek as if "designed by a Shaker splinter group"; a new website that had *just* beaten Aileen Lee's Gap site across the finish line; thirty prototypes to achieve that single, perfect new belt; monastically perfect Collection coats; shoots with fifteen models and three sailboats, bobbing along in the crystalline water of St. Barts; iconic American models (Lauren Hutton) and *Vogue* photographers (Arthur Elgort); fresh flowers in every store: it took big bucks to build that shiny J.Crew brand. Arthur and Emily had invested heavily in the golden halo that now encircled J.Crew, and it worked. But it also meant that the company cleared just $14 million in 1992. By '96 that had sunk to $12.5 million.[2]

On top of that, any investor who did their due diligence would not have had to dig deep to find the brand's HR issues. The company founder, after all, was prone to calling executives "goony birds." (Arthur once helpfully explained his go-to insult: "A goony bird is a bird that flies in decreasing concentric circles. Until it flies up its own ass!") This was no great secret: when a company spits out one executive after another, people tend to notice. J.Crew had shed Arnie Cohen, then head of retail Gary Sheinbaum, and now another C.E.O., Robert Bernard, had resigned days before the opening of the Prince Street store. It was also well known that J.Crew had come close to an investment deal before, with Bahrain-based Investcorp, which had stakes in Saks Fifth Avenue and Gucci. When that deal was shelved, it was reportedly because of J.Crew's "problems with management."[3]

They could have tried to sell a majority stake to a "strategic partner"—a parent corp, like Limited Brands or Gap Inc., which would have the in-house engine to power their long-awaited growth spurt.

Indeed, L.L.Bean and a couple of Japanese corporations had come in and kicked the tires, checked out the company financials. But a deal never materialized and, in truth, a strategic partner was a worrisome option: if J.Crew were absorbed into a large corporate stable, it was only a matter of time till the value of those fresh flowers and supermodels was called into question—why did a mass brand need that high-price gloss?—and corners got cut, making J.Crew less . . . J.Crew.

No, what Emily and Arthur were after was an investment firm. Someone to buy a chunk of the company, help them run it more efficiently, grow it fast—and then take it public, making back their investment (and Emily's, as a part owner) many times over.

Sounds simple enough, right? But J.Crew's on-again, off-again relationship with the venture capital firm Texas Pacific Group would prove to be longer and more convoluted than a Hollywood love story. T.P.G. came to Emily through a buddy of Cary Woods, a young gun in private equity named Tope Lawani,* who had heard Emily was looking for a way to buy J.Crew from her father—"she was interested in getting out from underneath his shadow," Lawani has said.[4] Emily once noted that the first time she set foot in T.P.G.'s San Francisco offices, with their airy light and blond wood floors, she felt a little zing of synergy. This place felt a bit like a J.Crew store!

Today, T.P.G. is among the biggest, most established firms in the V.C. world. But in 1997, it was a small, emerging firm said to be led by investors of a different stripe. Not unlike J.Crew itself, T.P.G. had a renown that exceeded its size, mostly due to founding partners David Bonderman and James Coulter, who met as investment advisors to billionaire Texas oil man Robert Bass and made their first big bet together in 1992, plunging $64 million into a Hail Mary on Continental Airlines. Then on its second bankruptcy in a decade and mired in a lengthy la-

* Now managing partner of Helios Investment Partners, the largest private equity firm in Africa.

bor dispute, Continental was "the least-admired company in America," Coulter once said,[5] and T.P.G. had taken it on at the worst possible time, when the economy was still digging its way out of the early-'90s recession. But T.P.G. was the only investor who showed up with enough capital to restructure an airline. It seemed crazy at the time, but the bet on Continental ultimately earned more than $600 million. "The very roots of our business were based on taking on problems that other people had perhaps seen but not been willing to take on," Coulter said. They called their approach "cautious contrarianism." They were into fixer-uppers—unafraid to take on industries in flux. As one reporter put it, the firm "thrive[d] by buying businesses no one else wants."[6]

But if T.P.G. was believed to be different from the standard "barbarians at the gate," that was also due to David Bonderman himself, who had a certain personal mystique.[7] "Bondo," as he was known, had once toiled in the Civil Rights Division of the Justice Department; studied Islamic law in Tunis and Cairo[8]; and in the '70s successfully argued before the Supreme Court to halt a wrecking ball poised to demolish the Beaux Arts facade of New York City's Grand Central Terminal. He made swashbuckling deals, but almost never spoke to reporters, who were left to draw their conclusions from his wardrobe choices (bright argyle socks that tended to fall down around his ankles[9]) and tales of the rock 'n' roll bashes he threw. Point is: The T.P.G. guys didn't look or feel like the standard Wall Street stuffed suits, and they weren't afraid of a company that had certain . . . complexities. Maybe they'd appreciate the nuances that made J.Crew tick?

T.P.G. was saying all the right things: It respected the J.Crew DNA. It wanted to keep Emily right where she was. It would simply pump in working capital and its own "operational value add"—that is, its financial SWAT team, which would come in, pop the hood, inspect the engine, and tell J.Crew exactly what it needed to repair to run more smoothly. And drive fast.

And, to borrow a line from *Jerry Maguire* (a recent hit), T.P.G. was about to *show them the money!* In a leveraged buyout, T.P.G. would buy a majority stake for $560 million.[10] The number to watch in a leveraged buyout is EBITDA, aka earnings before interest, taxes, depreciation, and amortization. It's a measure of cash flow that gauges a company's profitability, separate from the heavy debt J.Crew would take on in an LBO (more on that later). T.P.G.'s offer valued J.Crew at almost ten times EBITDA. This was generous; it arguably bordered on overvaluation. Such was the promise T.P.G. saw in J.Crew.

T.P.G. figured that it could boost J.Crew's annual revenue up $1.3 billion by 2000—enough to take the company public.[11] If all went according to plan, its big payday would be just four years away.

WITH A DEAL PENDING, ARTHUR ASKED MATT RUBEL—THE E.V.P. of the J.Crew Group and a member of Arthur's trusted inner circle, then based at the Popular Club offices in Garfield—to come into Manhattan for a meeting at J.Crew. Rubel didn't think much of it at the time, but when he arrived, he thought, *What am I doing here?*

At the table sat Arthur and Emily, with Marianne Ruggiero, J.Crew's HR director, and Dick Boyce, the founder of T.P.G.'s new Operations Group—the man leading T.P.G.'s fixer-upper effort at J.Crew. The question on the table: could T.P.G. start the search for a new J.Crew C.E.O., whose appointment would be announced soon after the deal closed? This had nothing to do with Matt Rubel. Eventually he surmised, "I was there to be Arthur's flank."

Dick Boyce was ready to start the search. Arthur was not. Arthur Cinader, the man who could see twenty angles on even the simplest issue, saw two thousand on this one. What if the deal blew up? Anything could happen. Rubel recalls, "He was not going to budge until the money had transferred."

But in a rare moment of visible discord between the Cinaders, Emily disagreed. She was with Boyce on this one. She was ready to start the search now.

In the upper echelons of J.Crew, some wondered if this was a long-simmering debate. Arthur, true to form, had been tormented throughout the dealmaking process. Occasionally, as it dragged on, he would come out to Rubel's house in Greenwich and spitball: What if he didn't sell the company after all? What then? Arthur did not like to feel boxed in. "He didn't want to be put in a position where he felt he *had* to [sell]," Rubel recalls.

But another former executive recalls a meeting years earlier that Emily and Cary Woods had set up with a V.C. firm, at which Arthur was not present. The arrangement under discussion—much like the one underway with T.P.G. in 1997—would have positioned Emily to buy out her father and take over. When the team returned to the office, Arthur asked this executive how it went. He appeared to have no knowledge of the dealmaking. "I chose not to tell him that this was what his family was cooking up," recalls the exec. He got the distinct impression that Emily was angling for a deal. Arthur, not so much. (Emily denies taking meetings about a possible sale without Arthur's knowledge.)

By the late '90s, though, if Emily was ready to run J.Crew without Arthur's interference, nobody would have blamed her. Emily ran cool, but she could be protective: The merchants, designers, and catalogue creatives who reported to her were rarely subject to Arthur's fits of pique. "She filtered the rest of the organization from him," says a longtime confidant who long suspected that behind closed doors, Emily absorbed quite a bit of Arthur's ire. Close watchers believed you could tell by Emily's mood if she'd recently had a run-in with her father. If she was short or explosive, "it could have been the stress of the business," the employee says. "But I think most of it was from Arthur." Says another observer, "I think she felt supported [by her father] at times. But also stultified, held back."

All this was conjecture, theory. What really went on between Arthur and Emily invariably happened offstage. But every person at J.Crew was a fly on the wall of the Cinader family dynamic. Rubel believes that Emily's diffidence, her siloed management style—dealing only with a handful of close recruits, keeping everyone else at bay—were shaped by her upbringing. "I think she grew up learning that it was better to hold your counsel than to speak too much, because Arthur was so precise," he says. "You had to be very thoughtful in when, and how, you could talk."

This meeting was the rare occasion where it was apparent Arthur and Emily were approaching the T.P.G. deal—and possibly the future of J.Crew—from different positions.

In the conference room, the conversation with Boyce quickly got heated. Arthur put his foot down. T.P.G. could put in a C.E.O. after it owned J.Crew—not before.

A DEAL ALMOST NEVER HAPPENED. BY FALL, J.CREW AND T.P.G. had at last made it to final talks when the third-quarter numbers came in. J.Crew had already taken a hit that August, when UPS shut down. In the strike of a generation, 185,000 workers walked off the job. *Armageddon*, the *Wall Street Journal* editorial board called it.[12] On the evening news, Americans saw picket lines across the country, and mountains of packages stuck on loading docks, going exactly nowhere. Who would order something from a catalogue if you had no idea when it would arrive? J.Crew lost nearly $9 million in revenue on the strike alone.[13] And that wasn't all: The Fall 1997 catalogue had *dud* written all over it. In September, same-store sales dropped nearly 14 percent. The sudden drop—though it was partially outside of J.Crew's control—was almost enough to scuttle the deal.

J.Crew was getting its first taste of the tricky relationship between fashion and corporate finance. V.C. firms invest in companies for their cash flow: any dip in that cash flow is a potential deal killer. But fashion, by definition, dips. A collection is off. Trends swerve. The back-to-school season turns out to be unseasonably warm, and nobody wants the thick wool sweaters you invested heavily in. Point is: Shit happens. Profits are inconsistent. Plus, as the *New York Times* would soon note, rather pointedly, in a story about the J.Crew deal—fashion companies can be hard for finance types to whip into shape: their "quirky management teams are known to micromanage down to the last buttonhole, and high-strung corporate cultures can get in the way of managing profit growth."[14]

Over just a few weeks, J.Crew suddenly became a shakier bet. Should that have been a red flag—a sign that this deal, which sounded so good on paper and promised to make all parties involved exceedingly rich, might not be everything it was cracked up to be? Depends on whom you ask.

Leveraged buyouts are in some ways similar to high-interest mortgages: homeowners put down their own money, usually 20 percent of the price, as a down payment, but 80 percent of the purchase is covered by the bank and, at the end of the day, it's really the bank that owns the house. Similarly, T.P.G. would put down $125 million on J.Crew—a relatively small percentage of the price—and finance the rest with a mix of bank loans and high-interest bonds. But unlike a mortgage, in an LBO the burden of that debt is not on the buyer—it's on the company that's been bought, which is now on the hook for fat quarterly interest payments, plus dividends to the new shareholders (in J.Crew's case, largely T.P.G.) and costly management fees (also to T.P.G.) for the work of steering its new purchase.

Critics of LBOs—and there are many—fundamentally bristle at this scenario, in which one day a company is clearing $12 million in profits, and the next it's $300 million in the hole, bogged down by so much debt that sometimes paying off debt is all it can do. The arrangement is almost like a sleight of hand: The investor acquires another company at almost no risk to itself—and that company is the collateral. If the company tanks and can't make its debt payments, the investor's company and personal finances are safe. But the acquired company is forced into default and bankruptcy. And LBO debt payments are often so hefty that a recession, or just a few dud seasons, can be all it takes to push it over the edge. Critics also say that because LBOs prioritize investors' short-term payoff—in T.P.G.'s case, a hoped-for public offering in 2000—the investor isn't incentivized to ensure the company's long-term survival. As long as J.Crew made it to the New York Stock Exchange and T.P.G. made out like bandits, what did it matter if J.Crew survived to dress a future generation of preps? The anti-LBO macro view: LBOs are a predatory system that pumps money into Wall Street pockets—maximizing shareholder profits while putting at risk companies that employ American workers.

LBO proponents, on the other hand, argue that J.Crew isn't the only one taking a risk here: The only way T.P.G. would get a return on its investment (other than those management fees and dividends) was by succeeding in making J.Crew profitable. From this perspective, investors *are* incentivized to do what's best for the brand—and while the risks for J.Crew are real, they might be worth it. T.P.G. had the money and the business know-how to do for J.Crew what the company had been unable to do for itself. The pro-LBO macro view: these deals make companies bigger and stronger, creating jobs and fueling the economy.

Early that October, after the UPS strike and the dismal quarter, T.P.G. asked J.Crew to drop its price. This time, it was Arthur who had to bend. With the deal in peril and the clock ticking, he lowered his asking price by $20 million. T.P.G. injected another $20 million to help improve the rating of the bonds that would finance the deal, and to appease the bank, and the wedding of J.Crew and T.P.G. was back on.

One morning in mid-October 1997, everyone at J.Crew was called together. Top brass knew what was coming, but to the rank and file—who'd had no chance to fear the implications of a sale, since they had no idea one was in the works—what came next was a total surprise. They were told a majority stake in the company had just been bought by a group called Texas Pacific. There was mention of other T.P.G. investments—Ducati Motors, Beringer wines, something about Continental Airlines. Most people had no idea what to make of this. "My first thought was, *Oh my god, the J.Crew catalogue is going to go in airplanes?*" says one employee, laughing ruefully.

Most of the staff learned the details the way everybody else did: in the newspaper. Emily retained 12 percent of the company, with the option to buy more. She was getting a $10 million signing bonus, plus a five-year contract for $5 million, which would double if business improved.[15]

As for Arthur, it seemed he had retired. No one I spoke with recalled a formal announcement of Arthur's departure. No going-away party, no goodbye speechifying. You'd have thought the man had just been laid off, not triumphantly sold the company he founded for almost $530 million. As far as most people could tell, soon after the deal closed, Arthur Cinader—a full-time presence since the day J.Crew was born—simply left.

This wasn't exactly surprising, given who Arthur was, but it also was not strategic. When Arthur vanished without acknowledgment—and without giving his formal blessing, toasting Emily at the helm—it was all too easy to believe the heated narrative that soon spread from desk to desk: that Emily, hungry for control, and sick of being under her father's thumb, had ruthlessly ousted Arthur. This, too, was conjecture, but many recall swallowing this version of the story whole, never pausing to question it. "It was all very hush-hush," recalls someone who worked closely with Arthur. "We came to the conclusion that it was hush-hush for a reason."

Emily, meanwhile, came out swinging. "The normally low-profile Woods," noted *Women's Wear Daily*, "is now front and center and talking like someone who likes being in control." J.Crew was finally about to reach its true potential, she declared, to become "everything I dreamed it could be."[16] There would be fifteen new stores in 1998; twenty more in '99. There would be new categories—a winter sports line; a range of body products (this happened; it was called "So J.Crew"). They were ready to rumble with the multibillion-dollar empires of Gap, Nike, Calvin Klein.

The reporters dutifully published these claims. But they also gleefully zeroed in on behind-the-scenes gossip: suddenly, Emily and Arthur's lackluster people skills were public knowledge. Writer Warren St. John opened his profile of the "Ultimate J.Crew Gal" in the reliably catty *New York Observer* with "the fucking pumpkin story."[17]

It was a humdinger. As the story goes, with Halloween approaching, Emily asks an assistant to fetch a small pumpkin for the office. The girl hits the streets, leaving no bodega unturned, in search of "the perfect J.Crew pumpkin—well proportioned, robustly hued and, of course, exactly 'small.'" After an extensive search, she presents Emily with a specimen not much bigger than a softball.

"You call that a pumpkin?" Emily reportedly sniped, before an audience of staffers. "That's not a fucking pumpkin!"

If J.Crew was hoping for a burst of sunny, full-steam-ahead public optimism, what they got was the opposite. "Given J.Crew's image as proselytizer for the sun-splashed, ruddy-cheeked American dream," wrote St. John, it has always been "a curiously grim place to work." He painted Emily as a leader as mercurial as her father (not true) who was deeply bogged down in the minutiae of every photo and pick-stitch (possibly true), casting shade on her ability to effectively lead a supersize J.Crew.

No one I spoke with recalled the incident of the fucking pumpkin. (Emily, for her part, did not respond to my request for comment on the pumpkin.) Her employees say it was not outside the realm of possibility—yes, Emily could be harsh. Still, some argue, is that even the point?

"I wonder how many times something like that has been said about some male C.E.O. who got half-and-half in his coffee when he really wanted milk," says Kelly Hill, the one-time James Madison University J.Crew fan, who went on to spend years at J.Crew as a top catalogue stylist. The business they were in—the work of nailing each and every detail, day in and day out, is "emotional sometimes," Hill says. Stress runs high. You don't always say the nice thing. No man who ran a company "down to its nooks and crannies" the way Emily did would be expected to play nice all the time. "What's wrong with saying, 'the fucking pumpkin'?" Hill says. "What's wrong with being tough?" Viewed through a contemporary lens, it seems conspicuous that the *Observer* story lacks any mention of the rarity of Emily—this young woman who, whether you knew her name or not, had changed the way a swath of America dressed—running an $800 million-a-year fashion company in the first place.

IN EVERY POSTSALE INTERVIEW EMILY MADE HER EXPECTATIONS clear: She would remain firmly in control of J.Crew. "Whatever transformations the company goes through in the future, I think of it as very much mine," she said. She didn't expect to see all that much of her new partners, really. "Texas Pacific is not a management company. It's an investment company."

That was odd, considering T.P.G. was known for its hands-on fixer-upper approach. And considering that T.P.G. muscle was already highly visible in the J.Crew offices. Dick Boyce had walked in on day one with an aggressive one-hundred-day playbook, determined to instill "discipline and predictability" in their product development process.[18] Bain &

Company already had boots on the ground, gathering data for a restructuring. Within what felt like minutes of the deal closing, this small but hungry pack of young M.B.A.s set up a war room at J.Crew's new home at 770 Broadway.

770 Broadway was the capacious, distinctly corporate new office space, just off Astor Place in NoHo, that J.Crew had moved to shortly before the sale. They had long outgrown 625 Sixth, expanding haphazardly, like a teenager careening through erratic growth spurts. Despite the vigilant release of office clean-up memos, that place had always been a bit messy, full of boards and samples and fabrics and stacks of boxes holding thousands of vintage textile prints. To the young and creative, it felt fertile, alive, like a starter apartment—scene of the scrappy but ecstatic early years of a marriage. And the spacious, serious 770 Broadway seemed an apt metaphor for their next chapter. To some, this was a good thing: J.Crew finally had a grown-up home befitting its place in the world—a place where all the appliances work and the sofa is plush, and you can feel comfortable inviting the boss over for dinner. Which was sort of what J.Crew had just done.

Others, especially those on the creative side whose inner ears were finely attuned to the nuances of "the moment," felt the loss of 625 keenly. To them, the delicate microclimate the Cinaders had bred, with its odd, obsessive work culture, was never quite the same after the move to 770 Broadway. At the new digs, some say, J.Crew never quite achieved that harmonic "all dancing, all singing" flow—right on the beat, in sync with the zeitgeist. To these people, the magic was already beginning to dim.

In late 1997, as its big opening act, T.P.G. handed out one hundred pink slips, axing 10 percent of J.Crew's workforce. Even those who were willing to accept this as a necessary evil—in a deal like this, heads will inevitably roll, and even nostalgists could admit that J.Crew needed to be streamlined, modernized—were alarmed by the speed with which T.P.G. moved. "They gave the list of names on Monday," recalls one former executive, "and these guys wanted to know why they hadn't been fired on Tuesday before noon."

As weeks ticked by, it was painfully clear that the numbers these suits had come here to crunch did not look good. It turned out that third-quarter dip that had threatened to throw off the T.P.G. deal was just an amuse-bouche for a dismal holiday season. There wasn't a lot J.Crew could do about this: In mass-market retail, the cycle is slow; new designs are finalized up to a year ahead of time, and manufactured on the other side of the globe. When a collection doesn't work, there is little choice but to wait it out. What was it we said before, about LBOs and fashion? Right: shit happens. As 1997 drew to a close, revenue was $25 million short of what J.Crew had forecast to T.P.G. Cash flow had suddenly dried up.

But at the company Christmas party, even with the layoffs and the general air of uncertainty, the mood was buoyant. Company veterans knew you couldn't get too upset about a one-season slump. J.Crew had weathered them before; every retailer does. And besides, '97 had been a momentous year. They'd launched the website, opened 99 Prince, been bought by these finance hotshots. Everyone was learning to pronounce this new phrase, EBITDA. J.Crew was finally about to realize its full potential. That was the whole point of this sale, right?

When one of the T.P.G. guys stepped up to give a toast, most didn't realize this was David Bonderman, their new Big Kahuna. They weren't thinking about the fact that this man was currently assessing the value of each and every person in the room. They were too busy staring at his necktie. This tie "was not to be missed," says a former executive. It was loud, garish. So *not* J.Crew. It seemed like a bad omen. *Oh my god,* this exec thought. *There it is. These guys don't get it.*

They assumed this T.P.G. guy was standing up to toast his new A-Team, the people who had turned a modest family company into an $800 million brand through sheer force of will. Instead, they got "Bondo," the razor-tongued trial lawyer known for shredding opposing arguments—the guy who'd just paid ten times EBITDA for a company that was earning nowhere near what he'd been promised, with a leader who was winning no popularity contest in the press. And now he had walked into this room to find a group of people partying, laughing, expecting to be, what, *congratulated*?

"The days of Mom and Pop running this business are over," is how one HR exec recalls Bonderman's brief but devastating speech. It was like some bad-joke version of the ghost of Christmas future: J.Crew had been inefficiently run, he told them, and things were about to change. Look around: "The people you see here, you're probably not going to see in a year from now." Happy freaking holidays. (Reached for comment, Bonderman denied having made a statement of this nature.)

Emily does not recall this speech. Is it possible she wasn't there? No one I spoke with explicitly remembered seeing her face in the crowd—surely the first place that any of these people, so attuned to her every facial tic, would have looked: *Oh my god, what must* Emily *be thinking?* It's hard to imagine Bonderman putting it that brutally, especially right in front of Emily, with whom he was still in the honeymoon phase. Surely even "Bondo" did not have the temerity to publicly humiliate *Emily*.

But for some members of Emily's staff, this became a moment they never forgot. If there was any lingering hope that T.P.G. would be a different, kinder, gentler investment firm, it died right there. They stood there staring at each other in a new kind of silence: *Is this guy for real?* "This is his message to a group whose blood, sweat, and tears were loyal to this organization?" recalls a top merchant. "We walked out of there with our heads down. In disbelief. Concerned. Depressed." Bonderman was all too right: many of the people in that room would not be there a year later.

CHAPTER 11

Swan Song

The Spring 1998 catalogue was peak J.Crew. Emily had gotten wind of a new TV show based on a premise that could have sprung from her own catalogue department: four fresh-scrubbed, hyperarticulate teens debate the meaning of life in a sun-dappled fictional Cape Cod town. Emily dispatched a team to the show's North Carolina set, to capture its cast of unknowns—Katie Holmes, James Van Der Beek, Joshua Jackson, and Michelle Williams—having some good old-fashioned J.Crew fun: treehouse-climbing, piggyback-riding, and plenty of picturesque, PG-rated nuzzling.

This was clearly a commercial swing, courting the exact demo Emily had spent the last decade trying to edge J.Crew's image away from. And it was a gamble: The catalogue landed days before the show even premiered. But *Dawson's Creek*, and that J.Crew cover starring Joey and Dawson and Pacey and Jen, crept into the millennial lizard brain. Fifteen years later, the issue would pop up on eBay for $124.99, juddering across the internet on a wave of nostalgia.[1] On glamour.com, a writer reminisced about the days when life "revolved around, like, six *totally* important things," among them babysitting, *Dawson's Creek*, "convincing my mom to let me wear burgundy lipstick," and "mail-ordering rollneck sweaters from the J.Crew catalogue."[2]

But back at 770 Broadway, when that catalogue dropped, the mood was far from playful. That February, Emily introduced J.Crew's new C.E.O., an affable, somewhat fatherly retail vet named Howard Socol. When Socol stood up and gave his new comrade a friendly slap on the back, the hair on the back of many necks stood up. It was like Bonderman's ugly tie: J.Crew had an incredibly specific culture, a protocol. This was not it. "You did not *touch* Emily," recalls a former catalogue creative. "And you certainly did not slap her on the back. I immediately thought, *This is never going to work.*"

Finding the right outsider to come in and run any family business is a matter of careful casting. Finding someone to run *this* company, alongside its ever-present yet elusive cofounder-slash-human embodiment? Tricky. Add in J.Crew's track record on retaining executives, and the very specific psychological hold the brand had on its customer? This should have been "a real kid glove operation," says a former HR exec. "Howard was . . . maybe the worst choice."

Socol looked great on paper. He'd just retired from running Burdines, the Florida department store chain that was a unit of Federated, where he'd worked since 1969. He was said to be one of Federated's best and brightest.[3] But his vibe, to his new employees at least, was a little "garmento," about as far from either '80s prep or '90s sleek—the twin orbs of J.Crew's Venn diagram—as it got. He wasn't a bad guy, but he did wear bad slacks. "I saw department store markdowns when I looked at Howard," one merchant says flatly. And he had "department store ideas," she says: He wanted to know why J.Crew wasn't making black shorts for men. *Black?* Everyone knew J.Crew was *navy*.

And why was Socol so . . . friendly? He walked into a room with a smile, greeting everyone. God, that was weird.

Socol wanted to tweak the stores. Emily's stark minimalist temples, so carefully considered, felt cold, he said. He wanted blown-up catalogue photos on the store walls—an obvious touch Emily had always forbidden. He told a reporter that the future of Collection was being "evaluated." Of course, by the time he said it, everyone knew Emily's baby was getting the ax: most Collection staffers had been laid off in T.P.G.'s first round of layoffs. Its head designer, Lena Youm, was out a month after Socol's arrival.[4]

There were some successes: T.P.G. introduced efficiency to J.Crew's processes, pumped money into fortifying the new website so that by the early 2000s, J.Crew.com was ahead of its competition in both tone and function. And early in T.P.G.'s reign, Matt Rubel architected the sale of Popular Club Plan to Fingerhut for $43 million, boosting the bottom line.[5]

But as 1998 wore on, it became increasingly obvious that the outcome of the T.P.G. deal was far from what Emily had envisioned. Her walled-off, secretive management style didn't make the transition any easier. She sometimes referred to the new finance guys dismissively, as "the bean counters." "This is conjecture," says Dave DeMattei, with empathy, "but I think she thought she was going to free herself from her father, and then realized she had a whole other set of issues to deal with."

People who had long made a study of the impenetrable Emily-Arthur dynamic were now trying to make sense of Emily-Howard. Who was really in charge here? "Although Mr. Socol politely refers to Ms. Woods as his partner, she is clearly no longer in the driver's seat," noted *Crain's*.[6] "Industry insiders suspect Mr. Socol has complete autonomy to run the business as he sees fit." A big-league headhunter weighed in: "At this point in his career, [Socol] wouldn't play second fiddle."

But at this point in *her* career, why would anyone expect Emily to be number two?

David Bonderman's Christmas prophecy played out just as predicted: within a year of the deal, many of the people at that surreal party were gone—including a handful of the business types Emily worked with most closely, the ones who really saw what she brought to the table. Dave DeMattei jumped ship, as did HR exec Marianne Ruggiero, trusted merchant Ray Attanasio, and a host of others.

Emily, watching the dissolution of her trusted inner circle and her airtight brand, needed to onboard the outsiders who were now walking the halls of 770—to get into their brains what this J.Crew thing *was* before it washed down the drain. For all its supposed "people problems," J.Crew had once been an organization in lockstep, where everybody "got it" and everyone was, a little mystically, on the same page.

Emily tapped Gayle Spannaus, the company's longtime model booker, to do a classic branding exercise. After all, nobody knows the essence of a brand like the person who chooses which beautiful people should embody its best self. Spannaus's assignment: construct a composite portrait of J.Crew. One by one, she tacked a series of items and photos onto a wall in the office.

If J.Crew was a writing implement, what would it be? *A No. 2 pencil.*

If it was a restaurant? *The insider-beloved Tribeca bistro Odeon.*

A drink? *Lemonade.*

A watch? *A Rolex. Maybe a Timex.*

A brand of soap? *Ivory.*

Dan Wieden, legendary ad man and founder of the agency Wieden & Kennedy, once said "brands are verbs." Marketing guru Marc de Swaan Arons put this into practice in an article for the *Atlantic*: Nike exhorts. IBM solves. Sony dreams.[7] J.Crew's low-key aspirational prep—its "tyranny" of ease—is hard to boil down to a single word. But its identity was clear enough to be conveyed by little more than a pencil and a bar of soap. After a decade steeped in the brand, this exercise was second nature for Spannaus. Like all the company's old hands, J.Crew's DNA was threaded in with her own. "We probably all had white dishes, slept on white sheets," Spannaus says with a laugh. "If you asked us our favorite sweatshirt brand, we're all going to say Champion."

Was the wall helpful? Unclear. Spannaus recalls that it did not stay up for long. It's easy to imagine how such a thing—tacked up by the people who "got it" to educate those who did not—might read to new arrivals. J.Crew was clearly potato salad, not coleslaw. Seriously? If this company was so clean and bright and *American*, why wasn't it Wonder Bread? On that one, Spannaus pauses to think: "I think . . . a torn loaf of fresh bread in a plain brown bag."

Emily remained as discreet as ever. But the tension with Socol was palpable, and some staffers felt caught in a tug-of-war. The merchant Carol Sharpe never forgot the time she sided with Emily on an issue instead of Socol (then her direct boss), and he snapped: *Why are you taking* her *side?* As odd as some things had been in the Cinader era, that would never have happened back then.

All along, designer Scott Formby believed that if anyone could steer them through this rocky transition, it was Emily. But in late fall, a new troop of management consultants appeared in the office. "When did I start getting nervous?" Formby says. "Definitely then." By then, J.Crew was used to Bain quants looking to squeeze every wasted dime out of their management process, but this batch of consultants was here for something different: they'd been hired by T.P.G. to question senior staffers on the issue of Socol v. Woods. *Do you rely on Emily Woods for X? Do you rely on Howard Socol for Y?* The underlying question was clear: Who was more essential?

Even Formby had to wonder, Who *was* more powerful? A new C.E.O. appointed by T.P.G., which now owned 85 percent of the company? Or the cofounder and company chairman, who had upped her stake to the remaining 15 percent?

Over the holidays, Socol phoned senior staff at home: he was leaving. Emily had won this round.

The tone of the press surrounding Socol's departure, after a mere ten months, was noteworthy, not for what it said about the C.E.O.—who was simply a bad fit for J.Crew; he soon went on to helm a golden era at Barneys—but for what it said about J.Crew. A year earlier, J.Crew had been celebrated as a glowing brand, full of promise, worthy of T.P.G.'s $528 million investment. Now, the *L.A. Times* identified it as "the ailing catalogue and retail company."[8]

NEXT UP: MARK SARVARY, A VERY NICE BRIT WITH A MOST PERplexing résumé. What J.Crew's new C.E.O. knew about retail, you could fit in a catalogue caption. Sarvary couldn't tell a knit from a woven. He asked questions like, "What's a polo shirt versus a polo sweater?" And no wonder: T.P.G. had plucked him from the frozen foods division of Nestlé. As a *Fortune* reporter observed, just a few months before he arrived at 770 Broadway, Sarvary had been "touting the improved Parmesan flavor in Lean Cuisine's chicken fettuccine."[9]

Sarvary was a former Bain analyst, a finance guy, which theoretically made him the right C.E.O. for Wall Street—which was where J.Crew was ostensibly still headed, A.S.A.P. He was billed as a bean counter in chief, someone who could open stores at a fast clip. This much, at least, was working: J.Crew stores were popping up at a rate the company could never have dreamed of in the Cinader era. There were sixteen new outposts in 1999 and twenty-three in 2000.[10]

Almost every J.Crew person I spoke with referred to Sarvary as "the frozen foods guy," except for one, who called him "Mr. Pepperidge Farms." Sarvary was likable enough, but his appointment felt like an insult to anyone who knew and respected the art of retail. Clearly T.P.G. did not have the slightest idea why J.Crew was lemonade, not iced tea—and didn't care, either. "What does this guy know about *Beowulf* allusions to a rollneck sweater," says a former HR exec, "in order to charge twice as much as you should be charging for it?"

There was arguably a method to T.P.G.'s madness. For one thing, by the mid-'90s there simply weren't that many great merchants on the market. The industry's most celebrated "merchant princes" had traditionally been forged in the training programs of great department stores like A&S and Bloomingdale's. But for two decades, those chains had merged and remerged, becoming highly consolidated in an effort to stave off the existential threat of specialty retail. The Great American Department Store wasn't that great anymore, nor was the pipeline of talent it once produced. The same three names were bandied about every time there was an opening at the top of a giant retail brand: Mickey Drexler over at Gap, Mike Jeffries at Abercrombie & Fitch, Rose Marie Bravo of Burberry. These stars could take their pick of top jobs, and J.Crew—now embarrassingly stuck in the weeds—was not the sexiest proposition.

But there was also a certain logic to shopping for a fashion executive in the frozen foods aisle: in the specialty retail boom, once-modest store chains had morphed into behemoths with hundreds of locations, and they were now galloping onto the web, too. These weren't simple operations where the person in charge just needed a great nose for next year's trends. By the aughts, good taste and reliable product weren't enough to make a company profitable; the C.E.O. of any specialty retailer had to manage international expansion, offshore manufacturing, burgeoning I.T. departments, and boardroom politics. These weren't skills one necessarily picked up in the jeans department of Macy's.

Who *was* suited to run these multipronged beasts? There was a growing sense that the answer was an experienced large-corporation exec. In '99, the top spot at Levi's was handed to a former chief exec of Pepsi. A guy from General Electric would soon be running Home Depot. And given the way that Howard Socol and Emily had tangled over merchandise, branding, and store aesthetics, there was a certain logic to seeking a generalist who could steer J.Crew toward that I.P.O. payday and stay out of Emily's way, leaving her to do what she did best.

Sarvary's appointment should have made Emily more essential to

J.Crew than ever. If T.P.G. was going to throw an M.B.A. with no retail experience into this equation, Emily—tricky as she could be to work with—should have been the glue holding this thing together.

But the first thing Sarvary did when he arrived was erect his own office with walls and a door—flatly rejecting the long-standing "J.Crew way," of open-plan culture. To his new employees, it seemed clear that after the Socol disaster, Sarvary walked in fully empowered by T.P.G. to do things *his* way. And most do not recall seeing Mark Sarvary interact with Emily, period. It was as if a thread had been cut. Emily was slowly drifting away.

Maybe it should not have come as a complete shock when she vanished altogether.

In February 2000, eight months after Sarvary's arrival, Emily poked her head into a conference room. Merchant Carol Sharpe was standing at the table, laying out samples for a holiday catalogue. As Sharpe recalls it, Emily said to her, "Let's take a walk." She knew immediately that something was terribly wrong. In eleven years at J.Crew, Sharpe had never seen the look that was on Emily's face that day.

Emily didn't say a lot. "Leadership," she said, not naming names, felt that she was a disruptive presence, redundant. Standing in the way of progress. No one knew for sure what had happened, but Sharpe was left with the impression that Sarvary had worked with T.P.G. to push Emily out. "They're letting me go," Emily told Sharpe. The pain of having to say it aloud was palpable. She asked Sharpe to look after things for her. Then Emily left the building.

Emily was thirty-nine. Three years earlier, she'd told the world that she intended to steer J.Crew through its next twenty years; that, despite the arrival of T.P.G., "I think of it as very much my own." Now, her era was over almost before it began. If Arthur's exit had been a relative tremor, Emily's felt like a shift in the firmament. This company had grown up alongside Emily, reflecting her tastes, her instincts, her obsessions, but also maturing as she did—catering to twentysomethings fresh out of college, and then thirtysomethings conquering the workplace, just as Emily herself graduated from one life stage to the next. She was the one who had made it "a catalogue that didn't feel like a catalogue." What was J.Crew without her?

Sharpe was stunned. After Emily left her standing in the hallway, she walked back into the conference room, where a meeting had gathered, and broke the news: Emily was leaving the company. That was it. To most of the team, Emily's departure was as elusive as her presence had always been.

That day, Scott Formby was out of town, called away to an off-site meeting. He'd assumed Emily would be there. Instead he was invited to an early breakfast, and given the news: Emily was leaving the company. Would he assume her creative duties? Formby was gobsmacked. "There was a handful of us who were family," he says. For more than a decade, she'd been his partner and protector at work. He was loyal to her, but also to J.Crew—the brand he had transformed into exactly what he and Emily had first talked about achieving. If he resigned, his team would be left in the lurch, possibly watching from the sidelines as some Sarvary appointee dismantled everything they'd built. So he took the promotion. But not without feeling like a traitor.

If Formby and Sharpe mourned Emily's departure, not every heart at J.Crew broke for her. Emily was the one who'd invited T.P.G. into their backyard in the first place—in the eyes of some, killing the magic of *their* brand. Now Emily had millions from the sale as a consolation prize, plus her dividend payments, while those who had served her were stuck holding together the pieces of a rapidly disintegrating brand.

Emily wasn't *gone* gone. By 2001, her ownership stake was up to 19.2 percent; she'd remain board chairman until 2003. But the woman who had shaped, inspired, or signed off on every item, every model, every shoot location, every last photo J.Crew made, had been reduced to a vote in board meetings. One voice among many.

Now Sarvary and T.P.G. were free to run J.Crew their way, which meant decisions based on data—analyses, studies, focus groups. Sarvary once described the process of launching a new frozen dinner at Nestlé: the company had spent a year and a half in focus groups on packaging design, "just to get the curl on the S in *Stouffer's* right," says Sharpe. "All of us were staring at him like, *Okaaaay*." In retail, merchants relied on data, but predicting what shoppers will want eighteen months or a year ahead of time is largely gut instinct. Under Emily, J.Crew had arguably given an edge to art over commerce—the subtleties and perception of the brand were paramount. Now, the question was no longer whether J.Crew was sourdough versus baguette, but how many pennies that loaf cost to make, how efficiently they could bake it, and what demographic was statistically proven to eat it.

J.Crew was now officially "merchant led," Sarvary said, issuing a string of market research–led dictates that sounded straight out of some reverse *Ab Fab*: The designers could no longer use orange—he didn't "understand" the color. Green, too, was out: men did not wear it. Light blue, on the other hand, was a bestseller. So he wanted light blue in every color palette, and in the Christmas windows, and on the front table of every store.

The day Gayle Spannaus told Sarvary that J.Crew was paying $15,000 a day for top models—a relative steal compared to the ad rates of other companies—he almost fell out of his chair. "*Why!?*" he asked, in genuine disbelief, when "there are so many pretty girls around the office?"

It was hard not to laugh—or cry. Sarvary just didn't get it. But on the balance sheet, his approach appeared to be working. By 2000, they were up to 103 stores. With the staff whittled down and every drop of waste squeezed from the production process, cash flow was up. That year, *Fortune* published a rave review: J.Crew—a year and a half earlier, you'll recall, the "struggling retailer"—had "emerged as one of the strongest clothing businesses around," on track for a likely I.P.O. in 2001, just a year behind T.P.G.'s initial forecast. One analyst called J.Crew "the envy of the industry."[11]

But that enviable balance sheet was the result of two-plus years of gradually cutting corners on quality, design, store design. One by one, the little upgrades that had made J.Crew different, *better*, had been erased. It can take customers a while to catch on to gradual decline: We assume, maybe that one piece was a dud? Maybe that other one was too? Until, hey now, *wait*. Suddenly clothes that were once simple have become plain. When that happens, there's no going back.

In April 2002, J.Crew's woes were outed in the *New York Times*. The headline said it all: "In a Race to the Mall, J.Crew Has Lost Its Way."[12] The company's "catalogues still arrive in the mail as regularly as utility bills"—yowch—but the truth was that J.Crew was on the brink of defaulting on the staggering debt load of its 1997 LBO. The article left no ambiguity about who was at fault: T.P.G. had been "running the company as if it were selling car parts or copier paper," draining J.Crew of all points of view. And the absence of Emily was sorely felt: Without her "laser-like focus on what the brand should represent," there was no one to be "keeper of the image." Mark Sarvary was out by May.

By late 2002, J.Crew had been diluted to the point that even its own employees couldn't walk into a store and find something that felt worth buying. They had doubled their store count over the past five years, but earnings had sunk to pre-LBO levels. Sales were in free fall, declining month after month.[13] They'd just laid off another hundred people. And though they had a new C.E.O., Ken Pilot—arguably their most qualified appointee yet, having spent thirteen years at Gap—with the S&P reporting that J.Crew was at "substantial risk of default," bankruptcy loomed. How much of a turnaround could Pilot be expected to engineer, under the circumstances?

T.P.G. knew it was time for a come-to-Jesus.[14] Was it time to cut bait on J.Crew? In the high-stakes betting game of venture capital, these moments came with the territory; not every bet can win. At the table were founding partners David Bonderman and Jim Coulter; Dick Boyce, who had been in charge of turning J.Crew around; and another senior player, Jonathan Coslet.

They'd already tried to offload J.Crew. Both Liz Claiborne and Abercrombie & Fitch had come in with initial offers between $600 and $700 million. But once those buyers got a chance to look under the hood, those offers evaporated. Now, there was one bid left on the table. American Eagle Outfitters had initially offered $650 million. But after due diligence, that shrank to $500 million—less than the company had been worth five years earlier, when it had almost a hundred fewer stores.

If T.P.G. took the American Eagle offer, it could cut its losses. It wouldn't earn a profit, but a sale was better than bankruptcy, which would have eliminated its equity in the company.

T.P.G. could chalk this one up to a lesson learned. Turns out you can't transform a medium-size catalogue business into a thrumming store business without hiring executives who actually *know* retail and respect it. Executives who deeply felt the specific alchemy of the brand, its identity, and also could envision how that alchemy might shape-shift into the next era—one that, by the way, would soon include a whole new existential threat, in the form of fast fashion.

Some on the T.P.G. side were ready to wave the white flag. Coslet would later note, "Part of me felt—and certainly some of my partners urged this point of view—that we had given this our best shot and it hadn't worked."

But there was another option. They could restructure J.Crew's debt—taking on an even higher interest rate—to give the turnaround one last shot.

A new, very strong, reason to consider this option had just popped up on the horizon: Millard "Mickey" Drexler. The most famous merchant in the business, renowned as the rare business mind who obsessed over design as fervently as the bottom line. Mickey's turnaround of Gap was widely believed to be the most dramatic makeover in retail history. A few years earlier, J.Crew could never have landed him. But Mickey had hit hard times at Gap, and six months before this meeting, he'd been unceremoniously axed. The best news for T.P.G.: he had walked away from a $2 million noncompete deal.[15] So the biggest guy in retail was a free agent. And, given his recent crash and burn—the first failure in his illustrious career—he also had something to prove.

PART TWO

CHAPTER 12

Rocket Man

J.Crew had never seen the likes of Millard "Mickey" Drexler. First and foremost, he was a dyed-in-the-wool stores guy, "a shopkeeper at heart," he likes to say. Arthur and Emily had been catalogue makers to their core, struggling to make their mark on the American mall. Mickey built his legend at Gap Inc. by putting a store in *every* mall and on what felt like every street corner in the nation. If you were looking for expansion, he was your guy.

But that wasn't the only reason Mickey Drexler threw every person at 770 Broadway for a loop. The man could have been bred in a lab to be the Cinaders' polar opposite: He was a loud, irreverent, neurotic New Yorker—cliché, but in this case accurate—congenitally afflicted, he says, with *shpilkes,* a condition he jokingly describes as "Yiddish for 'ants in my pants.'"[1] But *shpilkes* is more than that—it's a state of perpetual impatience, anxiety. And Mickey's *shpilkes* have a way of spilling out onto everyone around him. The Cinaders hated noise; Mickey was a walking disruption. If J.Crew's founders were like a matching set of padlocked diaries, revealing nothing of themselves and asking no personal questions in return, the company's new CEO has an almost confessional bent—disclosing the good, the bad, and the ugly about his own childhood, and asking everyone else their origin stories, too, all in an unreformed Bronx-ian squawk that is itself a dead giveaway of his own backstory. Journalists, future employees: he's as interested in their backstories as he is in their bona fides. He believes childhood is where every interview should start—after all, Mickey would be the first to tell you that his own childhood defined him, in many ways.

So, fine, let's start with childhood: Mickey Drexler's American Dream story started at the Mayflower, poetically enough. To children who grew up there, the six-story brick behemoth in the working-class Allerton section of the Bronx was a hometown unto itself.[2] But he remembers apartment 17A, on the ground floor, as a place devoid of warmth or emotion, where he grew up an only child, sleeping on a makeshift bed squeezed into the family foyer. Six days a week, his father, Charles Drexler, headed south to the Garment District, where he worked as a button and remnants buyer for Jill Jr. Coats, a manufacturer of women's coats.[3] Mickey is quick to correct the assumption that he followed in Charles's footsteps; he recalls his father as a bitter, angry man, a malcontent who craved success and money but never amassed much of either—a fact that pained Charles and his son, too. In junior high, Mickey ran errands for Jill Jr. Once, dispatched to the bank to deposit paychecks, he furtively opened his father's envelope to learn that Charles earned $15,000 a year. "I was fucking devastated,"[4] he has said—furious at the boss underpaying his father, but perhaps even more so at his father, for accepting less than the other guys at work whom he regularly disparaged. If anything, Charles was a model of everything Mickey did not want to become.

Mickey's mother, Mary Drexler, was diagnosed with cancer when her only son was an infant. Nobody talked about breast cancer in those days, and the nature of her illness was kept secret, even from Mickey, and referred to only in whispers. He surmised it was breast cancer only because she'd had a mastectomy. Mary survived to work full-time as a secretary, but spent most of her son's childhood either sick or depressed, ill-equipped to make up for what her husband lacked.

Back then, Mickey was far from the outsize presence who would go on to turn every company he ever ran into the Mickey Show. He describes himself as a shy, insecure kid—an observer, absorbing every detail. But not exactly meek. Mickey was allergic to authority. As a kid, the fierce, rebellious streak that would become all too familiar to his future employees simmered just beneath his surface. In junior high, he couldn't stand spending every Friday afternoon at yeshiva—after all, he figured, this wasn't real school, the kind you *had* to graduate from. After mouthing off one day, he was sent home with a punishment: Write "*Ikh vel zayn gut in shul*" ("I will be good in shul") fifty times. He returned to the next class with a single sentence spelled out on his sheet of paper: *Ikh vel zayn gut in shul X 1000*. This was a last straw. He got the boot from yeshiva.[5]

In his class of 230 kids, he was one of only five who passed the entrance exam for the Bronx High School of Science,[6] the magnet school also briefly attended by one Arthur Cinader. Bronx Science turned out to be both the greatest thing that ever happened to Mickey, and a fairly miserable experience. Surrounded by kids who were just as smart, if not smarter, than he was, the chip on his shoulder—no doubt instilled by Charles Drexler—began to throb. "I felt like I was the dumbest kid in the class," he has said. He had a B average. But to him it was torture, having to watch young Phillip Heller, who seemed to sit next to him in every class, get an A+ on every test.

Mickey had plenty of reasons to hate those years: When he was sixteen, Mary Drexler died of esophageal cancer. That bisected his high school career, and no doubt his life, into before and after. But Mary had pushed him to attend Bronx Science, succeeding in setting her son on his path, at least. At that school, college was a foregone conclusion. That certainty changed Mickey's life. He was the only one of his cousins to go to college, graduating from SUNY–Buffalo, then enrolling at Boston University for an M.B.A. And in grad school he discovered the twin loves of his life. One was a fellow student, Peggy, who like him came from a difficult family and had lost a parent, her father, when she was young. Peggy fortified Mickey. It had always been him against the world—craving love, siblings, a nicer home, a bigger family. With her at his side, he was finally part of a team. By twenty-four, Mickey was married. (Peggy Drexler, Ph.D., now a respected research psychologist and indie film producer, has written two books—both about father-child dynamics.)

Mickey's other true love? Retail. He was part of a generation of great merchants that rose out of the summer program at the legendary downtown Brooklyn department store Abraham & Straus (later absorbed by Macy's). The young men's jeans department suited his *shpilkes,* but also his talents. Mickey had the right-/left-brain command of a true merchant: an instant recall of sales figures, but also an eye for beauty and a nose for longing. He relished his influence over the customer. Just by choosing the right outfits for the mannequins, he could foment desire—*he* could decide what someone wanted next.

Mickey loved A&S. And A&S liked him back, though perhaps not enough. In a story he has told and retold, in 1968, they offered him a job earning $11,000 a year. But he learned that a former classmate—someone he'd recommended to A&S—had just been hired at $11,500. He'd worked there all summer, and already they were valuing Howard more than him? He was enraged. When Bloomingdale's offered $11,500, he took it. "I didn't want to be my father. I didn't want to be taken advantage of."[7]

Mickey is, was, and always will be obsessed with cool. He would never exactly *be* cool, though—he was too eager, too high-strung, to achieve that ineffable quality—but he has an uncanny ability to prognosticate "where the hockey puck is headed," another favorite expression. This gut instinct for the next It item—at one point: ultrawide-leg "elephant pants"—made him, he will tell you, the youngest, fastest-promoted buyer in the history of Bloomingdale's. In 1976, he skipped over to Macy's for $50,000 a year, enough to move the Drexlers to Park

Avenue.[8] The kid from the Bronx had arrived. But his love for department stores was waning. Mickey bristled at any hint of corporate bureaucracy; he also just didn't love working for other people. He wanted what Les Wexner had at the Limited: control over the feel and look of every aspect of a shopping experience—the clothes, the space, the vibe, the *smell* of the place. Perhaps most of all, he wanted to decide what everything cost. At Macy's he fumed: every time a competitor put their bathing suits on sale, he had to mark down his bathing suits, too. Infuriating! He wanted to set his prices without having to worry about what was hanging on somebody else's sale rack across town.

In 1980, he got his shot. At thirty-six, he was named president of Ann Taylor, then a lackluster, money-leaking chain of twenty-five stores.[9] Mickey saw its potential to be the right store at the right time, for some of the same reasons that, over in New Jersey, Ted Pamperin and Arthur Cinader were anticipating a catalogue boom: an influx of career women needed work dresses and bow-neck blouses, and had less time than ever to shop for them.

At Ann Taylor, Mickey established what would become his trademark takeover style[10]—the same take-no-prisoners process he would apply to Gap, and later J.Crew. "You can't wait," he would later say of the initial days at a new company. "You gotta run a business to win, not just to lose. So I did the surgery."[11] He calls it surgery for a reason: the process hurts, but it can save a company's life. In a flurry of change, he trashed the brand's existing clothes, image, design, and management, and built a new image from the ground up. For this he had one muse: Jacqueline Kennedy Onassis, then the chicest working woman in New York—a book editor at Viking Press whose look consisted of giant sunglasses, camel hair wrap coats, wide-leg trousers, and skinny rib sweaters.[12] Onassis never knew it, but everything Mickey did went through her filter. *Would Jackie like it?* Equally critical to the process: he shifted the company to vertical manufacturing and product development processes. The secret to specialty retail was unification, bringing the whole operation under one roof, as much as possible, and then closely controlling manufacturing through outside factories. Mickey is widely credited with "inventing" vertical retailing at the Gap. But in many ways his first attempt was at Ann Taylor, and that was built upon a path first charted by Wexner—standardizing the production and design of good-looking, affordable mass-market clothes. In three years, he turned Ann Taylor into a legitimately hot property, a go-to outfitter for the working woman.

This was just the kind of magic Don Fisher desperately needed over at Gap.

In the '60s Fisher had parlayed his father's contracting company into a semisuccessful San Francisco real estate business, when a tenant in one of the buildings he owned, Levi Strauss & Company, gave him a pair of jeans.[13] They didn't fit. When Fisher tried to exchange them in a department store, he ran into a problem a lot of people were having, now that Levi's were the hottest thing on the planet: he couldn't find his size. Most stores had a tiny selection and were always running out. In 1969 Fisher and his wife, Doris, opened a single boutique that stocked a single item: Levi's, in every style and every size the company made, plus a smattering of LPs to give their operation a whiff of countercultural cool.

It was Doris's idea to name the place after the "generation gap." "Don nixed 'generation' because he didn't want to pay for that many letters on the sign," says Mark Cohen, a retail professor at Columbia University and industry contemporary of Mickey, who worked for Fisher in the late '70s. "That's how compulsive he could be. He's a gazillionaire but, '*Generation Gap*—that's how many letters? How about just *Gap*?'"

Specializing in Levi's made Gap the original "denim store" at a time when jeans had just become the 24/7 uniform of American youth.[14] Gap soared through the '70s, a chain as groovy as the hip-huggers it sold, the envy of its competitors. By 1983 it was a roughly $400 million, publicly traded business with four hundred–plus stores. But it had lost its luster, along with its exclusive on its signature product. Now, anybody could sell Levi's. Fisher was playing whack-a-mole with jeans-focused stores popping up across the country. Plus, his original demo, the flower children, had matured into boomers entering their carpooling years. Gap was the overgrown teen who had failed to "adult."

By the time Fisher heard about the fast-talking guy who'd managed to overhaul Ann Taylor in a mere three years, Gap had churned through multiple fix-it men. Fisher and Mickey Drexler were not a natural fit. They had no shared philosophy or background—"no simpatico," Cohen says. Mickey was a short, hot-wired New Yorker who nursed a neurotic streak to rival Woody Allen's. Fisher was a rangy onetime college water polo player, deeply Californian, raised with money, and sixteen years Mickey's senior.[15] Mickey ran hot and shot from the hip, operating largely on gut instinct; Fisher was disciplined, methodical, and quiet. "Don believed in process," says Cohen. "He was orderly, organized: A leads to B leads to C."

But Fisher's company had lost its mojo just as the American mall had gone into overdrive. The specialty retail race was on—new contenders like Benetton and Esprit were on fire—and Fisher was just desperate enough to let Mickey take a swing.

In February 1983, Gap introduced a freshly minted president. For our tale, the timing was almost uncanny. With his close-cut fuzzy dark curls and round '80s glasses, Mickey showed up for his first day of work at Gap's nondescript, glassy office tower in the San Francisco suburb of San Bruno[16] precisely one month after twenty-one-year-old Emily Cinader first reported to the Garfield, New Jersey, offices of J.Crew—

and within weeks of the first J.Crew catalogue landing on America's kitchen table.

A YEAR AND A HALF LATER, ON AUGUST 15, 1984, MICKEY HAD his moment of truth. The exact date will forever be branded on his brain. He'd spent months in "surgery"—excising not just Gap's old inventory and most of its executive ranks, but also its entire visual identity. The signature bright-red store features had been erased. "Get the red out" was the order from on high. Mickey printed little signs to hand out around the office: *Simplify*.

For years, Mickey had been mentally percolating the brand he would one day launch. This being the '80s, it was inspired in part by Benetton—the brand's optimism and bold color, but also the *clarity* of its stores. Mickey liked that you could walk into any Benetton, snap up whatever you needed, and be out in ten minutes. He also had in mind the all-American kids' staple, OshKosh B'Gosh. He was seeking a simpler way to dress. And of course Ralph Lauren was also in the cocktail shaker in San Bruno, just as it was over in Garfield. It wasn't Lauren's idolatry of the preppy elite that informed Mickey's Gap, per se, but the core components of his casual look: classic, clean, and—there's that word again—*American*. Like the team that was building J.Crew, Mickey thought Ralph had a weak spot: too pricey. His motto, deployed at every brand he's ever run, was, "Good taste should not cost extra."

What would the new Gap sell? Mickey had the answers in his back pocket, literally. For years, on a sheet of scrap paper, he had kept a running list: bright color, fleece, pocket tees, washed (i.e., broken-in) jeans—all made for men and women alike. To him, these were the fundamentals of all-American, easy dressing. Well-made, all-cotton, stylish enough to appeal to anyone—and vanilla enough to alienate no one. Mickey figured the wealthy needed nice, solid T-shirts, just like everyone else; the middle class wanted good taste that was worth the money; and the aspirants would soon wear sweatshirts that read *GAP* as if it was the name of an elite alma mater—a symbol of middle-class acceptance.

Everyone at Gap who had watched Mickey parachute in, wipe out their old brand, lay off their former colleagues, and erect this new vision—never once appearing to second-guess himself—assumed the man was fearless. A kamikaze. But that day in August 1984, new merchandise was set to hit some 450 Gap stores that had *all* been simultaneously remodeled to Mickey's specifications—a feat that is almost unthinkable today. There was no soft launch, no trial and error, *nothing*. It wasn't that Mickey was fearless; it was that he thrived on fear. In fact he was scared shitless. Gap stock and revenue were tanking, and just as the all-important back-to-school season had arrived, he'd just killed off their back-to-school merch. Don Fisher was calling him at home, *What's going on?* (Fisher would later write that "betting the company on Mickey was easily the biggest gamble I'd ever taken in my life."[17])

But within days, it took off. Another Mickey-ism: *The business was like a rocket.*

By 1986 the *New York Times* was already calling Mickey's takeover "one of the most remarkable turnarounds in retailing history."[18] With Mickey leading product and image, and Fisher carving out deals with mall developers, the company doubled, tripled, quadrupled in size. Even bigger than its ever-growing footprint was its cultural influence—all because of that little word Mickey had printed on cards: *Simplify*. Well, that and the advertising.

Miles Davis wore khakis. Four words, superimposed over an old photo of the jazz great, sitting with one leg slung over the back of a metal folding chair, effortlessly hip—in khakis.[19] (Not *Gap* khakis, but who are we to split hairs?) Starting in 1993, a flood of black-and-white print ads led by in-house marketing whiz Maggie Gross made use of archival photos of the greats, wearing clothes that looked *almost* like

Gap's: Norma Jean wore khakis, too, as did Kerouac, Picasso, Warhol. And, soon enough, so would every desk-bound Clinton-era worker bee. These ads gave Gap something that no one but Mickey believed possible: actual cool. Fans ripped them out of magazines and peeled them off of bus shelters.

From the *Chicago Tribune:* "The ads have had such widespread recognition that 'so-and-so wore khakis' has entered mainstream conversations, has turned up in high-visibility 'Doonesbury' and *New Yorker* cartoons and has made khakis and Gap practically synonymous . . . David Letterman, who on his television show has been mercilessly poking fun at New York Gov.–elect George Pataki's name, introduced Pataki to read the top 10 ways to mispronounce his name—'Gap khakis' was one of them."[20]

The underlying conceit: nobody was too good for Gap basics. But it was Sharon Stone who really drove that message home. In 2021, gabbing with Naomi Campbell on a podcast, Stone revealed that one of the most memorable fashion moments of the 1990s was the result of a wardrobe malfunction. In 1996, she was up for an Oscar for the role of chinchilla-dripping goddess Ginger McKenna in Martin Scorsese's *Casino*. She had two gowns lined up, but one didn't work. And the other met an unfortunate demise beneath the wheel of a FedEx truck: "I finally made it to this big moment in my career and there's a big tire track down my dress."[21]

The view of this story from Mickey's office reads a little different: A day before the Oscars, Gap got a fax from Sharon Stone that read a little like a ransom note. It said that if the company would donate $250,000 to her sister's charity, Stone would wear Gap to the Academy Awards the following night: *I need an answer by noon.*

It wasn't the money that was the problem. Gap spent millions on advertising. But that was for carefully orchestrated productions—they knew what they were paying for. Mickey wasn't crazy about the idea of throwing a quarter mil at some cockamamie celebrity scheme that had a distinct hostage-crisis vibe. "Influencers" were still a long way off. It was a bit like Uma Thurman wearing J.Crew pants: Who knew if a famous lady wearing a cheap T-shirt would have any real payoff for the maker of that T-shirt? At his office that day, Mickey wrung his hands, debating it with anyone who'd listen. Finally, he agreed: *Oh, what the hell. Let's do it.*

The next night, Mickey and 45 million other Americans watched the Academy Awards on TV. There was Stone, glowing like an Oscar statuette in a slim, short-sleeved black turtleneck, under a velvet frock coat, with a Valentino skirt. She looked fabulous, of course. But there was no fanfare, no announcement. The rather crass "Who are you wearing?" was not yet a ubiquitous red-carpet question. Sure, Stone was wearing Gap, but how would anyone ever *know* it was Gap? Mickey was apoplectic. *Had he just been snookered into paying $250,000 for an actress to wear a T-shirt?* That night, he could barely sleep.

But the next morning, everything changed. The press was all over it. Decades later, images of Stone from that night regularly pop up on lists of the most iconic Oscar outfits of all time. For Gap, the PR value of that appearance far exceeded $250,000—indeed, its worth is almost incalculable. But the stunt also paid off for Stone. Wearing Gap to the Oscars rebranded her as a cool, canny risk taker—somehow above the fray of label-conscious Hollywood.

That moment was the apotheosis of the '90s craze for high-low dressing. As the writer Holly Brubach noted earlier, if your shirt cost $11.99 from Gap, it told the world you weren't a sucker. Now *that* was cool.

By 1997, the architecture critic Paul Goldberger would proclaim that Mickey Drexler had "greater impact on the quality and look of design in the past twenty years than anyone else in the United States."[22] Gap, he wrote, was "probably the most effective mass-market design engine in the world." By bringing good design to the masses, it changed the game of mass-market retail from one of sheer volume to one driven—à la high fashion—by image: "Buy the T-shirt, get the lifestyle."

The greatest success of Mickey's career, though, wasn't at Gap. Old Navy was born in 1993, after a rare lull in Gap's rise. In 1992, as Don Fisher once put it, Gap was getting "kicked in the pants," by a boom in bargains. Off-price chains like Marshalls and T.J.Maxx, which sold brand names on the cheap, had been gaining steam since the '70s. Then, in the '80s, outlet stores came into their own. And discounters like Walmart, Kohl's, and Target upped their game.[23] By the early '90s these stores were in an all-out price-war, syphoning off a "mass middle" that Gap did not serve. Half of all American families had a net household income of less than $45,000. These people were priced out of the kind of malls Gap dominated. Which was news to Mickey, who had always thought Gap was a steal. (Remember the subjectivity of *affordable*?) But in 1991, he took a trip to Target to check out Everyday Hero, a new range that looked a lot like Gap lite.[24] These were not terrible clothes, he realized. Why *wouldn't* shoppers switch to similar-looking khakis at a lower price?

Sometimes a good name was all it took to get Mickey's juices flowing. He and Maggie Gross had once spotted two words on the awning of a bar, while taxiing through Paris' Saint-Germain: Old Navy. The Gap Inc. board wasn't sure about this name. They called in corporate consultants, who suggested Old Indigo, Old Khaki, even Forklift—a hyperliteral stab at the income bracket they were aiming for, and maybe, a reference to the Home Depot–esque aesthetic Mickey had in mind for the new stores. But Old Navy stuck. According to Gross, it captured "the spirit of family, good times, basic values, and friendship."[25] And it was the one Mickey wanted.

Within four years, Old Navy was a billion-dollar brand. It earned

Mickey the reputation of a visionary, a seer. In the business pages, he became the "merchant prince." The notion of the all-powerful merchant can be traced all the way back to the Bible. The editors of *Women's Wear Daily* had long used "merchant prince" to describe a handful of retail executives. But once Mickey earned the title, it was as if he owned exclusive rights to it. The words might as well have been printed on his business card, as Don Fisher was well aware. In 1995, Fisher ceded the C.E.O. spot to Mickey, giving him dominion over not just Gap but also Banana Republic, Old Navy, and Gap Kids.

By the time *Fortune* put Mickey on its cover in 1998,[26] the annual sales of Gap Inc. totaled $8.3 billion—up 27 percent from the year before. The company had 2,237 stores, including those in Japan, the U.K., Canada, France, and Germany. Famously, Gap Inc. opened a new store somewhere on Earth *every day*. (For scale, recall that in 1997, at the time of its T.P.G. leveraged buyout, J.Crew had forty-eight stores.) *Fortune* compared a Gap T-shirt to a can of Coke: the only difference between the two, it said, was there was "no Gap formula hidden in some vault; there's only Mickey Drexler."

Fisher's two sons both worked at Gap. Still, "there is no heir apparent," an employee noted in the story. "There is nobody who is near [Mickey's] equal."

At company-wide town hall meetings, with everyone still riding high on the viral success of "Gap Swing"—that multimillion-dollar TV campaign featuring ecstatic khaki-clad youths dancing their hearts out to Louis Prima's "Jump, Jive an' Wail"—employees stood on their chairs, dancing like they were at a Prince concert, waiting for Mickey to appear. Some even cried. "That's how much love they had for the brand," says a former merchant. "That was the excitement Mickey created."

Even Steve Jobs wanted in. In 1999, Jobs was conceptualizing a sleek, happy home for his new tangerine-orange iMacs. The first Apple stores had to feel like Apple: playful yet slick, but not so slick they were intimidating. Mickey was "one of the few people in the world who were as successful and savvy as Jobs on matters of design, image, and consumer yearnings," wrote Jobs biographer Walter Isaacson.[27] And Silicon Valley's high priest afforded Mickey an unusually high degree of respect. Mickey helped Apple conjure stores that weren't all that different from Gap's own: glossy white surfaces, blond-wood floors, brushed-metal fixtures. "Think different. Dress casual. Whatever," wrote the *New York Times*, juxtaposing the ethos of two superbrands, Apple and Gap.[28]

FISHER CRONIES SAY THAT AS FAR AS HE WAS CONCERNED, AS long as Gap Inc. was minting money, Mickey could star on all the magazine covers he wanted. But Fisher had always struggled with Mickey's off-the-cuff behavior. Both men were alphas in their way; it set them up for an antagonistic, unhealthy relationship.

In 1999, bolstered by comparisons to Coke and praise of its unsinkable merchant prince, Gap Inc. went into hyperspeed, increasing its overall square footage by 28 percent. In 2000, it expanded stores by another 31 percent.[29] And then things took a turn. That year, sales fell, and then kept falling. Mickey, too, fell from grace with remarkable speed. Don Fisher responded without mercy.

What went wrong? Depending on who's doing the talking, Mickey either got too complacent or too adventurous. Either way, he was the one everybody blamed.

Forces far bigger than Mickey were churning on the horizon. We tend to think of "fast fashion" as a phenomenon of the late aughts, but when the Swedes of H&M landed on American soil in 2000, hawking $19 facsimiles of dresses that had just stalked the runways, Gap and every company of its ilk were watching closely. The specialty retail era had delivered good, solid design and wearability to the masses. Then Target,

Old Navy, and company had given us good-enough basics at a blue collar price tag. But this was something new—the optical illusion of *fashion*, but so cheap it didn't matter if it went out of style or fell apart tomorrow. If this week's $19 dress disintegrates, you'll have even more fun buying a new one next week.

The thing that was so inexplicable—you might say arrogant—about Gap's most recent burst of expansion was that the economy had weakened in 2000, and would fall into a full recession in the aftermath of 9/11, despite George W. Bush's exhortations to Americans to show their consumer patriotism. (The best thing Americans could do for their country? Go to Disney World, the president said: "Take your families and enjoy life, the way we want it to be enjoyed."[30]) The lull in spending hit specialty retail hard. Even Abercrombie, king of the late '90s, began to flatline. No one was calling the death knell of the mall just yet—that institution still had some fight in it—but its hold on the national psyche was slipping. America was beginning to see through the consumerist spell the mall had once cast.

And what of Mickey's good taste machine, the "veritable assembly line of esthetics" that Paul Goldberger said changed the way America looked and thought? When Mickey rebirthed Gap in the early '80s, that concept was totally new, unique. But almost two decades later, uniformity and sameness were starting to look a little . . . same-y. Going to a Gap to flip through the same T-shirts in every other Gap—and in lots of other stores, too, including Gap's own Banana Republic *and* Old Navy—was no great thrill. Les Wexner had wanted to make a clothing chain as uniform as McDonald's, and as ubiquitous, and Mickey had accomplished just that. But who wants to shop at McDonald's? Gap needed to shift gears, differentiate itself from its competitors *and* its own offshoot, Old Navy. And the arrival of H&M did turn Mickey's head. Could fashion be the answer?

So he tried it; for a few seasons, Gap swerved into trends. This was a huge mistake, though probably not as big as the press made it out to be: To blame the downfall of the mighty Gap on a brief spate of orchid-purple leather jackets and crocheted halter tops? No. The real problem, increasingly apparent in years to come, was that Gap Inc. was extravagantly bloated. In 2001, Gap Inc. had 4,100 stores,[31] including Old Navy's splashy four-story flagships at key urban intersections; those $8 tank tops were showcased in top-dollar real estate. Later, Mickey would call Gap's drastic expansion the biggest mistake of his career, claiming that—though he oversaw the growth—he was opposed to it. "I didn't fight the board hard enough to stop it. I should have fought harder."[32]

Mickey's style of micromanagement was not suited to the sprawling corporation Gap had become. Deep down, Mickey knew this. "The C.E.O. can't be the guy picking the fabric swatches at a company that size," Cohen says. Like T.P.G., plucking Mark Sarvary from Stouffer's, Gap, too, was beginning to wonder if its C.E.O. spot was better suited to a corporate type who spoke the language of I.T., global manufacturing, Wall Street—*not* a merchant prince. (Paul Pressler, who would be tapped to replace Mickey, came from Disney.)

THE THING ABOUT BEING THE HEIR APPARENT: WHEN THINGS GO wrong, there's no one else to blame. Around 9 P.M. on May 4, 2002, after nearly eighteen years of epic success and twenty-nine months of solid decline, Mickey was just getting home from what seemed like a perfectly copacetic dinner with the Gap Inc. board when he got a phone call. It was Steve Jobs.

By now, the men were friends. They had spent weekends together. Mickey sat on the board of Apple, Jobs on the board of Gap—an arrangement that was a little un-kosher, but that delighted Mickey. Jobs was a born rabble-rouser whose unfiltered opinions had a way of shaking up everyone else on the Gap board, which largely consisted of

Fisher's allies. That night, Jobs was once again going off script. "You're going to get fired tomorrow," he told Mickey.

Jobs was empathetic. He'd famously been through a similar ordeal in 1985, when he was ousted from Apple after a long power struggle with its board—after which, of course, he rose again to reclaim his throne. Jobs's epic redemption story could not have been lost on Mickey.

Mickey hung up the phone and dialed Don Fisher right away. "I have to see you," he said. But the boss refused to engage. "I'll see you at eight o'clock in the morning," he said. When Mickey showed up bright and early, Fisher merely handed him an envelope. Inside was a letter informing him that this would be his last day at the company.

Mickey walked straight into the conference room, where roughly ten board members were already gathered. No one would look him in the eye. "Where's your decency?" he asked them. "Your courtesy? Your sympathy?"

Ultimately Mickey did not leave that day. He elected to stay on and run the company until a replacement was found. For four months, to Fisher's amazement, Mickey worked harder than ever, determined to turn the company around. By that fall, he believed he had set them on the right track. But the decision stuck. On September 26, 2002, Mickey was out.

The design staff remembers watching Mickey's final walk to the elevator, exiting the company that, as far as they were concerned, he was singly responsible for building. "He passed by and we all gave a big golf clap," says a menswear designer. At Gap, "he was everything." To many people there, watching Mickey Drexler get pushed out was unthinkable, crushing. It felt personal. Says another staffer, "You felt like someone had betrayed him."

CHAPTER 13

This Is Your Captain Speaking

On a cold Sunday night in January 2003, Jenna Lyons phoned Gayle Spannaus at home. This call was unusual. They'd worked together for a decade, but had never been after-hours confidants. But Jenna had gotten a call at 7 P.M. that evening: J.Crew's latest C.E.O., Ken Pilot, was out. As the head of womenswear, Jenna was to come in early the next morning to meet her new boss, Mickey Drexler. Jenna's first thought was not: *The merchant prince is here to save us!* More along the lines of: *Geezus. Another one?*

At thirty-four, Jenna had toiled at J.Crew for thirteen years, her entire career. For most of it she had served loyally, with no regrets; she loved the job, the people, the brand. She didn't mind that J.Crew wasn't "fashion," or if she did, she never let it show. But for the previous five years—and especially the last eighteen months—working at J.Crew felt more and more like a never-ending season of *Survivor* (fittingly, one of the biggest shows on TV at the time). Jenna and Spannaus were among the last of the original cast still clinging to the island, bruised and exhausted, and beginning to lose sight of exactly what they'd been fighting so hard to save. Maybe it was time to admit defeat.

Spannaus had started in 1992 as the company's model booker and was now its fashion director. Jenna had risen from "an assistant to an assistant to someone else's assistant," as she sometimes jokingly put it, to designer, then director—touching nearly every part of the business along the way: Swim. Lingerie. Sweaters. Shoes. Sunglasses. Bags. In 2002, when Scott Formby, her mentor and the person who, for years, *had* been her after-hours work confidant, was finally pushed off of J.Crew's rapidly shrinking island, Jenna was crowned head womenswear designer, in a scene that echoed the one Formby experienced eighteen months earlier, when Emily was ousted, and he was handed her creative responsibilities. On the one hand, Jenna had just landed her dream job. On the other, she was replacing her friend on a ship that seemed to be inexorably sinking. "At the time, it did not feel like a dream job," she told me.

Jenna and her team had now completely redesigned J.Crew—no small undertaking—not once, but three different times, seesawing between C.E.O.s who did not have the first clue what J.Crew was about, and in some cases even how retail worked. They had abandoned the color orange at the behest of Mr. Pepperidge Farm. They'd endured a consultant who thought the big news in womenswear was the "shrug," that odd, scarf-like band women were wearing over their going-out tops in the early aughts. Everything about the shrug was so *not* "J.Crew"—but at that point, what *was* J.Crew?

"The trickiest part is I don't even know if *I* believed in what I was doing," Jenna has said. "You get into this weird situation: In order to keep my team, I had to keep it together. In order to motivate them, I had to drink the Kool-Aid."[1] Jenna was new to management, overseeing a large team, some of whom she didn't know well. She had a taste, for the first time, of what it must have been like all those years for Emily.

"You can never predict how challenging being the boss really is," she says. "It can be incredibly lonely, incredibly difficult." Everyone seemed to be looking to her: *Well, are* you *going to stick around?* She didn't want to lie. "These were some of the most creative, funny, inspiring people I have ever worked with," she told me. "That place was like family to me. It felt wrong to jump ship when things were bad."

Over the past six months, Ken Pilot had swung J.Crew in the direction of Banana Republic–sleek. That look didn't feel right to Jenna, but what could she say? She was hired help. And now . . . Mickey Drexler? He was industry-famous, but Jenna had only a vague notion of the so-called merchant prince. So she called her fellow survivor, Gayle Spannaus. That night they talked for hours, picking over the last crazy few years, hypothesizing about what might be next—and circling back, over and over, to a shared suspicion: *Yep, this is it. We're finally gonna get fired.* When they hung up just shy of midnight, Jenna was fairly certain her reign at J.Crew was about to be over before it had really begun.

MICKEY WALKED INTO J.CREW THE NEXT DAY WITH SKIN IN THE game. He was not just T.P.G.'s latest C.E.O.-for-hire, but a major shareholder, having invested $10 million of his own money for 10 percent of the company.[2] It was clear to his new team that he had arrived nursing a deep wound and a fiery grudge. Several people describe the animus in strikingly similar language: "Oh, he wanted to fuck the Gap." How? By making J.Crew cool.

Initially, there had been a half-hearted PR attempt to call Mickey's Gap departure a resignation, but Mickey isn't one to sugarcoat, especially when he feels he's been wronged. *They fired me*, he told interviewers bluntly. "The thing about Mickey is he wears his heart, and his business, on his sleeve," says the menswear designer Todd Snyder, one of the first Gap Inc. employees to follow Mickey to J.Crew. (Snyder was a J.Crew rehire: He and Jenna had been fellow newbies there in the early '90s.)

Silicon Valley startup culture, still nascent in 2003, had not yet rebranded failure as an anticipated stepping stone to success—proof of an entrepreneur's willingness to take risks and bounce back. For Mickey, being ejected from Gap "was a crushing blow," says a designer who became close to the C.E.O. "He took it very personally, like *he* had failed—and he doesn't like that." Years later, when J.Crew was on top of the world and Mickey was once again on the covers of magazines, he would admit that he still couldn't walk past a Gap store without feeling a bolt of anger. *Every time?* the writer asked. "That's right," he replied. "Every time."[3]

On paper, J.Crew was a shocking demotion for the merchant prince. By 2003, sales had dwindled to $766 million—about one-twentieth Gap's.[4] Mickey found a way to spin that as a positive. He had learned his lesson: "I don't do big well," he told a group of Columbia M.B.A. students early in his J.Crew tenure. "If J.Crew ever gets really big, I should not be running it." Whether he really believed that or not, it was true that J.Crew's size meant Mickey could run it his way: as if the whole organization were plugged directly into the 50-amp fuse of his own brain.

On day one, Jenna walked out of that first early-morning meeting with Mickey to find workers already stringing wire for a new office-wide intercom system. This way, Mickey could speak to the entire company at the press of a button. "I was like: are you kidding me with this?" she later recalled thinking.[5] Not in the least.

"*Jim Larkin. Jim Larkin. Can you please come to my office?*" Larkin was then editor of the catalogue, a rehire from the Emily days. He was also the first J.Crew employee to receive the call of God—er, Mickey—as the boss's disembodied Bronx accent boomed around the office. The first time he heard it, Larkin cracked up. Were they all being pranked? Everything about Mickey was surreally different from the J.Crew way.

Was the intercom Mickey's megalomania run amok? Sure. But it was also expedient. J.Crew had grown up gradually around Emily—it was both her offspring and her sibling, in a way—but Mickey was an outsider, dropping into the middle of a crisis. He needed to establish himself as the command center, the literal voice in their heads. And he was impatient. He didn't know who these people were or what each of them did, and he had nonstop questions, ideas, and demands. No way was he going to leave a message on someone's voicemail and wait for the answer to trickle up to him.

With the intercom, he kept hundreds of people both on their toes and adrift in his own stream of consciousness, like it or not. "Don Fisher would have cut his head off if he'd tried to pull that at Gap," says Mark Cohen. But for the first time in Mickey's career there was no Don Fisher. T.P.G. stayed relatively hands-off. As far as anyone on the ground could tell, Mickey was the final word.

He staked out a corner of the open-plan office space for his desk, which was really a large conference room table. If new recruits didn't like being interviewed in front of the whole cast of J.Crew, tough luck. ("I don't have an office," he later said. "I had one of those at the Gap."[6]) Anyway, Mickey didn't stick to a desk. He had a way of being everywhere, all the time. He called spontaneous meetings wherever he happened to be, stalked the halls, firing questions at everyone from the designers to the folks who delivered the mail. "Wherever Mickey was, that was the center of the company," says a web exec. "It was as if he had cameras on him at all times."

By now, when it was time to "do the surgery," Mickey had his system down pat. He did what he had done at Ann Taylor, Gap, and, to a degree, Banana Republic. Step one: "Get rid of the ugly." Or, to use another Mickey-ism, cut the "schlock."

It wasn't Mickey's style to do this discreetly, in the privacy of a few trusted deputies, as Emily certainly would have. No, cutting the schlock was his favorite kind of theater. On day two or three, he gathered every style J.Crew currently stocked, plus all the samples of what was on order for the upcoming season, *plus* much of the company staff in one room.[7] The employees would present the goods, item by item, and he would decide what to keep, or cut. The process was triple whammy: Mickey could simultaneously size up the wares and the people presenting them, while affording everyone a good view of his own thought process and point of view.

Some fifty people gathered to watch the big review. Under any circumstances, this would be a slog—as a catalogue company, J.Crew stocked up to three times more items, or stock-keeping units (better known as S.K.U.s), than a traditional store retailer. And it was nerve-wracking: What, and who, was he going to like or hate? Everyone in the room was keenly aware they were being sorted like fruit at a market stall, handled, sniffed, inspected for damage. Mickey had said so himself. In his first meeting with a bunch of employees, he had pushed back his chair, propped a foot on the table like he'd never felt more at home in his life, and announced, "You're all interviewing for your jobs."[8]

Jenna stood on the edge of the room, stomach in knots. Privately, she shuddered at some of the clothes that lined the room—the slinkier new stretch pants and leather pieces they'd produced at the behest of Ken Pilot were neither to her taste nor, in her opinion, right for J.Crew. But as the head womenswear designer, Jenna was the one who had to answer for the existence of these clothes. Was she really going to tell the new boss—and the entire company—that clothes she herself had overseen were . . . crap?

What happened next has become the Cinderella story of *Jenna,* a woman who emerged from the nameless, faceless ranks of mass retail—from the unglamorous bowels of a catalogue company, no less: unheard-of!—to become a bona fide fashion star.

Mickey didn't like the merchant who started to present the women's collection. He asked Jenna to take over. The first thing she did was pick up three pairs of skinny pants off the rack. For a moment, she stood there, staring at them. "Okay, which ones do you like?" Mickey asked. This was her moment of truth. If she told him what she really thought, it might be her chance to finally be heard. Or it might get her fired. She took a deep breath, and let 'er rip: only one of the three was worth keeping, she said. Mickey did not flinch. "Fine," he said, "throw the others on the floor."

Next was a trendy sweater made of curly, poodle-like fur. The thing sold like crazy; Jenna thought it was godawful. Dump it, Mickey said. Jenna worked her way around the room, ruthlessly editing, a mountain of rejects piling at her feet. "I was so confused, and I was scared, but I was also a little bit excited, because all the things that I liked and I thought were brand-right, he was leaving up on the wall," she later said. "Is that good, is it bad? I don't know."[9]

Jenna also didn't know that Mickey had already been tipped off by Todd Snyder, his trusted menswear designer at Old Navy, to look out for this woman, Jenna Lyons. Now, in Mickey's gut, a familiar excitement was building: the thrill of locking in on a core member of his future team. To Mickey, identifying people who had the right ideas, the right temperament, to take a company forward—*his* people—was more memorable than adding another industry trophy to his pile. And as Snyder had said, Jenna had *It*. Her instincts were spot-on. She was decisive. She had vision. And she knew, deep down, what was J.Crew and what wasn't—perhaps the most valuable skill of all, for someone in Mickey's position.

As far as Mickey was concerned, this company was a shitshow. But he knew there was something worth salvaging here, a nugget of gold buried deep in the mess: the brand itself. Even in his Gap days, when he was crushing the competition, Mickey had kept an eye on J.Crew. The catalogues were regularly spotted on his desk. He loved the relaxed styling, the *ease*—that imagery, no one did it better. J.Crew had often provided inspiration, and yet remained a little untouchable. Indeed,

Mickey admired the broken-in wash of J.Crew chinos so much, he tried to replicate it. Even with Gap's deep-pocketed R&D budget, they never quite nailed it.

Unlike his "get the red out" siege at Gap, Mickey was not out to eradicate J.Crew's past. If anything, he wanted to rewind the tape back to the feeling the brand once conjured. Soon, he would designate a "heritage team" of Emily-era survivors—Jenna and Gayle Spannaus were key members—whom he could page over the intercom when some item was on the chopping block: Should he kill it? Or was it true to J.Crew? Mickey's HR team would soon be calling up ex-Emily-era employees: Would they come back? Also: Did they happen to have any old J.Crew clothes lying around? "People were running around creating an archive," says an executive who got such a call, "so Mickey could figure out: what was the secret sauce?"

He wasn't trying to reverse engineer the perfect Barn Jacket so much as re-create the culture that bred the jacket—the team of competitive, deeply bonded believers; those tireless twentysomethings thrilled to come to work every day at their weird New Jersey startup. The people who got it. Now, Jenna was first on his list.

In the conference room, after the racks had been thinned and piles of clothes littered the room, Mickey gave Jenna the green light: "Okay, get on a plane. Go to Hong Kong, start developing new product, and re-present."

JENNA RECALLS MICKEY'S ARRIVAL AS A SWEET RELIEF, "ONE OF the happiest times in my life." It was not as rosy for everyone.

In a replay of his rough landing at the Gap, he axed the schlock with apparent glee—cutting lackluster clothing and downmarket parts of the business with equal abandon. As far as he was concerned, the clothes sucked, the stores felt strangely empty. Worst of all, in Mickey's estimation, was that J.Crew had become a place where nobody paid full price. The emails J.Crew sent out, offering customers 20, 30, 40 percent off, infuriated him. "Why is the whole place on sale?" he crowed in meetings. He took two fingers and snapped them onto his forearm like an addict tapping for a vein. "Pull out the needle! Get rid of these promotions!"

Nobody there *wanted* to be selling schlock, least of all those who still recalled J.Crew's glory days. But Mickey's rat-a-tat commands put the business side in a bind. Even with Mickey's $10 million cash infusion, bankruptcy loomed. How were they supposed to keep the company afloat *and* cut the things that still made money? When Mickey learned that J.Crew clothes were being sold through third-party retailers—other, not-so-hot websites—his orders were unequivocal: "Kill it. I want the entire thing dead right now." But those affiliate sites accounted for 10 percent of all online sales. The "poodle" sweater that had ended its days in a pile at Jenna's feet? A million-dollar business, gone. That cut into J.Crew's bottom line but, for those whose compensation was tied to performance, also into their own paychecks. But Mickey moved like a freight train. Who was going to step out in front of him?

CHAPTER 14

Panning for Gold

All eyes were on Mickey, of course. All eyes were always on Mickey. Whose own eyes were zeroed in on a wall of cashmere sweaters. Why were these so *boring*? he wanted to know, now staring murderously at the staff gathered around a conference table. Where were the colors? The orange? The green! The yellow! "I don't understand what you guys are doing!" he said, chucking the offending knits to the floor one by one. "Go get those colors!"

Mickey had cashmere on the brain for a reason. Even now, with the company a shadow of its former self, "J.Crew people" still considered themselves J.Crew people. "I've never seen that kind of customer loyalty to the *idea* of a brand," he had told his employees on day one.

He needed to send up a flare to those people: a single focal point that would tell them J.Crew was credible, covetable, even aspirational again. What one item could do that? As Arthur Cinader once put it in a "J.Crew haiku" worthy of a *New Yorker* cartoon: "Cashmere . . . spun of cashmere fibers from the necks of goats in Mongolia's finest herds."

Cashmere has been a cornerstone of the well-to-do wardrobe—synonymous with wealth, status, unimpeachable taste—since Empress Josephine racked up hundreds of shawls in the late 1800s.[1] And cashmere is baked into prep, of course, the collegiate fifties sweater set being the age-old companion to a demure pearl necklace and itchy tweed skirt.

But in the mid-aughts, with a wide range of grades of cashmere newly available, a "pashmina" was now draped on every shoulder, and cashmere was having a *moment*—still a staple of the rich, but also proudly sported by the not-so-rich year-round, in every ply, weight, and hue.

Mickey wanted to sprinkle some of that fairy dust over his beleaguered brand. But the people in his conference room were having a hard time picking up what the boss was putting down. And no wonder: Several months into Mickey's tenure, it still seemed like someone was getting fired every week. The pressure was "bone crushing," one Mickey veteran told me, and the office politics were dog-eat-dog: factions were forming, and Mickey seemed to enjoy it. The new Gap hires were skeptical of the J.Crew team, who thought it was a big deal to sell in a month what Gap sold in a weekend: What did they know about building a superpower? But the J.Crew people were equally skeptical of Gap arrivistes: they knew how to sell T-shirts by the boatload, but what did they know about the rarefied identity J.Crew had (at one point) perfected? Were these people going to turn *their* J.Crew into another bland empire of khaki?

Both sides were unnerved by Mickey, who could turn on a dime, finding an employee fascinating one day and icing that same person out the next. Some joked that he should keep a *Vanity Fair*–style "in and out" list on his door, to make it easier to keep up with where they stood with him on a given day.

Mickey adhered to "the Socratic method of management," a former creative jokes. He treated every interaction, whether it was the office, the stores, in a restaurant, or on the street, as a roving focus group—questioning anyone about anything, at any time. He never hesitated to put someone on the spot: *What do you think of this shirt? What would you pay for it?* At other retailers, C.E.O.s were being hired to pore over data and spreadsheets, but at J.Crew it worked somewhat in reverse. Mickey largely trusted his deputies to stay on top of the number crunching. The nitty-gritty of customer relations was Mickey's job, perhaps his greatest skill: eventually he would print his own email address in the catalogue.[2] He wanted to hear from everyone.

This was nice in theory, but could be a nightmare in practice. In meetings, you could never let down your guard, lest you were next up in the hot seat. Mickey was disarmingly nice to the customers and mail guys he quizzed. But members of his own team who failed to supply the correct answer to one of his constant queries—that is, the one he wanted to hear—might find their response dismissed out of hand. Or they might be shamed later over the intercom: "Finance team! Come in here and tell marketing what they're doing wrong."

"I don't think I can call anyone who ran a meeting like that a 'genius,'" says an Emily-era merchant who survived a year under Mickey. "That kind of thing overshadowed anything he did that was so great."

In the conference room, as he continued to rant about colors, a race ensued to racks in the hallway, where all the items the staff had previously weeded out—things that seemed too challenging to sell, or too expensive to produce—were grabbed and hauled back in. As the store visuals expert John Valdivia (one of Mickey's first Gap Inc. recruits to J.Crew) recalls it, by the end, a rainbow of twenty-plus hues was spread across the wall. *Now, this!* Mickey said, *This is what I want.* This *is exciting.*

A couple of brave souls murmured dissent: *Uh, Mickey, aren't these too expensive? How will we ever get a decent margin?* But he wasn't listening. He was adding and subtracting sweaters from a pile on the table, lost in some Willy Wonka knitwear fugue, muttering to himself. Finally, he stepped back to admire the assortment he'd created, and looked up at them, triumphant. But everybody stood there, deer in the headlights, gawping at him. It seemed to finally dawn on Mickey: these people were too paralyzed, too fearful of him, and whatever he was about to do next, to catch the adrenaline jolt he was trying to transmit.

In the Cinader era, silence had been required, and prized. With

Mickey, silence simply never occurred. There was no "low" on his dial. He processed externally. When he liked something, his enthusiasm was unbridled. "Oh. My. Gawd!" he'd exclaim about, say, a great pair of men's brogues. Or he might fake a swoon, as if to say, *I love this so much I can't* stand *it.* When he hated something, he was equally emphatic about that, too. Mickey's a showman. Showmen do not like a dead audience.

As Valdivia tells it, Mickey took matters into his own hands. The merchant prince, age fifty-six, climbed up on the table, lay down, and began to drape himself in sweaters, rolling around like he was bathing in knitwear. "I *looooove* these colors!" he shouted.

It was absurd. For the Emily-era people in the room, it was beyond that: unthinkable. But at last, the tension was broken. A few people started to laugh. That moment "was a huge unlock for everyone," says Valdivia. Looking around the room, you could see twin realizations begin to dawn. The first was that part of their jobs—perhaps the most critical part—was going to be keeping Mickey himself excited, engaged, entertained. The second was that anyone who cared this deeply about cashmere, of all things, was not planning to turn J.Crew into wall-to-wall tees and khakis. The relief was palpable: *Phew. He's not trying to turn us into Gap.*

TO ANYONE WHO WAS LOOKING TO SEE WHAT MICKEY WOULD DO with J.Crew, the Spring 2003 catalogue provided the first clue. It came out six weeks after his arrival. Among the many things Mickey had unceremoniously tossed out was the photo shoot intended for that cover. He hated it. Casting about for a solution, Mickey fixated on a little stuffed dog someone had brought into the office. It was made of patchwork madras—the kind of upscale tchotchke you might find in a

Martha's Vineyard gift shop. Instead of a laughing blond cavorting in the surf, Mickey put that dog on the cover of the catalogue. The image was just a few inches tall, perched in the bottom right corner of a bright white page, beneath the J.Crew logo. That's it. It was cute, hypersimple, playful, and optimistic. Very Mickey. It was also as preppy as preppy could be.

Funny thing about Mickey's big dig in the annals of J.Crew—his "heritage team"; his top execs, sitting around studying old catalogues: all of it was leading to a place that J.Crew, despite appearances to the contrary, had never actually been—true, unadulterated prep. This made sense for the times. Menswear in particular was back in one of its cyclical love affairs with popped collars and boys' school blazers. The cult Japanese style rags that the J.Crew menswear team looked to for inspiration were obsessed with vintage J. Press and Brooks Brothers. Abercrombie's notion of prep was still huge in middle America. And in 2004, Ralph Lauren would launch his "preppy with a twist" line, Rugby,[3] pairing distressed denim with old-school rep ties and blazers bearing loud, fake-school crests.

Like any spike in interest in prep, America's uniform of belonging, this one could be traced to bigger-picture forces: Given the financial insecurity that followed the recession of 2000, and then the earthshaking events of September 11, 2001, some saw it as consumers clinging to an imagined past—a time when things felt safe.[4] Others saw just another pendulum shift in the wake of two trends that J.Crew had, for the most part, sat out. Grunge was finally dead: now anything distressed or "dirty" felt passé. And after the sexed-up Paris Hilton–lewd of Y2K—lower-than-ever, bum-skimming jeans; swagged peek-a-boo necklines—suddenly a popped collar looked somehow cheeky again.

But this time around, prep came with a new accessory: a wink. The legacy of the '90s was that fashion—so self-serious for so long—

now had a sense of irony. It arguably started when Seattle rockers with matted hair and dirty Converses took to the stage wearing thrift-store grandma cardigans and pearl necklaces. Theirs was a fashion statement born of necessity: these hipsters were flat broke. But it also reflected a jaded Gen X eye roll, which gradually built into its own self-referential form of elitism (and ageism): *I'm in on the joke—aren't you?* Clothing would never exactly be "straight" again. Now that prep was coming back out of storage, the best way to shake out that whiff of mothball was by adding a little side-eye—a sense of nostalgia, but also a knowing nod at the look's elitist roots.

Mickey wasn't so concerned with side-eye. For his purposes, preppy was a convenient cultural shorthand. Gold-buttoned navy blazers and grass-green cable knits radiated J.Crew values Mickey wanted to reinstate (well-made, classic, upscale) plus a lot more that it didn't hurt to insinuate, either: authentic, old money, patrician.

This was Mickey's ethos: simple, digestible. To a degree, obvious. Early on he asked Valdivia to design a window for the Fifth Avenue store that telegraphed a message any passerby would absorb with a single glance. At the time, Valdivia had neither new designs to work with, nor any extra budget. He was coming from Old Navy, where $5 T-shirts were shrink-wrapped like T-bone steaks and sold out of old-fashioned freezers. And he had just inherited the team that helped craft Emily's "mini-Barneys." What *was* the message he was supposed to be telegraphing? Even Mickey didn't know that yet. But the boss knew what he didn't want: every time Valdivia presented a quiet, tasteful concept that seemed "very J.Crew," he was sent back to the drawing board.

Finally, he hit Mickey's sweet spot. He proposed a line of mannequins in collegiate navy blazers and Nantucket-ready "critter pants"—the same cutesy embroidered lobsters, whales, and anchors that Emily had loathed—in front of a bright blue backdrop that read, *Catch a crit-*

ter! He even blew up oversize images of these critters, that looked like they were scurrying across the background.

You could almost hear Emily's groan echoing down from her new Connecticut digs. Valdivia had met J.Crew's former empress only once, but in those days her ghost was still palpable in the hallways of 770. As he began to paint store walls neon green and cyan yellow, breaking one Emily rule after the next, "I'm thinking, *She fucking hates me!*" he says with a rueful laugh.

But Mickey didn't have Emily's hangups about cliché prep. If anything, he seemed to have a thing for WASP culture. When he learned that one of his designers had grown up in Greenwich, he ribbed the guy constantly: "Hey, where's the summer house again?" (The designer didn't have a summer house. Mickey, on the other hand, a millionaire many times over—in the sunnier days of 1999, *Forbes* estimated his on-paper value at a billion[5]—collected oceanfront real estate like a kid amassing baseball cards.)

Mickey loved those windows. "That was it for him, he was *flying*," Valdivia recalls. "He goes, 'Oh my god, oh my god. This is what we're doing.'"

Catch a critter! was as succinct as *Miles Davis wore khakis*. The shift in language was another one-eighty for J.Crew—not that anyone paused to notice, in the relentless churn of Mickey's takeover. Arthur Cinader had artfully seeded confusion, littering the catalogue copy with not-quite-puns and obscure references to Renaissance musical instruments. But Mickey was about *simple*. At Gap, he had zeroed in on a single message, then hammered it home, telling customers exactly what to buy. *Khakis Swing:* Two little words. "Nail it," he always said. Be clear. Say it straight.

It didn't hurt that the Fifth Avenue store, where those windows debuted, was right across the street from Gap's New York offices. Within months of touching down at J.Crew, Mickey made sure his former colleagues—whose fortunes had not improved—could not avoid knowing exactly what their famous ex was up to.

CASHMERE WAS HIS FIRST REALLY BIG SWING. TWO OF MICKEY'S earliest questions for Jenna had been "What's wrong with our cashmere? Why are our colors so dull?" The only way to get better colors was to source better quality cashmere "tops," aka the raw material, she told him, thoroughly prepared for him to laugh off the suggestion. Their finances were dire. In board meetings, the talk was of cutbacks. John Valdivia was overhauling Fifth Avenue windows with foam core and a bucket of paint. But Mickey did not laugh. He asked: "Well, what would be the best quality?"

That would be Loro Piana, the century-old firm based in the village of Quarona, at the foot of the Italian Alps.[6] Most people know Loro Piana as the maker of $1,000 sweaters sold at Neiman Marcus—sweaters as soft as angel wings and, for most mortals, about as accessible. But, for decades, Loro Piana also (quietly) operated a thriving wholesale arm, selling wool to Brioni and Brooks Brothers. These appropriately pricey companies stitched the curlicue script of the Loro Piana logo right beside their own, inside their garments, doubling the wow factor. But for years, Loro Piana had also sold cashmere to J.Crew. Scott Formby and Arnie Cohen had flown to Quarona to negotiate a deal back in 1989. But then in the T.P.G. years, rarefied yarns became a relic of J.Crew past.

Within months of Mickey's arrival, despite its budgetary crisis, J.Crew was again investing in Loro Piana cashmere—and selling curiously soft cashmere crewnecks, V-necks, and turtlenecks at $178 to $228, a fraction of the cost of the brand name, in "some of the most vibrant, lush colors anyone had ever seen," Jenna says. (One clue as to how they managed to pull this off: These yarns may have been spun in

Italy, but from there they took a sharp left to the Far East, where they were stitched together. The cashmere was from Italy. The *sweater* was from Hong Kong. "It was kind of a bait and switch," says an employee.)

The deal had always been that J.Crew could sell Loro Piana, as long as they didn't tell anybody it was Loro Piana. And for years, Emily's J.Crew had complied, content to let quality speak for itself, never shouting about the provenance of its goods.

But ten months after Mickey's arrival, this covert relationship rather strategically "leaked" to the *New York Times*: "Women with more lust than budget for high-end cashmere should note that this year's crop of sweaters at J.Crew are made of cashmere from the Italian company Loro Piana."[7]

For years, Mickey's J.Crew would whisper that this "leak" got them in trouble. *The Italians were not thrilled with this big reveal!* Poor Neiman Marcus was still trying to move $1,000-a-pop knits—they didn't need everybody knowing you could get *four* J.Crew sweaters for the price of one. Loro Piana's U.S. president, Pier Guerci, told the *Wall Street Journal* he gave Mickey a wrist slap: "I told them, why don't they just put in the ZIP Code?" he said. "They could have a little map, with an arrow pointing to the factory."[8] Of course, the same article revealed Guerci was a buddy of Mickey's who sometimes borrowed his Hamptons house—and also that J.Crew was far from singular in its access to the best: LP supplied cashmere to Bloomingdale's and other middle-market brands, too. But the idea that there had been a contretemps between J.Crew and Loro Piana protected the luxury brand's interests while burnishing the mall brand.

In the new era, Mickey was standing on the roof of J.Crew with a bullhorn, broadcasting J.Crew's once-quiet relationships—not to mention taking credit for them. (No one happened to mention that Mickey was reinstating the marriage of J.Crew and Loro Piana, not inventing it.) He had installed a full-scale PR and marketing department, something Emily once actively spurned, which would soon extol other rarefied suppliers, including silks from Ratti, the famous Italian textile house. This kind of publicity would be a masterstroke. Loro Piana cashmere, reintroduced less than a year after Mickey arrived, put J.Crew's new-sounding (if not wholly new) mantra, "affordable luxury," on the map. Like flipping a switch, it gave a company that had been suffering a slow death months earlier a quiet but real cachet. The message was loud and clear in exactly the right corners: "Everybody in America knew Mickey was the first guy to do inexpensive cashmere in tons of colors," says longtime retail analyst Richard Jaffe, who was keeping tabs on J.Crew for Wall Street. "That was brilliant."

MICKEY'S FAVORITE PARLOR TRICK WAS PLAYING CARNAC THE Magnificent, the "seer, soothsayer, and sage" that had been a favorite Johnny Carson bit on *The Tonight Show*. Carson would put on a turban as wide as a bicycle wheel, close his eyes, hold up a closed envelope, and magically divine whatever information was in the envelope. Mickey's Carnac would put his hand to his head like he was holding up an envelope, and magically spit out the season's buy. "Not just the top line, but what each percentage color would be," Jenna recalls. "It was pretty fascinating to watch." Mickey had perfect recall of numbers—to this day, he can remember the exact dates he started at both Gap and J.Crew—and the ability to process past sales information, plus gut instinct about a new collection, to bet on *exactly* how many of an item to buy. "It was uncanny," Jenna says.

They were all in awe of Mickey's legendary gut. "He could look at an assortment on a wall and pick the home runs," Todd Snyder recalls. And when Mickey saw a winner, he didn't just buy 10 percent more of it—he bought twice as many. "That's what set him apart," Snyder says. "(A) he picks the right things, and (B) he really goes for it."

But left to his own devices, Mickey would spin out. He was both the guy at the top, with the big-picture ideas, and the one at the very bottom, chasing every detail like a human pinball machine. What he was *not* doing was the day-in, day-out focused work of keeping a company on track. For the first eight months of his reign at J.Crew, Mickey charged ahead topsy-turvy, running in every direction at once, until everyone around him was ready to pull out their hair.

But in late 2003—with a flood of rainbow-bright cashmere set to arrive in J.Crew stores—he brought in a hire who many saw as critical. "What really changed the trajectory was when he hired Tracy Gardner," says Snyder. "In my opinion, she was the secret sauce."

Gardner had worked with Mickey at Gap Inc. since she was twenty-five, most recently running the Gap brand. She was straight-shooting and hyperfocused, and she happened to look not unlike an early J.Crew model: bright-eyed, clean-cut, blond. Unlike many there, Gardner was experienced in managing Mickey. As Snyder puts it, "She wouldn't overlisten to Mickey." No matter how many times a day he paged her over the intercom, how many debates he pulled her into, she could not be goaded into chasing the pinballs he sent spiraling off in every direction.

Gardner brought a new calm to Mickey's operating room, and rounded out the team. In addition to Jenna, Snyder, and new head of marketing and PR Margot Fooshee, Mickey's coven included Jeff Pfeifle, the former head of Old Navy; Jennifer Foyle, the master merchant with a sixth sense for what customers would love; operations expert Valerie Vanogtrop; and Jen Myerberg, a savant of distribution.

There's a point to mentioning all of them by name: Mickey and Jenna—and *only* Mickey and Jenna—are famously credited with leading J.Crew into a new golden era. But there was a team of heavy hitters behind them, and most of these people hailed from the mighty Gap Inc. These were people who had fueled the epic launch of Old Navy, opened stores by the thousands, and fostered pop-culture moments like Khakis Swing—they were there for the last true golden era Gap would ever have.

With them in place, by early 2004 the people at 770 Broadway were erecting what was really a new company—product by product, catalogue by catalogue, store by store. It bore the name and some of the genetic material of the original J.Crew, but under the hood, the engine was all Gap. And while the look and vibe of Mickey-era J.Crew is widely (rightly) chalked up to remarkable design talent, it was also co-engineered by Gap-educated merchants who knew how to craft items that would sell, sell, *sell*: over the years, this would give us the skinny Jackie cardigan, the Washed mens' shirt, the French bikini top, the cropped Minnie pant, the trim Tippi sweater. The CeCe ballet flat, at $98, that skipped right off the catalogue pages. This team brought that single-minded Gap-khakis focus to J.Crew hero items: If chinos were the big bet of the season—the $100 million MVP—chinos were front and center in stores, in the catalogue, on the home page. And chinos landed in the right stores at the right time, something these Gap people say J.Crew had never quite nailed. The science of planning and distribution isn't as sexy as designer sketches and fabric-sourcing jaunts to Italy, but it's what makes retail tick. One merchant describes it thus: "You have to take 900 S.K.U.s, and buy them right, month after month, season after season—at a margin, and not create markdowns. Do you have any idea how much skill that takes?" Gap people, accustomed to keeping an empire of *four thousand–plus* stores in lockstep, did.

They knew how to turn Mickey's rapid-fire brain waves into full-fledged businesses. Flipping through a back catalogue one day, he stopped short: "Holy shit, *CrewCuts*. I love that!" Like Old Navy, a great name was sometimes all it took.* J.Crew relaunched children's

---

* Never too late to give credit: the CrewCuts name was originally invented by '90s accessory designer John Ascher.

wear. A customer service operator at the call center in Lynchburg had noticed something odd was going on—women were ordering certain beach dresses five at a time, in different sizes—she suspected they were for their wedding parties. When Mickey got wind of it, he launched bridal.

By June 2004, a little more than a year after Mickey's arrival, sales were up dramatically. Remember when Emily vowed that anything "too Connecticut" was out? Ha! Now, shoppers were loving J.Crew's "Greenwich look" of patchwork-madras jackets, critter pants embroidered with dogs and geese, and rubber Wellies printed with bumblebees, Scotties, and hunting dogs. Was the design team thumbing its nose at Mark Sarvary—the C.E.O. who banned the color green—by introducing not one, not two, but *nineteen* shades of green, including clover, pear, and parakeet in a single season? Whatever the reason, as the *New York Times* noted, "While some other merchants play down their preppiness, J.Crew revels in it. 'We're over the top,' Mr. Drexler said, laughing."[9]

CHAPTER 15

Redemption Day

June 28, 2006. The dual redemption of J.Crew and Mickey Drexler was official. That morning, standing on a podium just above the melee of the New York Stock Exchange, looking unusually corporate in a wide-stripe rep tie and navy jacket, Mickey rang the fabled bell. Trading was officially open on J.C.G. Standing by was the boss's young son, Alex, looking like a teenage mini-Mickey in black frame glasses. Beside him, the joint chiefs of Mickey's administration: Jeff Pfeifle, Tracy Gardner, Jen Foyle, Todd Snyder, Margot Fooshee, and Jenna Lyons. This team took in the spectacle—the crush of traders waiting to get their hands on J.Crew—and looked at each other in amazement. *We did exactly what we set out to do.* From a shambles to an I.P.O. in three years flat.

To Jenna, seven months pregnant at the time, it was like she was birthing two babies at once. "It felt like the world was opening up," she says. She'd been at J.Crew for sixteen years. "I never believed [going public] would actually happen."

Even as they stood there, though, this I.P.O. was far from a sure bet. Mickey's turnaround had been dramatic, but its track record of success was brief: The company had shown a profit for the first time in ages just one year earlier, in 2005. The J.Crew they took public was heavily leveraged, strapped with $590 million in debt—twenty-four times its $25 million in cash.

Mickey had woken up that morning with his *shpilkes* in full effect. Would the I.P.O. fall short of expectations? Would something go wrong at the last minute?

In truth, the main thing J.Crew had going for it that day was not Mickey's turnaround, but rather Mickey himself. Investors were sympathetic with his plight: For seventeen of his nineteen years at Gap, the man had consistently pulled the rabbit out of the hat, making the Fisher family wildly rich in the process, only to be spit out. It was widely believed that the merchant prince deserved better. Plus, Wall Street loves a comeback. In the days leading up to the I.P.O., analysts predicted Mickey would add a few points' valuation, just because of who he was.

And by the end of the day, it was clear this was true. J.Crew's I.P.O. was a landslide victory. At the time, the second richest opening day of any retailer ever to go public in the United States. J.C.G. had been projected at $15 to $17. It closed its first day at $25.55.[1]

T.P.G. wasn't the only one laughing its way to the bank. Three years after Mickey put $10 million down, his investment had just leapt to $136 million.[2] But the team standing with him on the platform that day recall watching Mickey experience something even richer: vindication. "Having seen the hardship at Gap toward the end—I mean, that was his baby—and having to retreat . . . ," says the merchant Jen Foyle, recalling the emotion of that day. "And then watching him build a brand again? It was magical."

The merchant prince was back: Mickey was once again "the Babe Ruth of retail," squawked the *New York Post*.

Now that J.Crew had made it to the I.P.O., Emily—still a board member and part owner, and now at least $100 million richer herself—could make a clean break. Which she did, six months after the I.P.O.[3]

In four years away from J.Crew's day-to-day, Emily's life had changed radically. She never returned to a full-time job. Now divorced from

Cary Woods, she had built a new life with a new husband, Tom Scott, the cofounder of Nantucket Nectars. This time around, her husband *did* look like a member of the J.Crew-isphere: blond, brawny, born for the prow of a schooner. Emily and Tom Scott were a pair of improbably good-looking entrepreneurs with a combined fortune from the sale of their (rather compatible) brands, and a new kind of business to attend to: a pair of young sons.

This was the final break between the Cinader family and the company they founded. Mickey never met Arthur, who would die in 2017, and his relationship with Emily was cordial, but distant. To Mickey-era employees, Emily was an impenetrable presence, perfunctorily polite but decidedly cool. While to the employees of her own era, that natural reserve had made her all the more fascinating, to Mickey's regime, it just made her cold. The Emily era wasn't all that long ago, but by 2006 it was so deep in the rearview, her exit made barely a ripple in the press. To her inner circle, the erasure was disturbing.

Brick by brick, Mickey had erected a bigger, louder J.Crew that towered over Emily's quiet empire until, eventually, it blotted it out. The press was itching to cover anything the merchant prince said or did; in a matter of months he generated more column inches than the Cinaders had in their whole careers. By the mid-aughts, when Cinader-era employees went on job interviews, they found themselves having to explain—even to industry colleagues who should have known better—that, yes, there was a J.Crew before Mickey Drexler. No one seemed to remember that old J.Crew, too, had been a phenom. This was a bitter pill to swallow. Mickey was building on DNA that Emily had established, often even reinstating (albeit on a far grander scale, and much more profitably) ideas her team had pioneered: Cashmere? CrewCuts? Shoes not-so-secretly made in the same Italian factories as designer? Mickey's publicity machine never got around to mentioning that these were resurrections, not inventions. Through the grapevine, Emily-era people heard Mickey and his people spoke condescendingly, at best, about the business Emily and Arthur had built; they referred to it as "a great brand that had no idea how to make money." But in the '80s and '90s, their team had taken this unknown from $75 million to $800 million in less than ten years and made the catalogue that Mickey himself had revered. That wasn't nothing.

"Arthur and Emily got lost," says Scott Formby. "Or maybe the better word was *forgotten*. That was hard to see. This company, the first twenty years of its life, were just shoved aside."

ON I.P.O. DAY, THE FIZZY *THWOP! THWOP!* OF CHAMPAGNE CORKS rang out in the offices of 770 Broadway. These people had a lot to celebrate! But as far as Mickey was concerned, what the I.P.O. brought was an even-more-amped-up pressure. Going public was no time to relax. It was time to get aggressive. J.Crew had shareholders to keep happy now, and if Mickey's time at Gap had taught him anything, it was that shareholders don't buy into a company (or a famous C.E.O.) for what it is on I.P.O. day, but for what it will become. Shareholders want growth. And moola.

But the place where Mickey had always found growth before—the mall—was becoming an increasingly risky bet. In 2007, for the first time since the mall's invention in 1956, not a single new mall would be built in all of the U.S.; by 2008, *Newsweek* would ask, *Is the American shopping mall dead?*[4] Mickey had spent his early years at J.Crew not opening new stores, but rather shuttering a handful of low performers and working relentlessly to turn around the existing fleet. Post I.P.O., he planned to get a little more ambitious with store openings, but he'd learned the lesson of overgrowth the hard way. "We were maniacal about real estate," says one former exec.

If growth couldn't come from footprint, it had to come from demand. It was no longer possible to stand out from the crowd just because you had the softest chinos around. J.Crew's former niche as America's classic, pared-down, upscale outfitter for office and weekend? *Zzzzz.* Minimalism felt boring, suburban, the *same*. And shopping itself had changed: high-priced fashion was going ever higher; low-priced fashion, ever lower. Mickey spied a "white space" J.Crew could occupy, nestled between designer and mass.

By the mid-aughts, the prices for designer fashion had become truly mind-boggling. Call it the *Sex and the City* effect. "It's not a *bag*, it's a *Birkin*," said the salesman in "Coulda, Woulda, Shoulda," an iconic episode from 2001. The cherry-red bag Samantha Jones was ogling cost $4,000—enough to make even shock-proof Samantha flinch. But by the time J.Crew went public, that kind of sticker shock was almost quaint. Designer fashion had gone wide. Labels once flashed only in rarefied zip codes were now clocked and craved by "regular" women everywhere. By 2012, the opening price for Samantha's Birkin would have shot up to roughly $9,000, "with no corresponding upgrade in materials or craftsmanship," Elizabeth L. Cline reported in *Overdressed: The Shockingly High Cost of Cheap Fashion*.[5]

The clothes these luxury goods firms made were mostly window dressing; their profits came from logo-laden shoes, bags, eyeglasses, and fragrance. The "It bag," in particular, was "one of the biggest scams in the retail world," Cline reports, marked up ten to twelve times the cost of production. A pair of Gucci heels that might have cost Carrie Bradshaw $350 in the late '90s had ratcheted up to $650 a decade later. Yet, somehow, as prices doubled and even tripled, women kept buying. Mickey, Mister "good style should not cost extra," didn't get it. "The prices aren't logical," he told *Fortune*.

And then, on the flip side, *le cheap, c'est chic!* The steamroller of fast fashion had arrived: H&M, Mango, Forever 21, Uniqlo, and of course the ominous Spanish galleon Zara—already the largest fashion company on the globe by 2006—had taken root in America. Zara alone was a rather terrifying force: Everything about this company was an existential threat to any specialty retailer like J.Crew, which designed its clothes a year in advance.[6] Zara was a massive corporation built to pivot on a dime, with factories automated like car-manufacturing plants in which robots cut and dyed fabrics night and day. It had a vast design team and a new kind of infrastructure that enabled those designers to spot a trend and get it into stores in two to three weeks flat, start to finish. Zara changed everything, even the quantities of product it sent to each of its stores: By stocking as few as three or four copies of a new dress in its thousands of locations, Zara re-trained its customers, who knew they had to snap up whatever they spotted at full price, rather than waiting for it to go on sale, lest it sell out. And they knew that, to get the good stuff, you had to keep going back, shopping constantly to catch each new style. J.Crew and its old school brethren could not touch that.

Internally, the chiefs of J.Crew debated how to face the threat fast fashion posed: are we going to try to compete with *that*? It was theoretically possible, though prohibitively costly, for a company like J.Crew to speed up its design and manufacturing process. But it would have required an entirely different business model. And for what? According to a study done in 2009, most fast fashion garments were built to last no more than ten wearings.[7] That was antithetical to everything J.Crew had always stood for, and especially to the upscale identity Mickey was pushing. They couldn't switch to a fast fashion model without cheating the product. "We were never going to discount to that level. We would never reduce quality," says a former executive. "We just weren't *that*."

But what J.Crew could do, better than any other mass retailer—and far better than a fast fashion operation—was consistency, quality. And great storytelling. By 2006 that ability had never been more valuable. As an article in *Buzzfeed* joked that year, in a new era of "authenticity," even a company marketing a new brand of pickle had to come up with a compelling backstory: It had to announce that it came from "an old-country recipe from the Romanian hills, using heirloom cucumbers grown upstate and fresh dill from the factory's rooftop garden, and [that] it was crafted only two miles from here in a facility that used to make No. 3 pencils."[8] Millennials who had grown up in Mickey's Gap Kids togs were now credit card–wielding adults, and their generation wanted to purchase stuff that reinforced their self-image—they wanted the things they bought, wore, and ate, to tell the world (and themselves) that they were creative, discerning. Not just like everybody else.

The new "authenticity" was the polar opposite of the mentality that had shaped specialty retail, in which every aspect of a shopping experience was uniform, and every rough edge had been meticulously buffed out. Indeed, at Mickey's '80s and '90s Gap, every new shipment had arrived in stores with an explicit blueprint from central management, specifying exactly how and where employees should fold, stack, and hang each item. It was all highly regimented—which at the time was a breakthrough: it meant no Gap store would ever have the messy, haphazard, depressing-looking array of togs you might find in a regional department store.

But *authenticity* was all about rough edges. Literally. Reclaimed wood paneling. Edison light bulb fixtures. An elderflower cocktail served in a mason jar. On cue, corporate consultants were riffling through back catalogues in search of "realness"—that is, elderly brand identities that could be reinvented for the nouveau Pabst Blue Ribbon set.

As usual, Mickey had one in his back pocket. If J.Crew wasn't opening a fleet of new stores, it *was* expanding—and keeping shareholders happy—by following the gold-plated example of Old Navy: launching an offshoot, this one aimed squarely at millennials.

In 2004, Mickey had acquired the rights to the intellectual property of a defunct workwear manufacturer.[9] Once again, a great name started everything: *Madewell,* written in a curvy script reminiscent of the Peterbilt truck sign, carried a whiff of the real American factory workers who had once made stiff denim coveralls in a New Bedford, Massachusetts, factory. Of course Mickey had no intention of replicating these coveralls, or of giving anybody in New Bedford—where the ghost of the original brick factory still stands—a new factory job. The backstory was mere pixie dust. Mickey leased the Madewell trademark to J.Crew for $1 per year and used the founding date of the original factory, 1937, in the brand's early signage and web address.

The first Madewell store opened on lower Broadway, in Soho, in 2006, soon after the I.P.O. It was near the J.Crew offices, which allowed Mickey to do constant check-ins on his little test kitchen. The store had all the hallmarks of the day—raw wood paneling, pipe fixtures—and the small-batch vibe of an indie boutique. To the naked eye, there was little to suggest that the cute new hipster on the block was in fact the well-funded little sister of a publicly traded empire of upscale prep.

JENNA LYONS COULD BE A SWEETHEART, A CHARMER, QUICK WITH a joke, always self-deprecating. But she was not a pushover. And she could see that the era of "authenticity" had wiped out fashion's brief dalliance with prep. Except for diehards who would always live by the code, by 2006 preppy had become passé yet again. Indeed, as the trend cycle began to churn ever faster in the era of fast fashion—egging on an increasingly manic schedule of international Fashion Weeks, as the industry pursued constant novelty—prep would start to spin in and out of fashion not by the generation, but by the season, flying "in" and "out" like any other subculture that had been commodified into a marketable "look." Grunge, hippie, boho, minimalist, prep—they all cycled in and out. Rinse, repeat.

It wasn't that Jenna hated prep, exactly. But her idea of an argyle sweater didn't come with trousers, loafers, and a beret. A Jenna argyle was exploded into an oversize pattern and paired with camo pants.

J.Crew, like every other brand that cyclically drags the old codes into a new era—whether it's Ralph or Tommy or Abercrombie—has relied heavily on the phrase "preppy with a twist" (each brand acting as if it's the first ever to have uttered it). But Jenna's twist was more like a one-eighty. She loved the soigné midcentury world of Slim Aarons photos, where everyone has a drink in hand and the party is just getting started. Straight country club prep? *Ugh.* Like Emily before her, she envisioned J.Crew as a club where anyone was welcome—and perhaps more than Emily, she was sensitive to the ways in which it was not.

Jenna had a set of uncanny, almost Carnac-like abilities all her own. She could walk into any store, see a mishmash of good, bad, and weird, and know exactly what to eliminate to bring the whole thing into focus. It came naturally to her—the DNA was in her bones. She could also go toe-to-toe in Mickey's constant game of double-dutch. She seemed to get his rhythm. "You had to be able to read the wind with him, and Jenna could," says a witness.

"Jenna completely charmed Mickey," says a former creative. "He was mesmerized with her and her ability. She has a way of getting you exactly where she wants you. I remember thinking at one point, well, she's got Mickey."

And Jenna had real style, that je ne sais quoi that Mickey's J.Crew needed. Gayle Spannaus recalls a meeting when the boss paused midthought to take in the spectacle of Jenna's own outfit. Spannaus can still spit out exactly what Jenna was wearing that day: cargo pants, navy blazer, striped men's shirt, high heels. An amalgam of references and genres—utilitarian, preppy, masculine, glam—all at once. The "Jenna look" that a generation of American women would soon emulate. In Spannaus's memory, it hit Mickey all at once, a true light bulb moment: "Wait," he said. "You're the coolest-looking woman ever. Why aren't you just doing *you*?"

Jenna laughed. "I'd love to do me."

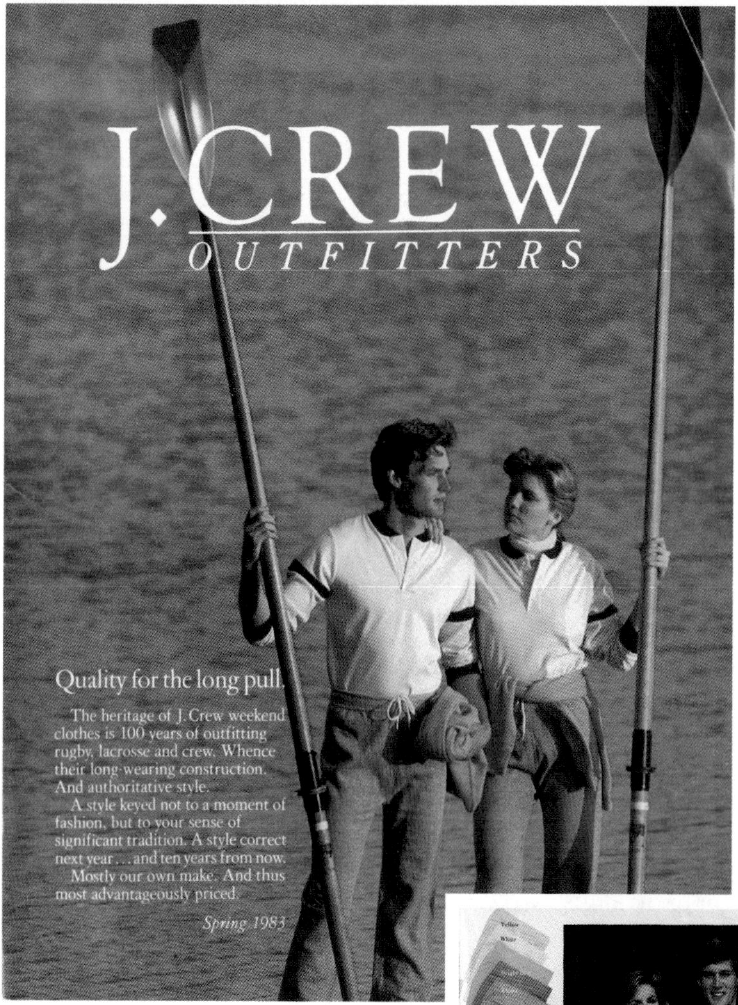

J.CREW

OUTFITTERS

Quality for the long pull.

The heritage of J.Crew weekend clothes is 100 years of outfitting rugby, lacrosse and crew. Whence their long-wearing construction. And authoritative style.

A style keyed not to a moment of fashion, but to your sense of significant tradition. A style correct next year . . . and ten years from now.

Mostly our own make. And thus most advantageously priced.

Spring 1983

Vive Le Bateau!

Thomson's for men

Men's even sizes 30-40.
0552 $27.00

Thomson's for women

Women's even sizes 6-16.
0551 $27.00

True prep? The debut issue of *J.Crew Outfitters*, as the catalogue was originally titled, launched in January 1983—the same month Emily Scott (née Cinader) arrived at her father's company straight out of college, and at almost exactly the same time Millard "Mickey" Drexler landed at the San Bruno, California, headquarters of Gap Inc. *Photographed and produced by Michael Belk*

J.CREW
OUTFITTERS

The pull. The strain.
The hard endurance.

And the spirit.

J. Crew weekend clothes embody the solid quality that means long wear. And the spirit of sporting tradition.

Hence a style correct not just this year, but next year…and ten years on.

Mostly our own make, and thus most advantageously priced.

Fall 1983

By the second catalogue, Fall 1983, J.Crew was already a modest hit. The idea, according to one early employee, was to look "like a party everybody wished they had been invited to."
Photographed and produced by Michael Belk

The indomitable father-daughter duo that made J.Crew tick: Cofounders Emily Scott *(left)* and Arthur Cinader (seen below at the opening of J.Crew's first brick-and-mortar store with then-CEO Arnold Cohen). *Emily, Fernando Bengoechea, c/o Getty Images. Arthur, photographed by John Sotomayor for the* New York Times, *1990*

A few of the young go-getters who invented instant J.Crew classics. *Clockwise from top:* Lisa Anastasi, designer of the original rollneck; Sid Mashburn, originator of the Barn Jacket and the cult-beloved anorak; and Claire McDougald, creator of countless rugby stripes—including the ones seen here. *Photographs and original painted works, here and at right, courtesy of Claire McDougald*

By the late '80s, the color-blocked J.Crew rugby was a cult cool-kid must-have. For years, sketches were hand-painted, cut out, and pinned on boards for Emily's review. (As a young designer, Jenna Lyons would log countless hours hand-painting color options.) When Emily moved to L.A., designs were sliced down the middle, and one half was FedExed across the country. No matter where Emily was, no detail escaped her eye.

Above: Fall 1989, a breakthrough cover: The hottest supermodel on the planet, shot by a *Vogue* photographer, for . . . *J.Crew? Sacré bleu! Linda Evangelista, photographed by Arthur Elgort, 1989*

Right: Elgort went on to shoot for J.Crew for years, including a long collaboration with a new "J.Crew girl," American icon Lauren Hutton—seen here with Elgort's son Warren. *Photographed by Arthur Elgort*

J.CREW

In 1992, the Elgort family was given free rein with a box of J.Crew clothes. *Inset, above left:* Wife Grethe Holby wears the ultimate J.Crew combo, a Barn Jacket and maillot. Son Warren *(top)* makes an even bigger impression, wearing nothing at all. *Photographed by Arthur Elgort*

J.Crew pioneered its own kind of lifestyle photography, with high-energy, familial-feeling shoots in outdoorsy, aspirational (but not "country club") settings—where the people behind the camera looked a lot like the people in front of it. Photographer Tierney Gearon, who saved these behind-the-scenes snaps from a 1991 beach shoot, recalls "huge crews, big productions, like a film scene. And it was all about feeling good." *Right:* A model grabs the camera to shoot Gearon (center) and the J.Crew "crew," including (in black swimsuit) longtime stylist Eve Combernale. *Above, left:* The two Tierneys of early J.Crew, Gearon and fashion director Gifford Horne, on location.
Photographs courtesy of Tierney Gearon

8 25 '91

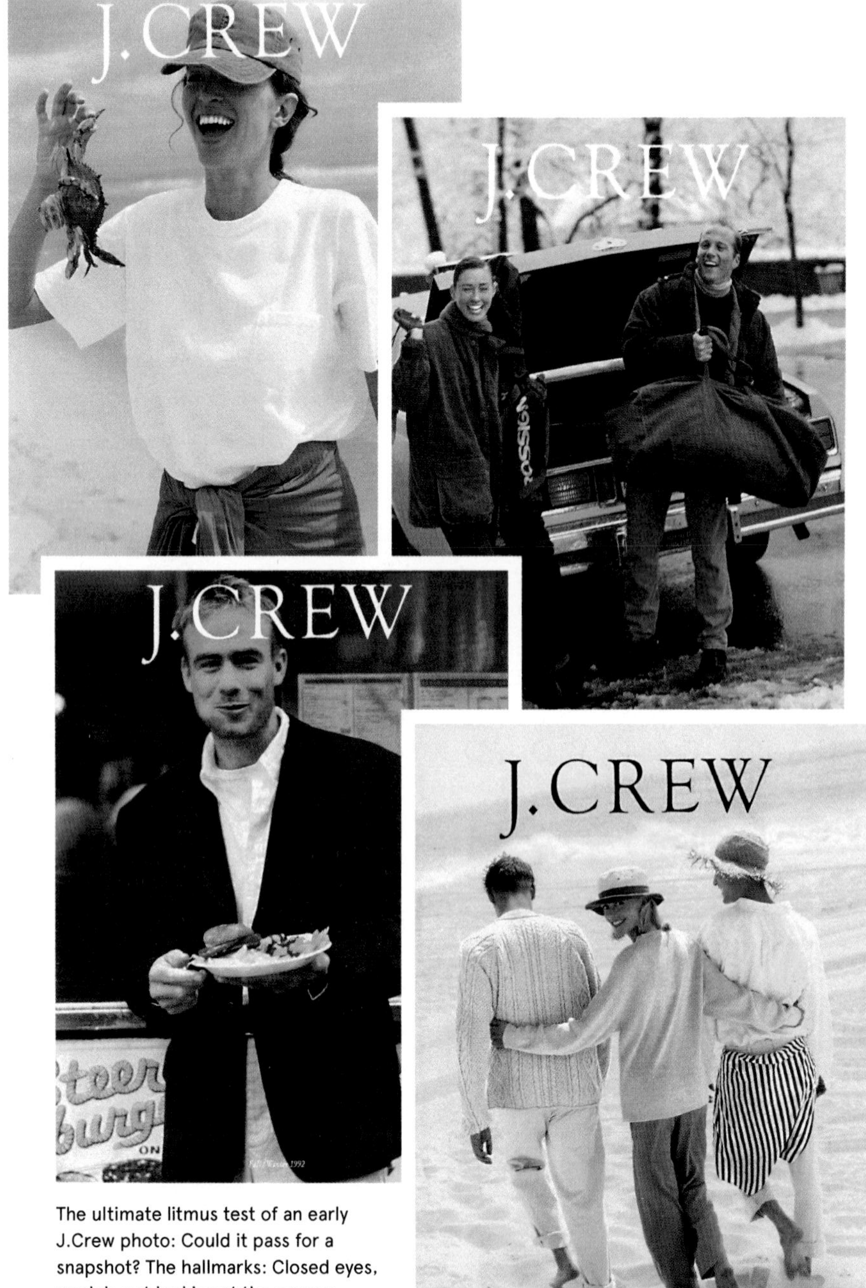

The ultimate litmus test of an early J.Crew photo: Could it pass for a snapshot? The hallmarks: Closed eyes, models not looking at the camera, inclement weather, food that had actually been eaten, and always—always—laughter.
Photographed by Jean-Luc Fievet

You know a brand has hit a nerve in the culture when it starts to be mercilessly spoofed. In 1995 *Spy* magazine produced "Crew," using the visual language of the ultimate preppy catalogue to market—with ultimate political incorrectness—what it called the "gangsta" look.
Courtesy of Sussex Publishers, LLC

The same year, Middlebury College students produced a full-size glossy, *J.Crewd*. Among other things, it zeroed in on J.Crew's heavy layering with this "none-in-one" masterpiece: "Are you fat? Try on a three piece. Like to sweat? Then go for the bulk."
"Nine-in-one" photographed by Ray Diorio. "Rollhead," model: Clint Bierman, photographer: Nicole Shore

Photographer Ben Watts famously creates scrapbooks using behind-the-scenes Polaroids that capture the raw energy of his fashion shoots. Here, two pages of Watts's snaps from early-2000s J.Crew catalogue shoots. *Photographed and collaged by Ben Watts*

SURF
THE FRAME KILLER
RAINY DAYZ IN
MITT STORA HJÄRTA
LIVET ÄR HÅRT!
SNOPP!

In 2003 the "merchant prince" Millard "Mickey" Drexler arrived to save the day!
Photo: Brent Lewin/ Bloomberg via Getty Images

In January 2009, Mickey and Jenna Lyons's J.Crew 2.0 made it to the Capitol. Michelle Obama (in green J.Crew gloves) holds the Lincoln Bible as Barack Obama takes the oath of office. Malia *(second from right)* and Sasha Obama look on in custom CrewCuts, designed in a top secret fashion mission.
Photo: Chuck Kennedy/AFP via Getty Images

With Jenna Lyons at the helm, the J.Crew look is radically redefined. For women: a glitzy, spontaneous-looking mix-and-match aesthetic that eventually went all the way to Fashion Week. Seen here: the fall 2013 lineup.
Photo by Simon Russell/WireImage

For men: dark-denim "urban woodsman" authenticity meets natty *Mad Men* polish—as epitomized by J.Crew's tiny, influential Tribeca space, the Liquor Store. Seen here: Designer Frank Muytjens with his fall 2010 Collection for J.Crew.
Photo by Shawn Ehlers/WireImage for J.Crew

One, two, three Jennas? In May 2016, Jenna Lyons attends the annual Costume Institute Gala at the Metropolitan Museum of Art with Jenni Konner *(left)* and Lena Dunham—cocreators of HBO's *Girls*—all suited up in the trademark "Jenna" look. *Photo by Venturelli/FilmMagic*

CHAPTER 16

The Tao of Jenna

Jenna's memory holds no black-and-white "you do you" Mickey moment. In her mind, the transition wasn't that clean, like turning a page from one phase to the next. She recalls the evolution from the straight prep of Mickey's early years to a J.Crew look that was nuanced, more modern, and distinctly new as a process of trial and error, littered with hits and failures. But she does remember Mickey teaching her to follow her gut—much the way he followed his own: "He believed in instinct."

For Spannaus, who fast became Jenna's chief deputy, there *was* a definite moment, like a flash-forward, that distinguished "before" from "after."

Soon after Mickey green-lighted Jenna to develop a new look, she took Spannaus under her wing: *Okay, we've got to figure this out*. Spannaus, you may recall, was the longtime model booker Emily once tapped to educate T.P.G.-era outsiders on what J.Crew "was" and "wasn't"—a woman who *got*, deep in her bones, why J.Crew was a No. 2 pencil and a bar of Ivory soap, but absolutely *not* a loaf of Wonder Bread. And like Jenna, she also had a sense of how times were changing. How they could loosen up the backbone of strict J.Crew simplicity that Emily had instilled in them both to create something new, something . . . fun.

For Spannaus, that something new crystallized one morning in 2007, roughly a year after the I.P.O. That day, she was just about to walk out of her apartment en route to a J.Crew photo shoot when she remembered a specific tube of lipstick lurking in her makeup stash. It was L'Oreal #43, an "old-lady coral," she says. A definitively uncool shade suited to a '60s debutante, or to the perma-tanned Florida retiree that debutante aged into—picture the well-worn Magda in *There's Something About Mary*. The color had never looked right on Spannaus, but she'd always thought it was just "off" enough to look interesting on a model. *Why not?* she thought, and dropped it into her styling kit.

Telling this story, Spannaus laughs. Lipstick seems like such a trivial thing. But at the old J.Crew, lipstick—visible makeup in general—had been verboten. It was a sign of vanity, artifice. Makeup was *trying too hard*, and that was a no-no, innately uncool. Spannaus still vividly recalls a moment in the mid-'90s when she was standing in the ladies' room of 625 Sixth, brushing her teeth after lunch. A woman walked in and began to reapply her lipstick. The woman was new—Emily had recruited her from a fashion magazine. She joked, "This is the only place I've ever worked where no one ever reapplies their lipstick. They all just brush their teeth." Spannaus thought, absent all malice, *Oh dear, you'll never last*. And she was right. The woman was gone before long. If you didn't get the no-makeup thing, you didn't get Emily's J.Crew.

But bright, obvious makeup—the kind that's not trying to fool anyone—would prove essential to Jenna's J.Crew. Just as Emily had built J.Crew up around her, an extension of her tastes, her history, her worldview, now Jenna was making it her own. And the first rule of Jenna's world was that anything too "correct," too "perfect," felt wrong.

Emily *was* perfect; or at least she projected it—polished and sleek and born gorgeous, with those bright white teeth and that shiny dark hair. Anybody who wakes up looking like Ali MacGraw doesn't *need* makeup to look or feel good, and Emily always seemed to slightly disdain those women who did. Jenna was a very different animal. Which was exactly what made her so relatable. *Authentic*. In adulthood, Jenna presented as an enviable character—at a lean, lanky six feet tall, with mile-long limbs, striking bone structure, and an innate sense of cool, she was the kind of woman who was not afraid to wear stilettos, no matter how tall she was. But she didn't have the personality expected of a woman who looks that way. Jenna knew what it was to feel ugly—worse than that, to feel like "a freak," she has said[1]—and she never forgot that feeling. That, paired with her sense of humor, was a kind of superpower: For a woman so striking and successful, to also be so real and vulnerable? It made it easy to fall for her. To want to *be* her.

She was born Judith, a Californian by way of Boston. When she was four, her family moved to Palos Verdes, a town perched like a cake decoration atop tall red bluffs, surrounded by limitless Pacific blue. The kind of beach town where the sand is machine-combed every morning, manicured as a zen garden. Where it's great to grow up, as long as you fit the mold: tan, buxom, blond.

Judith was none of these. She had been born with a genetic condition, incontinentia pigmenti, that all but erased her eyelashes; striated her skin with patches of light and dark, a little like vitiligo; and left her with conically shaped teeth and bald patches on the back of her scalp.[2] But it was her height, as much as anything, that plagued her. By sixth grade, she stood six feet tall, a head above anybody else in her class. In the schoolyard, boys chased her down and hit her. "I was officially gross," she later wrote, on Lena Dunham's short-lived website *Lenny Letter*. "I started wearing long sleeves and pants every day in the hot California sun. I stopped smiling. And when I couldn't help myself, I covered my mouth in shame."[3]

It sounds like a fairy tale, too saccharine to be true, but fashion really did change her life. Well, if you can call a skirt of floor-length yellow rayon sprinkled with a giant watermelon print *fashion*. She made it for herself in seventh grade. She'd reported in to Home Economics for the same reasons as everybody else—to learn how to balance a checkbook, hard-boil an egg. But the class also required her to learn how to sew. The first thing she made was the watermelon skirt. It was born of necessity: she wanted something long enough to cover the scars on her legs. She could never find pants that fit. Sometimes she wore her father's old suit pants; other times, she bought a size 14, the only size that was long enough. To make the skirt, she started by measuring her body. Because she was so tall, she had thought of herself as *big*—but now, suddenly, she realized how slim she was. How, when clothes actually fit, she looked great in them.

The first day she wore the skirt, a popular girl passed her a note in Social Studies: *Love your skirt. Where did you get it?* That note imprinted on Jenna's brain. Like Mickey's makeshift bedroom in the foyer of his Mayflower apartment, that skirt, and the note, would become the fuel for Jenna's ascent, the story told over and over again. Someone had confirmed a talent in her—a kind of beauty, a worthiness. Eventually that skill would open up an escape hatch. "It was the first time I had positive feedback on something that I had not only worn, but I actually made it myself," she has said.[4] When she told the girl she'd sewn it, a response came quick: *Would you make me one?*

That was it. Her grandmother bought her a sewing machine and a subscription to *Vogue.* Her first issue, in 1982, had Isabella Rossellini on the cover in a haze of purple eyeshadow, and an article inside on Japanese designer Issey Miyake.[5] Jenna memorized the names of designers and models, even the editors on the masthead. She read that magazine like it was a guidebook to her own future.

Jenna's single mother already stretched a piano teacher's salary to cover Jenna and her younger brother, Spencer. Yet she found a way to spring for private lessons in sewing and drawing. In high school, the drawing teacher, Mrs. Webster, introduced Jenna to *Antonio's Girls*, the louche, gestural drawings of iconic '80s fashion illustrator Antonio

Lopez. Here was the crimson-lipped Tina Chow, long and leggy Jerry Hall, riotously curly-haired Marisa Berenson—all gorgeous, all sexy, all so *different* from one another. *Wherever this idea of beauty is,* Jenna thought, *I want to go.*[6]

At eighteen, she made it to L.A.'s Otis College of Art and Design, which would prove to be a pit stop before she transferred to the more prestigious Parsons in New York. On day one, she shed the name Judith like a snakeskin. A teacher asked if anyone went by a name that was different from that on the official roster. A girl sitting in front of Jenna, hitherto known as Christina, spoke up: "Oh, I go by Sebastian." *Holy shit,* Jenna thought. *All bets are off.* She wracked her brain. In that split second, the only sound in her head was the voice of her little brother, teasing her: *Gen-na, gen-na, gen-na-talia.* When the teacher got to her, she threw out a name she had never used before: Jenna. It stuck.[7]

When Jenna joined J.Crew, it was because she wanted to make clothes for real people, not just rich women who could afford Donna Karan. But lingering within her was always the girl who devoured *Vogue* like a meal, who was fascinated by the undiluted sex appeal of *Antonio's Girls*, who recalled the sensation of borrowing a slinky high-priced Azzedine Alaia dress (size 6) from a rich roommate at Parsons and reveling in the way *real* fashion felt on her body—and the new way people looked at her when she wore it. ("I was staggered, just staggered by the reaction," she would later recall.[8])

Most people at J.Crew back in the '90s would never have guessed Jenna would become *Jenna*. She was talented, but then weren't they all? But at least one thing about her was notably different from the rest. "We all liked fashion," recalls a designer who worked closely with her back then. "Jenna was more amped up about it." On inspiration-shopping excursions in Europe, Jenna wasn't just buying samples for J.Crew inspiration. She shopped for herself. In the mid-'90s, she came back from the annual Paris fabric shows kitted out in head-to-toe Helmut Lang—the look du jour, soup to nuts: black short-sleeved tee over white long-sleeved tee, with Lang's signature splash of neon. This was an a-ha moment for colleagues: the rest of them were content in their artful interpretations of J.Crew. Jenna had designs on being a fashion person.

TOGETHER, JENNA AND GAYLE SPANNAUS TURNED J.CREW'S CATalogue styling area, aka the "styling cage," into their laboratory. And indeed, what they were doing was a little like chemistry: reconstituting what were in many respects the same clothes J.Crew had always sold—chinos, T-shirts, cardigans, button-downs—into an amalgam that felt fizzy and new. But not so new that it would blow up in their faces and scare off their customers. Jenna and Gayle were themselves an amalgam: Jenna was the tall, true fashion lover, whose look was a little more polished. Spannaus was the petite, expressive stylist with quirkier, more casual taste. They joked that in Emily-era parlance, Jenna was "classics" and Gayle was "durables."

In some ways the mixing and matching they were experimenting with was a look that Jenna, inveterate magpie, had been honing since middle school. "My grandmother lived on the East Coast and would send me these really preppy clothes from Bergdorf Goodman," she has said. "I remember getting a navy blazer, and wearing it the first day of school in eighth grade. It was a hundred degrees and I was sweating bullets, but I paired that with my Cure T-shirt and my dolphin shorts." She liked the mix. "I loved the way those two things looked together."[9]

"It wasn't a strategy," Jenna says. "It was just all I knew. I didn't feel comfortable when things were too polished or prim, but when things were opposites." For Jenna and Spannaus, the question in their heads was never "What is the J.Crew woman going to like?" but rather "What do *we* like?"

But in fashion, what "we" happen to like rarely comes out of a vacuum. And what they were making was very much a product of its time. By the mid-aughts the hot tickets of New York Fashion Week were a bunch of downtown kids: Proenza Schouler, Rag & Bone, Phillip Lim, Joseph Altuzarra. Hip, young (and almost all male), these designers had skipped the long slog of working one's way up in a storied *maison* or at some Seventh Avenue powerhouse, and instead opened their own labels, sometimes straight out of design school. "Young designer" was a retail category now, jockeying for space not only in the usual chi-chi department stores but in a profusion of indie boutiques. New York had Scoop NYC, Intermix, and Big Drop NYC. Even Brooklyn, no longer the fashion hinterlands, had Bird and Butter. The name of the game in these stores was "curation." For the young and creative, head-to-toe designer fashion was distinctly uncool (and fiscally implausible). It was all about pairing your Isabel Marant jacket with overpriced denim, a vintage belt, and maybe a cheap-and-cheerful eyelet top from Zara. This, too, had a perceived authenticity: stirring together a little of this and a little of that felt "real," spontaneous.

But so far, this look existed in fashion photos and on runways, and on the streets of a handful of fashion capitals. No one had found a way to market "personal style" to the masses. Yet.

If Emily had been a minimalist, painstakingly deliberate in the placement of every line, Jenna was a joyful maximalist. She loved shiny things and jolts of neon, revered the work of Cy Twombly, preached that "the beauty in the mess is the best part." Emily's office had been eerily spotless; Jenna's was curated chaos, framed art stacked on the floor, walls papered in postcards and tear sheets. In Emily's day, catalogue photos had to feel like snapshots—every detail of the happy "family" cavorting on the beach had to ring true. In Jenna's day, catalogue shoots were fashion shoots. The fun was heightened, the locations remote, the props ironic. The models did not look like the girl two doors down in your dorm—they looked like models. They *were* models: established faces like Anouck Lepère, Carolyn Murphy, Liya Kebede.

During the Mickey transition, Jenna had not only saved her own hide from his slash-and-burn restaffing but also shielded much of her team, including a long-running trifecta of talent. Designer Cynthia Ng Villaluz had a taste for cool denim washes and relaxed, worn-in chinos. Tom Mora brought in a refined femininity and loved a good Liberty print. Marissa Webb added rock 'n' roll sex appeal. Each supplied a piece of the puzzle. "Put them together in a blender, and you've got that crazy aesthetic, very sort of sweet-salty, feminine, preppy-but-not," says a former colleague, who pointedly notes that in the early days, "it wasn't about *fashion,* it was about style."

This was a heady time. On office dress-up days, they chose a theme—winter white, camo, stripes, khaki—and the creative side trooped in wearing their individual takes on it. The night before big presentations, they worked late, blasting Beyoncé. Jenna was by most accounts excellent at working with creatives. She was supportive, explained her demands in detail, and she did not have a blasé bone in her body. She and Mickey shared a capacity for unbound enthusiasm. And she laughed all the time. "It was so exhausting, but so fun," says Spannaus. "It was like all we did was play. It was so easy."

In some ways, though, Jenna's apple had fallen not so far from Emily's tree. Both were relentless perfectionists. Both demanded one iteration after the next. There were those who thrived on this—who, just as in the old days, believed it was the secret sauce, the only way to achieve greatness—and, predictably, there were those who did not. "One time she wanted to find the right white. It needed to be *warm,*" says an ex-Gap colleague. "Do you *know* how many shades of white there are?" The relentlessness echoed not just Emily, but Arthur, some twenty years earlier, shutting down construction on the Westport store until a single beam could be moved sixteen inches to the right.

When I interviewed Jenna in 2017, she was at, or near, the top of a very short list of the most famous women in American fashion. We sat in the Soho apartment she'd spent two years renovating during the darkest time of her career. Most people who had been living through the kind of maelstrom Jenna was back then would have pulled the covers over their heads and deputized the detail-management to some high-priced interior designer. Not Jenna. She knew the life story of every paint chip, doorknob, and (custom) light switch in the place. Naively, I asked which, of the many thousands of details that went into this place, she'd had to compromise on. Was anything too costly, too labor intensive, too much of a pain? She scanned the room for a moment, then slowly shook her head. "I don't think I let go of a single thing," she said. This was what it was like to work for her, too: She knew what she wanted. And pushed until she got it.

But in the inevitable comparison of the two matriarchs of J.Crew, Jenna had the gentler bedside manner. "The difference was, Jenna would say, *I think it would look better this way*," says a former catalogue editor. Emily would say, "You got it wrong."

The look that emerged from Jenna's laboratory was a balancing act of equal but opposite forces. It looked utterly spontaneous. But, though this was not immediately visible to the naked eye, it actually followed an inescapable law of the universe: what goes up must come down. If something was *high*, it had to be paired with something *low*. The new J.Crew woman paired her menswear-style tuxedo jacket (masculine, formal) with jeans (casual) and a sequined heel (femme). If her dress was sparkly, she tied a jean jacket around her waist. If she wore something wild, like a floor-length tutu, she paired it with a sweatshirt, maybe a chambray shirt—often borrowed from the men's department.

(The mens'-side bestsellers began to include extra-smalls that women ordered for themselves.) Sequins went with mohair went with puffy parkas. Nerdy turtlenecks dated feathered skirts. The genius, from a sales perspective, was if you deconstructed these outfits—which seemed so advanced, far beyond the way most people knew how to dress—you got basic building blocks, with a little something for everyone: dressed-up sparkle for the glamorous, boyish chinos for the understated.

The number one rule was that when it was all assembled, something had to be a little undone. That gave it sex appeal. "You can't have perfect hair, and clothes, and makeup," Jenna would later say. "You need an element of imperfection to make you feel like there's a person behind it all."[10]

As it happens, this was faithful to the source material—not just of Emily's "throwaway" ideal, but also to the studied negligence of those 1930s Princeton rakes, with their scuffed Bucks and rumpled flannels. Jenna's twisted take on prep—carefully calibrated to retain that all-important J.Crew ease, lest one appear to try too hard—fell right in line. Her dressed-up/dressed-down ethos echoed "the Eastern Establishment virtues of being dressed down from a formal perspective, and dressed up from a casual one," as *Ivy Style* founder Christian Chensvold put it.[11] *Wabi sabi*. Sprezzatura. The hint of imperfection—even if it's a carefully crafted illusion—that makes it cool.

BACK TO THAT CORAL LIPSTICK. THE DAY GAYLE SPANNAUS dropped it into her kit, she was not headed to just any old J.Crew shoot. She was working on the company's first lookbook. This in itself was a turning point: Lookbooks are like mini-catalogues, made specifically for the fashion editors and stylists who might "pull" J.Crew clothes to use in editorial shoots. Lookbooks are standard practice for any label that relies on fashion coverage. But that wasn't a kind of attention

J.Crew had explicitly courted before. Mass brands occasionally made it into fashion magazines, but until now, J.Crew had relied mostly on its lone (and very effective) advertising vehicle, the catalogue. Now they were betting the new Jenna look would land J.Crew in fashion pages usually dominated by altogether different labels.

Since the lookbook would be for press, not consumers, Spannaus didn't have to work so hard to keep it real. She had to make J.Crew *exciting*, fresh, even to a jaded fashion eye. On set that day there were racks full of the usual maritime stripes and natty wool coats, but also marvels never before seen chez J.Crew: tufts of feathers here, a splash of sequins there. Stacks of big, fun, unabashedly faux jewelry (another Emily no-no, thrown to the wind!). One of the assistants had even concocted a flowery wreath. But when they perched it on the messy updo of the model, a Swede named Mona, it called for a final touch. That's when Spannaus remembered that tube of L'Oreal #43. Patted onto Mona's lips and cheekbones, it leant her skin a sweetly false Technicolor flush.

Spannaus skipped out of the shoot on a high—as exultant as when Therese Mahar left the offices of Elite in 1989, waving a signed contract for Linda Evangelista. She called Jenna on her cell: "You're going to *die* when you see these pictures."

Jenna told her to hurry back to the office: "Get in a taxi! I have to see it!"

When she shared the photos, Jenna did not react with a quiet smile, as Emily had once done. "We were screaming," Spannaus says. "Jenna literally cried." The design team came in, and everybody celebrated. It felt like a corner had been turned. "It changed the game," Spannaus says. "It happened right then and there."

CHAPTER 17

Mad Men and Brooklyn Loggers

Next to the new, cool J.Crew girl, the J.Crew guy—still idling in Prepsville—was starting to look like a fuddy-duddy. "Why aren't the women dating the men?" Mickey wanted to know. "Why don't these two things have anything to do with each other?" He dug into the question at one of his usual breakfasts with Roger Markfield. Mickey used every meal as an information-gathering session, whether he was breaking bread with Michael Bloomberg or plumbing inspiration from his favorite young pups from the office over a plate of fried artichokes at his usual table at Morandi. Markfield, then C.E.O. of American Eagle, was a retail know-it-all who got a kick out of serving the merchant prince, king of all he surveyed, the kind of bluntness permitted only among old friends.

Later, Markfield told a mutual industry friend what he had said to Mickey over that breakfast. As the friend recalled, Markfield bragged, "I told Mickey, 'It's all shit. Don't kid yourself—there's no value in anything you've got hanging on those racks.' I really let him have it."

Men's fashion was gearing up for its biggest about-face in recent memory. As the waxed and plucked metrosexual of the early aughts was slowly replaced by, shall we say, the twenty-first-century *lumbersexual*, "it suddenly became more acceptable for 'normal' guys to be interested in their appearance," says menswear consultant Michael Williams, whose site ACL would emerge in 2007 as one of a new crop of menswear bloggers with real clout. The new ideal was traditionally masculine—handy! hairy!—but also evolved. Sensitive enough to raise the kids *and* capable of rewiring the house. And able to read a blog post about the right way to cuff his pants without worrying his manhood would be called into question. This guys' guy had a new kind of cultural permission to geek out on clothes the way his forebears collected cars and watches—as long as those clothes had a baked-in integrity, lest the lumbersexual be accused of superficiality or abject consumerism. The "right" clothes to love came from sturdy, Made-in-America "heritage" labels.

Following his breakfast with Markfield, Mickey came into the office even more fired up than usual—which is saying something—though he didn't quite use his crony's choice of words. "I had breakfast with Roger," he told menswear designer Todd Snyder. "He thinks we're too 'dandy.' We need to pivot." In Snyder's recollection, "Mickey turned on a dime."

Mickey started routinely cruising through the menswear department, barking at Snyder: "We gotta be cool! *Buzz it up! Buzz it up!*" Music to Snyder's ears. He already had a look in mind. He and his creative team—along with most of young, creative New York—had logged many a late night at Freemans, the downtown restaurant that was the new unofficial HQ of the lumbersexual.

Founded in 2003 by Taavo Somer and William Tigertt, a pair of budding hipster-preneurs, Freemans was the epicenter of aughts "authenticity." It had the cozy, ramshackle charm of an old ski lodge, flickering with firelight and plush with taxidermy. And its enviably cool waitstaff exemplified the look of the moment: turn-of-the-century mustachios, navy watch caps, deep-cuffed raw denim, scuffed Alden boots.

This was what Snyder wanted to try at preppier-than-ever, clean-cut, gold-buttoned-blazer J.Crew? Yep. "Out went the Kelly greens and shocking pinks," recalls Frank Muytjens, a Dutch menswear designer with a taste for aged denim, who'd arrived at J.Crew by way of Ralph Lauren. In came "clothes that we, the design team, would like to wear." (If this sounds familiar, that's because it's exactly what motivated Sid Mashburn and his fellow early designers in the '80s.) The colors got earthier, the fabrics more robust. The revamped J.Crew menswear was among the first brands Michael Williams ever covered on ACL. In Williams's view, J.Crew packaged the look "better than anyone," and far better than other mass brands. They nailed the styling, the rolled and cuffed dark denim, the workwear vibe. Most of all, they had the right accoutrements.

By now shoppers were used to "collabs" between designer and mass fashion, mostly thanks to Target, which first invited industrial designer Michael Graves to bring his witty, curvilinear *objets* to middle America in 1999, and had since attracted card-carrying fashionistas to its fluorescent-lit aisles with a slew of limited edition collections by *Vogue*-approved young designers. But when Todd Snyder called up Red Wing, the century-old Minnesota bootmaker, he had something different in mind: he didn't want a J.Crew version of their sturdy lace-up work boots. Why try to make what might turn out to be a poor imitation, when you could just get the real thing? He wanted to stock Red Wing boots, at a Red Wing price, in J.Crew stores.

"What Snyder did was figure out how to sell a real fashion moment to skittish guys who were used to thinking of their closets as a series of checkboxes meant to be ticked," Sam Schube would later write in GQ.[1] "How do you get skeptical guys to trust your clothing? You pair them with things they already trust." That article was titled "The Man Who Taught Men to Love Clothes."

But early on, not everyone at the home office was convinced. Red Wing made boots for hunters and log splitters that cost upward of $300.

How much log splitting was J.Crew's mall-shopping prepster really doing? And what made Snyder so sure a J.Crew guy would spend twice as much for Red Wings as he paid for J.Crew boots? But Snyder knew that Red Wings had a kind of cred that a J.Crew label could never bestow—something for which guys would be willing to pay. Yes, *authenticity*.

Mickey thought the idea was worth a shot. The other J.Crew merchants played along "just to shut the designers up," Snyder says with a laugh. The first order was tiny: one hundred pairs. Those blew out within a week. They ordered three thousand more for the holiday; before Christmas was anywhere in sight, those were gone, too. That December, Snyder made a plea to the president of Red Wing: *What can you do for us?* The company chased up another three thousand. Which sold out.

"Suddenly Mickey's going, 'What else we got?'" says Snyder. Next came Timex watches; then New Balance sneakers—Mickey wore them constantly; then tailored shirts by the English firm Thomas Mason, founded in Lancashire, England, in 1796. Polished brogues by Alden, of Middleborough, Massachusetts—the last surviving manufacturer in what, 150 years earlier, was a teeming New England footwear industry. These guest stars came to be known as "In Good Company" collaborations. It mostly wasn't about profit: Selling twenty-five pairs of handmade Alden Revello Cordovan Longwings at $710 a pop did not fill the coffers. But it cast a halo. Just as Target was the only big-box store in America with a whiff of real fashion, now J.Crew was the only store at the mall with a whiff of the small-batch specialist—and a cost-efficient way to hold on to relevance: Should Red Wings fall out of fashion, no problem. On to the next "heritage" find.

AT MOST J.CREW STORES, WOMENSWEAR—THE CASH COW THAT accounted for some 80 percent of their sales—got pride of place. The men's department got the dregs, usually hidden away downstairs or tucked in the back. It irked Mickey, the born shopkeeper: what was the point of having an amazing new look without a proper boutique where it could all come together—where customers could see it in context, soak in the sum of its parts? But according to Snyder, the board kept talking him down. They knew Mickey could get carried away. *Keep your eye on the ball,* they told him. For a while, he listened.

When he could stand it no more, he asked Andy Spade to drop by the office. Spade is a branding expert—cofounder, with his late wife, Kate Spade, of the eponymous brand and the men's accessory range Jack Spade. And like Mickey, Spade is a born stores guy, a master of the immersive in-store experience. Mickey surely knew what he would get from Andy Spade, who took one look and declared, "You *gotta* have a store!" "I knew it!" Mickey crowed.

That day, Spade took Mickey and Todd Snyder on a field trip. He knew the perfect spot: a tiny, grimy out-of-work bar on a crooked corner in Tribeca. The original bar was still intact, down to the bourbon bottles, and the little neon sign in the window: *Liquor Store*. Even the old cash register was still there. "It was a no-brainer," Snyder says.

Mickey, a man who once opened a new store in America every day, spent months carefully honing the concept of a nine-hundred-square-foot shoebox. Back at the office, he staked out a separate space for editing what the Liquor Store (the name, and the original sign, stayed) would stock. Only a handful of employees were allowed in. This was an exercise in precision, and he didn't want too many voices muddying the vision. Between the various washes and fits, J.Crew produced some thirty different chinos. The Liquor Store would sell one. One kind of T-shirt, one kind of jean. The interior would feel clubby, almost cluttered, and dense with product—but the edit would be exceedingly clear. Men did not want too much information, Mickey said. The mantra: *simplify*.

In the back of the store, there would be a separate room for suits. Really, *a* suit. For the first time in decades—arguably since Mickey himself had helped foment the dereliction of taste known as "business casual" in the '90s—young men had rediscovered the suit. On the flip side of the lumbersexual, we had Don Draper. *Mad Men* premiered in 2007, and skinny ties and charcoal-gray, slim-cut suits loomed large in the collective unconscious. Over on Planet Fashion, designer Thom Browne had pioneered the most radical reinvention of men's tailoring since the leisure suit. GQ dubbed him "the incredible suit-shrinking man."[2] Browne's high-water tailoring freed the ankle, and even, for the extra-daring, the furry knee. These suits were both too fashion-forward and too pricey for the J.Crew guy, but their influence trickled down. Snyder knew *the* Liquor Store suit had to be lean, clean, and narrow. It also had to flatter the twenty-first-century mainstream American male who, sadly, bore little resemblance to Don Draper.

It took Snyder and Frank Muytjens two years to tweak the Ludlow Suit to perfection. In the end, it was deceptively simple looking: a skinny, two-button jacket and tapered trousers, which got its name after "the Tribeca" proved too difficult for J.Crew's lawyers to trademark. What made it work so well "is still sort of a mystery," admits Muytjens. "I've never seen a suit that fits so many body types off the rack."

That one suit would more than double J.Crew's tailoring business,[3] becoming so ubiquitous that the *New York Observer* dubbed its followers "the Ludlow brotherhood."[4] In 2020, the *Wall Street Journal* said this single, $650 suit changed the game for a generation of "fresh-faced 20-somethings wading into the workforce for the first time." The suit became "a covetable commodity like a can of Coke or a pair of Nikes." Can you think of another suit you know by name—other than perhaps Brooks Brothers' No. 1 Sack Suit, *the* ur-suit of the twentieth century? Or of another one that has held its currency for more than a decade and counting: in 2021, Prince Harry chose a pale gray Ludlow—princely, yet relatable—for his and Meghan Markle's fateful post-Megxit sit-down with Oprah Winfrey.[5]

Andy Spade had a theory about how to make a company like J.Crew feel cool: "the bigger you get, the smaller you act."[6] When the Liquor Store opened in August 2008, even the bottles of bourbon behind the bar were still intact. Old-timey bowling balls and oil paintings of toy dogs were strewn among the clothes. The speakers emitted the crackle of an old hi-fi. Spade's own toy soldiers lined the mantel. There were stacks of books from the landmark bookseller the Strand, and a mug of pencils prechewed by writers—somewhat less terrifying in a pre-COVID world, but still decidedly weird.

Over at Freemans, owners Taavo Somer and William Tigertt, who by then had opened a clothing store of their own, were said to be less than thrilled. "They copied us down to the shade of the paint colors," their sales director grumbled.[7] But wasn't that the ultimate compliment? Mickey had once designed a fleet of stores that were both inescapable and instantly recognizable to any American citizen. Now he had one singular store that a man could stumble into, and have no clue he'd just entered J.Crew. Such was the evolution of the consumer that this was considered a victory. J.Crew might have been mass—inherently lame, from most tastemakers' perspective—but it could code-switch at will to pass as small, indie, *special*.

The whole time the Liquor Store had been gestating, the board grumbled. *Why the hell was Mickey wasting this much time and money on one microscopic store?* But when it opened, none could deny its success. The Liquor Store never made a ton of money, but that wasn't the point. It put J.Crew menswear on the fashion map. And provided a gold mine of data. Now they had granular detail on exactly what they were selling, and to whom. When size 36 suits started flying out, they knew they had tapped the elusive skinny style arbiter: suddenly, the J.Crew guy was giving the J.Crew girl a run for her money.

A month after the Liquor Store opened, Todd Snyder handed in his resignation; he was turning forty and was hankering to start his own company. Mickey was furious. "We're on the launch pad," he yelled. "We're ready to take off! And you're *leaving*?" Snyder has no regrets,* but he admits that none of them could see, at the time, that they had just introduced the new uniform of the style-conscious American male. "I didn't see how big this was going to be."

---

* Snyder's eponymous brand is now among the most influential in American menswear. In many ways, his award-winning label bears the stamp of work Snyder pioneered at J.Crew—including a reputation for limited edition collaborations, such as those with Timex, New Balance, Champion, and L.L.Bean.

CHAPTER 18

The *J* in J.Crew

A little past 11:45 P.M., October 27, 2008. Jenna was in Brooklyn, in bed next to her husband watching *The Tonight Show*, when she gasped and jolted up. "I almost took his eye out," she recalls. Michelle Obama had just walked onto the set. "I knew instantly she was wearing head-to-toe J.Crew." A shimmery pencil skirt, a silky print shell, and a bejeweled cardigan—all signatures of the Jenna look—all in a mélange of sunny yellows. Jaw dropped, Jenna watched Obama wave to the crowd and sit down, smooth her skirt, and look to Leno expectantly. Practically the first words out of his mouth: "I want to ask you about your wardrobe."

In October 2008, the audience knew exactly where this was headed. *Moneymoneymoneymoney*. It was a constant refrain. Americans were defaulting on their mortgages in record numbers. Six weeks earlier, Lehman Brothers had collapsed. Soon, GM and Chrysler would get an epic $80 billion bailout from Uncle Sam. Mickey was as terrified as any multimillionaire would be. Now, over his lunches with his Upper East Side cohort, he wondered aloud: *Are we gonna lose it all?* J.Crew's stock dropped to $8 a share. Their stellar I.P.O. suddenly looked like a distant memory.

Meanwhile, a story had just broken on Sarah Palin, the gun-toting Alaska governor who could see Russia from her house. *Politico* was reporting that, in the middle of a recession, the Republican National

Committee had blown $150,000 at Saks and Neimans to gussy up John McCain's surprise V.P. pick for the campaign trail.[1] If asking a political wife about the clothes on her back seemed antediluvian at first blush, Leno's question was also topical. He nodded at Obama's look: "I'm guessing about sixty grand? Sixty, seventy thousand for that outfit?"

More like $414. "Actually, this is a J.Crew ensemble," she replied, as the audience erupted in cheers. Turning to them, Obama arched a pointy eyebrow and offered one of her now-famous between-us-girls asides: "Ladies, we know J.Crew. You get some good stuff online. . . . When you don't have time, you've got to click on."[2]

Oprah once joked that the day she saw Michelle Obama appear in J.Crew, "the first thing I did was pick up the phone and buy stock in J.Crew."[3]

In late 2008, any retailer in the world could have used the endorsement of a woman like Michelle Obama. But J.Crew desperately needed her vote. The threat to the company was "terrifying," one executive recalls. And the hit they took was real: sales dipped, net income dropped 44 percent, stock plummeted 77 percent.[4]

And they'd been hit by the recession at a vulnerable moment. Every other retailer across the country was slashing price tags. But J.Crew had just completed its grand makeover in the opposite direction—toward Mickey's white space, just left of designer. The Liquor Store had opened in August, with $49 knit ties jostling up against $1,200 plaid mackintoshes.[5] Then, in September, the women's side had planted its flag in old money terrain. The new Upper East Side boutique housed the brand-new—er, brand-new-all-over-again—brainchild, Collection. The parallels with Emily's Collection were evident: Once again, the high-end range was seen as the "baby" of the woman in charge. But true to Jenna, this time it wasn't just hyperrefined wardrobe staples, but also limited-run showpieces, the kind of stuff you'd expect to see in the neighboring designer boutiques on Madison Avenue. On opening day, the first item customers spotted as they walked in the door was a mannequin dressed in a cropped sequin jacket hand-painted to resemble tortoiseshell. For $3,000.[6]

Behind the scenes, of course, J.Crew was doing exactly what every other retailer was doing: slashing prices to move inventory. But by all appearances, they were all about $400 snakeskin flats, rings with real pearls, dresses of Italian silk. At the dawn of a recession that many feared was about to slide into a full-blown depression, was this the most tone-deaf move a mainstream retailer could make—a shift away from their faithful customer? "J.Crew Gets Uppity," sniffed the *New York Times*: the Collection store had opened during "just about the worst week in financial memory."

Or did the up-leveling make a mysterious kind of sense? Within J.Crew, there was a strategy at work. For the worker bees who now depended on it, J.Crew was still making "regular" stuff—but the new upscale addition sprinkled a little extra fairy dust over the rest, making it feel a little better, a little *richer,* than what you could find at J.Crew's competitors. Meanwhile, for wealthy shoppers whose Loro Piana budgets had just been Madoffed, J.Crew was now fashion-adjacent, and a heck of a lot more affordable than the Prada they usually bought.

The thing is, J.Crew needed people to *believe* in its new uphill image—to believe its high-end clothes were worth their elevated price tag. "We were frustrated," recalls an executive. Internally, *they* knew J.Crew made jackets out of some of the same tweeds as Chanel! *They* knew these clothes didn't just fall off some Chinese assembly line (okay, some did, but whatever): "We wanted to say to the customer: Do you know that these beautiful things that you love, they're *designed?*"

The "empathy economy." That's what design guru Michael Rock called the relationship consumers had come to expect from their favorite brands. It was all about feelings. "Everything from your razor blade to your public library to the I.R.S. needs to have a relatable personality," Rock said.[7] Who could give J.Crew a believable—even lovable—personality? Who could wear a J.Crew jacket with so much style it looked as good as Chanel, or close enough? Who could put a human face on J.Crew, make it feel designed? Who could satisfy the new, rabid consumer curiosity about what went on behind the curtain of fashion?

They had just the woman. By late '08, Jenna was president and creative director of J.Crew, reportedly with a signing bonus of $2 million and a base salary of $675,000. With Todd Snyder out and Jenna in a new position of power, if J.Crew was going to have a "face," it was going to be hers.

But the "making" of Jenna was not a thing that happened lightly, or by fluke. It was a corporate decision, the subject of internal debate. "We pondered it," says the same executive. "Was it a good idea? Was it a bad idea?"

In 2000, Joan Didion described "the perils of totally identifying a brand with a single living and therefore vulnerable human being," in the *New Yorker.*[8] She was talking about Martha Stewart—the living and, at the time, invulnerable-seeming founder of a billion-dollar brand that had just gone public. Today, now that pretty much everybody is a "brand," it's hard to imagine any misgivings about the idea of taking Martha Stewart Living Omnimedia public. But at the time, it was unorthodox: publicly traded corporations were rarely so closely aligned with a single human being. Time Warner, the previous owner of Stewart's media empire, had resisted expanding Martha Inc. for exactly this reason. What if Martha lost her Midas touch? Or fell out of favor? Or, you know, died? There was also "the related question," Didion wrote, quoting from the list of official I.P.O. "Risk Factors" in the company prospectus: What "if Martha Stewart's public image or reputation were to be tarnished"? What would that mean for the brand she embodied?

But as the J.Crew higher-ups debated the possibility of making

Jenna their "celebrity designer," the fear wasn't that Jenna would overtake the brand. It was that people simply wouldn't *care* who designed J.Crew. Ask yourself: Who designed your $19.95 Gap pocket tee? That trusty Ann Taylor shift? (No, "Ann Taylor" is not a person.) Fashion fans idolize people who front luxury houses and cool indie brands. The folks who churn away for eighteen years at companies like J.Crew? Never heard of 'em.

Before Michelle Obama ever walked onto the set of *The Tonight Show*, her stylist, Ikram Goldman, made a prediction: "The first question he's going to ask will be about your clothes." Obama was skeptical. *Seriously?*[9]

But Ikram Goldman has a way of being right about these things. The owner of Ikram, Chicago's most influential source of high fashion, Goldman is said to be a fashion soothsayer, able to dress a woman to "tell the story she should be telling." Back when Michelle Obama was a Harvard-educated hospital exec—before she was the wife of a U.S. senator, and well before the White House was a glimmer in her husband's eye—their friend Desirée Rogers (later, President Obama's social secretary) had made the introduction to Goldman.[10]

Sparkly $79 mall cardigans were well outside the usual Ikram wheelhouse. But the clothes of the woman who could be America's first Black First Lady needed to tell a very specific story. "I didn't want her to look fragile and untouchable," Goldman said. "I wanted women to know that they could look like Mrs. Obama." And on that night in October 2008, her clothes also needed to artfully jab at Sarah Palin and the profligate R.N.C. Ikram talked that appearance through with her husband: What American label was glossy enough for TV, yet down-to-earth enough to be on message? Had to be J.Crew. Goldman went to a J.Crew store in Chicago and bought an armload of clothes.

For J.Crew, the Leno appearance seemed like a onetime gift from the gods. But a week later, Barack Obama was elected the forty-fourth president of the United States. Now there was an inauguration in the works. Goldman oversaw Michelle Obama's wardrobe like the invisible hand of a future queen—with state-secret level discretion, and a clear agenda. She tapped diverse, small-batch talents like Isabel Toledo and Jason Wu, a kind of designer who had never before been in the running for an inauguration. And she tapped J.Crew—even more unlikely to touch that pedestal. Jenna's team got a top secret request for sketches of "happy, approachable" looks for Michelle and her daughters, Sasha (then seven) and Malia (ten). They churned out options, sent them off to Ikram, and then they waited. Nobody knew if the clothes Ikram had commissioned would make the cut.

On the bright, cold morning of Tuesday, January 20, 2009, the J.Crew team watched the black car carrying the Obama family to the Capitol building with bated breath. As soon as the door swung open, they spotted bright pops of sapphire blue and bubblegum pink—*their* coats for the Obama girls! Malia's bright blue befitted the older sister; Sasha's pink was pure fun, paired with an orange scarf and red tights—classic J.Crew color blocking. For once, the children of a First Family were not dressed like tiny adults, somber stuffed-shirt royals. They looked like actual children. But wait, *there was more*: Michelle had paired her lemongrass-green Isabel Toledo dress and jacket with olive-green J.Crew gloves. That night, at the inaugural ball, the new president's ivory silk bowtie was custom J.Crew.

Oscar de la Renta, outfitter of every First Lady since Jackie Kennedy, had submitted a dozen sketches to Goldman, but "never heard another word."[11] J.Crew hadn't just made the cut, but had been worn by every member of the Obama family on perhaps the most historic inauguration day ever? Unthinkable.

The website crashed. Emails flooded in from customers jubilant to have something in common with a First Lady. The company stock—though still in the gutter—briefly jumped 10 percent.[12]

And then, to everyone's astonishment, Obama *kept* wearing J.Crew, mixed with Azzedine Alaia belts and Manolo Blahnik heels. She made a point of regularly wearing clothes any middle-income voter could buy—something no predecessor had done before.

"Not everyone listened to all of the speeches or read the analysis or considered the context," wrote fashion critic Vanessa Friedman in 2017. "But everyone paused for a moment to assess the visual. And a couple who had spent their entire lives being scrutinized as pioneers understood what that meant, and instead of bridling at it, leveraged it. If you know everyone is going to see what you wear and judge it, then what you wear becomes fraught with meaning."[13]

Boy did we eat it up. For six years, style blog *Mrs.O*—likely the first blog devoted to the style of a politico—chronicled every bejeweled cardigan and State Dinner gown. Obama's "astonishing influence" on the stock value of the companies she wore was the subject of a *Harvard Business Review* study titled "How This First Lady Moves Markets." In 189 public appearances in less than a year, it estimated Obama racked up $2.7 billion in total value for twenty-nine companies, J.Crew chief among them.[14]

When America's first Black First Family pledged allegiance to J.Crew, one element went curiously undiscussed. The Obamas had alighted on a brand synonymous with prep, one that still, on some level, "oozes Anglo" out of every pore, just as Lisa Jones had written in 1994.[15] As Jenna put ever more twist on J.Crew prep, remixing the canon, this new mix-and-match formula seemed to lightly thumb its nose at its own country club roots—implying that these clothes weren't just for blue bloods. *Implying.* Never stating. Yes, the number of people of color in the J.Crew catalogue gradually ticked up slightly; the model Liya Kebede, in particular, would become a recognizable figure in J.Crew Land. But the company never directly addressed its underlying whiteness. Mickey often referred to Michelle Obama as "the gift that kept on giving." Arguably her biggest gift to J.Crew was a free pass into an era of "change we can believe in," as the campaign slogan went. Without ever doing the hard work of addressing the cultural foundation J.Crew was built on—or making any significant overtures to a population it had never explicitly wooed—for a shining moment, J.Crew found itself hand in hand with the progressive future, and an evolving "American beauty." How could "so J.Crew" still mean "so white" if it was the house brand of the Obama presidency? What a lucky break.

TO MICKEY'S EX-GAP STALWARTS, THE THRILL OF WATCHING Michelle Obama hold the Lincoln Bible in J.Crew-gloved hands as her husband was sworn in carried a sense of déjà vu. This was how it had felt when the world lost its mind over Sharon Stone's Gap turtleneck: Like they were at the white-hot center of a major cultural moment. The usual fashion hierarchy had been upended. It was suddenly clear what was *the* American brand. Soon, you couldn't walk a block in any upscale city neighborhood in America without bumping into an instantly recognizable uniform: a guy in dark, cuffed jeans and a gingham-checked shirt; a girl in skinny cropped pants, a slim belt wrapped around her bejeweled cardigan. The J.Crew look.

The last time "the" American brand was anointed, all praise had been directed at Mickey. This time the spotlight swerved in a different direction: directly onto Jenna Lyons.

For many in the world outside of J.Crew, the first time Jenna really came into focus, she was sitting on a corner of her own bed, in her Brooklyn brownstone, on a 2008 cover of the interiors magazine *Domino.*[16] Jenna's decor was an exercise in juxtaposition, grand but also comfortable, elegant, and consciously imperfect. She paired brass bathroom fixtures with cement walls; a rough farmhouse table with shiny geometric chrome chairs. It was just like the catalogue styling: approachable yet nearly impossible for regular people to pull off. With her head on her husband's shoulder, and their blond-curled toddler, Beckett, on her hip, Jenna was the picture of New York career achievement *and* domestic bliss. This scene would figure into countless strangers' reveries of a new kind of aspirational existence: the artsy-affluent Brooklyn life. The story sparked a craze for limoncello-colored velvet couches. It came out years before Pinterest launched, yet somehow became one of the site's most-pinned interiors. Years later, Jenna would visit the home of U.K. prime minister David Cameron and spy a familiar-looking mix of black cabinetry, yellow upholstery. Yes, Samantha Cameron confessed: she'd been inspired by Jenna's house.

When the higher-ups first decided to pull the trigger on publicizing Jenna, it was largely because of how she dressed. Her own colleagues were in awe of her style. "Every outfit she put together, I would just *die*," says a former high-ranking exec. "There's nothing not to love." She was the perfect poster girl for their new look. What they never saw coming was the effect of Jenna herself, the total package.

"What would happen if one woman told the truth about her life?" wrote the poet Muriel Rukeyser in 1968.[17] "The world would split open." A few years before women like Lena Dunham and Amy Schumer would define the era of the overshare, in which confessional young female voices would fearlessly expose both their bodies and their innermost vulnerabilities, Jenna told *Vogue* the kind of things that designers seeking entry to fashion's inner sanctum do not say. That her teeth were fake. That she felt "like a giant." That she'd been bullied as a kid. That her trainer was working on her "thutt" problem, "trying to separate my thighs from my butt."[18] She talked about her skin disorder, and the bald patches on her scalp—details that she could easily have hidden or skated past. The media doesn't demand bare-it-all candidness from women in her position. Jenna offered it up of her own accord. Had she learned this confessional tendency from Mickey, who discussed the privations of his childhood in distinctly non-C.E.O. language? Or, as a former "freak," as she has put it, did she feel a sense of obligation to the girls out there memorizing the pages of *Vogue*, as she once had—a duty to be frank and honest, instead of trying to perpetuate a myth of perfection? Or was this simply the only way Jenna knew how to be? Whatever the reason, she was unedited, funny, unerringly *nice*, and just "flawed" enough to be a deeply sympathetic character. In a historically chilly fashion landscape, Jenna Lyons was a humanizing blast of warm air.

Fashion is about self-expression! It's about being yourself! That's what the industry has long preached. But really, it depends which "self" we're talking about here. Fashion was long fueled by the assumption that to be beautiful, to be *It*, flaws, real or perceived, should be fixed, masked, or vigorously denied. The very short list of fashion-world icons who have embraced their own cosmetic idiosyncracies—legendary *Vogue* editrix Diana Vreeland, with her strong profile and Kabuki makeup, comes to mind—did so with almost cartoonish imperiousness. Frank self-deprecation? Not so much.

Plus, for all her confessions, Jenna *looked* stunning: Slim as a No. 2 pencil, tall as the Empire State, better dressed than most models. She talked about flaws we couldn't actually see: by all appearances, she fit the mold. But the way she described feeling she *didn't* was believable . . . authentic. That was a powerful one-two punch. Like her mix of sequins and sneakers, denim and tuxedo jackets—Jenna wasn't *too* perfect, or too imperfect. She was the right fashion person for the right time.

Today, Jenna bristles at the suggestion that she became famous overnight. "Maybe from the outside looking in, it looked like it was overnight, but it just wasn't," she told me. "I don't even know if I could piece together how it all happened."

But back at the office, it felt lightning fast. The inauguration flipped a switch. After that, "there always seemed to be new people dropping by the office," checking out what was going on inside of J.Crew, recalls a stylist. "Every magazine wanted to do a story on Jenna." Soon, the outside world seemed to think J.Crew *was* Jenna.

Predictably, not everyone was thrilled by this perception. Jenna had long been a standout on the team, but the arduous turnaround had been a group effort; she had not been its queen bee, or its sole driving force. But then came her promotion and, at almost that exact moment, newfound fame. Now, here she was on *Oprah*, the crown jewel of an episode about "dream jobs." And there she was on a best-dressed list next to Alexa Chung and Rachel Zoe and Kate Middleton—two TV personalities and an actual royal. *Vanity Fair* wanted to know which flowers Jenna preferred (New Zealand peonies in a highly specific shade of coral), what she ate for dessert (her husband's homemade ice cream).[19]

J.Crew had wanted a celebrity designer. What they got was a full-blown celebrity. Emily had, with a few rare exceptions, gone out of her way to avoid this turn of events. But from what her colleagues could tell, Jenna loved it. "She became her own creation," says a colleague. "And she wanted it badly. She wanted to be exactly what she became—the attention, the accolades." The girl whose life was changed by one classmate's appreciation of a single watermelon-dappled skirt was now getting a steady stream of positive affirmation, and so was J.Crew. That was a good thing, right?

CHAPTER 19

Everyone's an Expert

Just as Jenna shot into the stratosphere, word around the J.Crew offices was, *Have you heard about this guy, the Sartorialist?* Photographer Scott Schuman had begun stationing himself not inside the great tent of fashion but outside it, on the sidewalk, where he snapped whomever struck him as well dressed, posting his photos not in magazines, but on his own blog. The "street style" photography of Schuman and fellow snappers Phil Oh and Tommy Ton shook the fashion universe. In theory, anybody with a great look could be in their photos, and anybody could opine on them in the site's comments section. The most exciting source of style inspiration was not Brazilian bombshells stalking the runways, but "real" people—well, real*ish*: the people who looked so great in these photos were often from the trenches of fashion—who dressed themselves.

The tight cabal of fashion magazine editors employed by publishing houses like Hearst and Condé Nast—the people who had historically decreed what was in and out—were watching their advertising revenues and page counts tank in the recession, and facing serious competition from a scrappy band of self-declared style arbiters: bloggers. Suddenly these outsiders, like Bryan "Bryanboy" Yambao; *Style Bubble*'s Susanne Lau; and even the opinionated eleven-year-old "Style Rookie," Tavi Gevinson, had a real voice. Readers loved their straight talk, which in the early days seemed untainted by the murk of advertising. Now, in the comments section of their favorite blogs, "anonymous users could scrawl graffiti on fashion's bathroom wall," as one writer put it. "Fashion is subjective," said *Interview* editor Keith Pollock, voicing an opinion that many legacy editors would have considered terrifying at the time. "I don't see how a fashion editor's perspective on a Prada shoe is more valid than that of a teen blogger in Evanston, Illinois."[1]

For years, high fashion had dragged its stilettos about joining this brave new world, the internet. People had been buying *clothes* online since the '90s, sure, but that was different from *fashion*, which seemed inherently analog. How could its thrills be transmitted via screen? Surely customers had to touch the cashmere, or at least stroke the glossy magazine page it was depicted on, to really *feel* it. And what about the expertise of a great salesperson, or the joy of trying on that dream dress in a dressing room? You couldn't get that in a FedEx box! And besides, deep down, fashion was wary of a universe that had no velvet rope. The internet was so *egalitarian*. Yikes.

But by the dawn of the Obama era, it was time to get on board. With broadband internet service now widely available—making it possible to shop the web faster, with fewer glitches, than ever before—in 2008, clothing was second only to books in the number of purchases made online. Even high end holdouts were climbing aboard Yoox and Net-a-Porter, sites that had the prestige of the Barneys of yore, plus a reach that was instant, and global.

"This is how we shop now," Eva Wiseman would write in the *Guardian*, marveling at the rise of Net-a-Porter. "We use our screens for window shopping. We scroll quickly through a season's worth of evening wear in a minimized window below our inbox, we click to enlarge, we add to basket."[2]

The convenience and accessibility of the web paralleled that of those glory-days catalogues of the '80s, shoppable 24/7. And then there were the *prices*. During the Recession, when retail sales dropped to their lowest rate in thirty-five years, stores stayed alive by slashing price tags, not just by the traditional half-off but by as much as 80 percent. Shoppers got used to those sale signs—especially online, where they could compare prices like never before. And when the economy improved, that discount mentality stuck. So much for customer loyalty—even a retailer's longtime fans would stray to its competitors, if the price was right. But J.Crew had a reason for brand loyalty that others did not: Jenna.

In the first flush of Jenna's tenure as president and creative director of the J.Crew brand, "everything changed," recalls menswear designer Frank Muytjens. She restructured the creative side of the company, pooling the teams for the various divisions—women's, men's, kids—and bringing in a wave of new hires. It put everyone on the same page, at the same team. Whether you worked in design, store visuals, internal presentations, styling, the catalogue, or the website, "it felt like we all had the same point of view," Muytjens says. "Everyone was there to make everyone else look good."

Jenna knew that every piece of the J.Crew puzzle had to tell *one* story. In marketingspeak, they needed "emotional coherence."[3] Walk into any Apple store and you can feel it immediately: the iPhones, the logo, the shiny white surfaces, the diverse, just-hip-enough sales force—it all aligns. At peak Emily, J.Crew had achieved almost perfect emotional coherence, largely because of Emily herself: The single filter through which clothes, images, stores, site, logo, and branding had to pass. She was like the famous "menders" at the Loro Piana factory, who spent all day poring over cashmere, literal tweezers in hand, ready to pluck on any imperfection. Nothing escaped her eye.

Now, Jenna was that filter. "I don't care if it's an employee handbook or the layout of the nursing room," she said, the whole thing had to say "J.Crew."[4] Not only did she oversee all the big things—store interiors, web design, perfectly layered catalogue looks—but also, to an almost impractical degree, she saw the little stuff, too. Every last email blast to the customers required Jenna's sign-off. And she gave notes. The stores, for one thing. They looked "like a modern house with tons of shit in it . . . it really doesn't look so pretty."[5] Jenna wanted better than pretty. She wanted $8,000 Serge Mouille chandeliers—a staple of design magazines—for J.Crew boutiques.

Todd Snyder, now observing J.Crew from the outside, says with Jenna in the driver's seat, "there had never been better creative in a company. The stores never looked better, the catalogue never looked better, the product never looked better. When she got in charge, everything made sense."

Among her first projects: overhauling the catalogue. The "empathy economy" and the era of the blog put an interesting pressure on brands like J.Crew. They needed more than a vague sense of authenticity; they needed "personality," *voice*. Content! A website stuffed with articles that had nothing to do with the stuff they made, to wrap the hard sell inside a fuzzy blanket of storytelling. This content created a chatty intimacy with the customer, er, *reader*. It implied J.Crew wasn't just some cold, consumerist selling machine, but a friend, a fun source of inspiration, information, and, yes, also some nice clothing!

Now, Jenna had the clout to pump up the photography budget, demand better models and more exotic locales, and even to rework the logo: No more *J* swooping low in front of *Crew*. Now the letters were aligned; in the era of "collabs" it made the name easier to "lock up" with other words. A former *Domino* editor was hired to develop the voice of the new *Style Guide*, aka the catalogue, which had a new kind of heavy lifting to do—now that it was an instruction manual to the J.Crew life. The *Style Guide* had the feel of a fun travel magazine. Mr. and Mrs. J.Crew went on high-dollar, far-flung expeditions to India, Africa, Iceland, Japan, and they took with them a barrage of styling how-tos: how to roll your sleeves the "Jenna way," how to partial-tuck that shirttail, how to nail the right proportion of sequin to denim. This didactic approach was at least in part a Mickey brain wave. His instructions: *Don't make it secretive. Show people things they can do.*

The biggest hit in the new *Style Guide* was "Jenna's Picks," which looked like a page ripped from *InStyle*: every month, Jenna's "fave" bubble necklace, her new lipstick hue. The pale-pink ballet flat "I'll be wearing this fall," accompanied by snapshots of Jenna on vacation, Jenna holding Beckett, Jenna at her hot pink desk in the office. It was the bestselling page of the catalogue. Anything she wanted, we wanted.

IN JUNE 2008, A PART-TIME ACTRESS AND VOICEOVER ARTIST named Marika Casteel walked into her local J.Crew store in Walnut Creek, an upscale suburb of San Francisco, and stumbled upon a gem: the Astrid, a cropped jacket trimmed with small fabric balls, like clusters of berries. Casteel already had an Astrid in gray. But this was a new shade of pale blue, and Casteel had spied it *before it was even online*.

Casteel was one of the "Crewlade" drinkers, a new breed of J.Crew superfan. To her, the specialness of Jenna's J.Crew—ribbon details, sparkles, little clusters of fabric balls—recalled the ruffled socks and flounced dresses of childhood, fancy clothes that "sparked joy," as Marie Kondo might say, before adulthood came along to crush our spirits with credit card bills and performance reviews. Jenna gave grown women permission to wear clothes that felt *delightful*. Who says only kids wore glittery Mary Janes? Why save that jeweled top for the special occasion that might never arrive? "It was an invitation to make magic with clothing," Casteel says. "Jenna told tens of thousands of women, Don't wait to wear your good stuff!" From the revamped *Style Guide*, Casteel would quite literally learn a new way to dress: how to mix a polka-dot shirt with a low leopard heel and dark jeans to achieve a look that felt of-the-moment but still worked for a working mom. "Jenna gave a lot of these gifts to women."

When Casteel spotted the rare blue Astrid, she could not keep this news to herself. That day, she went home and started building her own style blog. She named it *Gigi's Gone Shopping*, using her nickname. Almost instantly, a commenter popped up: "Thank you! So helpful! What's next?"

Blogging had shaken up the media establishment, but it also changed things for the other side—the fans. By definition, ardent fans had always been obsessive. Recall the coeds of James Madison U., inventing racy dialogue for J.Crew catalogue models in 1988. But the internet allowed superfans to connect, forming sprawling communities around entities like *Star Wars* and Rihanna. They also united around brands, and not just fancy ones. There were fan blogs for IKEA, Trader Joe's, Lululemon.[6]

More than a dozen blogs and Tumblr accounts would eventually pop up to worship J.Crew. But only one of these was considered "the mothership." In May 2008, a slender, dark-haired Connecticut mystery woman named Alexis—a professor by day, who keeps her surname and identity secret online—launched *J.Crew Aficionada*.[7]

Aficionadas obsessed over J.Crew the way sneakerheads slaver over the latest Nike "drop." A "tissue tee" bearing a large ribbon design in the shape of a rose drove them "berserk," says Casteel. It sold out, then popped up on eBay at two and three times the original price. A *T-shirt*.

But the bigger the fan, the greater their sense of ownership over the object of their obsession. Beyoncé's "Beyhive" would happily follow her into the flames of hell, and ruthlessly descend upon anyone who dared speak ill of their chosen queen. But brand fans are different. J.Crew Aficionadas loved J.Crew, but they also expected more from it. They went deep on the company's inner workings; some even tuned in to Mickey's quarterly state-of-the-union calls with financial analysts, gathering in the comments section to parse his tone of voice and duke it out over issues of operating income and product differentiation.

From the earliest days of the site, JCAs took issue with J.Crew's fit, its shipping policies, its fabrics. Why the heck was the website still so glitchy? In 2008, it seemed to crash at least once a week. More than anything, they got riled up about price and quality. In 2009 one commenter wrote that she'd stuck a Post-it to her J.Crew credit card: *Do not buy J.Crew cashmere!* JCAs were dubious about the high-end Collection stuff.

Q: Was anybody out there actually buying $358 snakeskin heels from J.Crew?

A: Only if found on deep sale.

J.Crew knew about this laundry list of grievances. A few months after the *J.Crew Aficionada* blog launched, Alexis emailed Mickey directly, partially to put to the test the much-lauded legend that he emailed customers back directly. He lived up to the hype, emailing her right back. In a post titled "Mickey Drexler = AWESOME," she quoted the C.E.O. himself: "totally and very much aware of your blog—we read it daily."

But was J.Crew *listening* to the JCAs? Hard to say. At the time when these online superfans began to coalesce, J.Crew was whipsawing from one big development to another. From mid-'08 to early '09 alone, the pace at 770 Broadway was relentless: They swung from Jenna's *Domino* cover; to the opening of the Liquor Store; to the departure of Todd Snyder; to Jenna's ascent to creative director and president. Throw in the financial collapse. The stock plunge. The opening of the Collection boutique. The *Style Guide* overhaul and launch of "Jenna's Picks." Mrs. Obama on *The Tonight Show.* Election. Inauguration. That first flush of intense Jenna fixation. *All* of that transpired in one big whoosh, and most within a single, blinding six-month span. "That time is somewhat of a blur," Jenna says now. "It was really intense."

Maybe there wasn't time or bandwidth to fret about online complaints, especially coming from a group that identified as J.Crew's biggest fans. Could anyone who shopped J.Crew for sport and spent considerable time pondering it online really think the company was so bad? And besides, was this online fan—the one swapping discount codes and scouring sale racks—really "our girl"? Wasn't "our girl" in fact the chic creature in Mickey's mind's eye, who occupied that designer/mass white space and relished the way *Loro Piana* rolled off the tongue?

You can't keep all the people happy all the time, right? And at that point—even as they were doing fancy footwork to avoid a financial meltdown—J.Crew seemed to be keeping an awful lot of people happy a lot of the time.

CHAPTER 20

Let's Make a Deal

R*iiiing riiiing.* Everybody in the office knew what that tinny sound meant: here comes Mickey. By 2010 he'd taken to winding around the gray-carpeted office corridors on a Gary Fisher Simple City bike. Someone had brought it in to show him one day. He liked it so much, he kept it. Now it was a set piece of the Mickey Show, rolled out when there was press in the office, as the boss pedaled from one department to the next.[1]

That bike was so Mickey. It was well designed, solid, not too slick or tricksy—obviously nice but not gold plated, not ostentatiously fancy. And inherently egalitarian. What could be more down to earth than a bike?

But a bike in an office? It had to be the most attention-seeking way to get from point A to point B, short of a rickshaw.

The Gary Fisher Simple City said, *I'm not like those other* C.E.O.s. Mickey never wanted to be perceived as the kind of guy who thinks of himself as a big shot, the kind who hands down dictates from his corner office. Mickey wore jeans and sneakers to work, talked to everybody, ran J.Crew like the guy behind the counter of his '50s drugstore—boots ever on the ground, the minutia of keeping the customer happy very much his direct responsibility.

But Mickey *was* a big shot, of the variety one might see on *Billions*: the C.E.O. who wears a vaguely Euro-looking scarf around his neck, not a tie, and who will go deep on the subject of the best Chinese takeout in the neighborhood, and also happens to have a box for the Boss at the Garden (he's a Springsteen superfan) and regularly lands in the real estate pages for casually picking up another $20 million estate. Mickey had homes in Martha's Vineyard, Sun Valley, the Bahamas, Napa. When he made his unannounced drop-ins on J.Crew stores all over the country—surprise!—he did it in his own Gulfstream IV, which had interiors by Thierry Despont, the architect tapped to restore the Statue of Liberty and the Ritz Paris. Mickey and Peggy Drexler had never been big on the social circuit, but their circle included Ian Schrager, Larry David, and *Rolling Stone* founder Jann Wenner.

By 2010 the list of dignitaries who dropped by the office to kiss Mickey's ring was both shiny and delightfully random, from Kate Hudson to A-Rod to Jimmy Buffett. Mickey sent a batch of Ludlows over to his new bud, Coldplay front man Chris Martin (when the young women in the office were more excited about Martin's then wife, Gwyneth Paltrow, he was cool: "I don't get what all the fuss is about," he shrugged). Barefoot Contessa Ina Garten dropped by the office with samples of a new packaged food endeavor. What did Mickey think?

Who wouldn't want a little of that Mickey magic? In the downturn, J.Crew had appeared to be headed for the gutter along with everybody else, but in 2009, they shot right back up to the surface: profits jumped 40 percent, revenues hit $1.57 billion—twice what they'd been when Mickey arrived at J.Crew.[2] Things were less rosy for the competition. Long after unemployment was back down and consumer confidence back up, the numbers at Ann Taylor and Banana Republic were still dismal. What appeared to be the difference? Mickey Drexler.

By 2010 Mickey's own J.Crew stock and options were valued at more than $270 million. He landed the cover of the *Wall Street Journal*'s magazine, *WSJ*, next to the cover line "Welcome to the Church of Mickey Drexler."[3] He got the twelve-thousand-word treatment from the

New Yorker—the highbrow-media equivalent of a lifetime achievement award.[4] So, yeah, you could roll your eyes at the guy, riding high on his Gary Fisher, eating his $10 peaches flown in specially from Georgia. Plenty of his employees did. But you could not argue with his success.

In the summer of 2010, Tracy Gardner told Mickey she was stepping down as president of J.Crew Group. Gardner's job had a much bigger purview than Jenna's: she was president of J.Crew, plus Madewell, and the fast-growing outlet division, J.Crew Factory. It was Gardner who had brought a much-needed sense of order to Mickey's bone-crushingly intense initial turnaround. And it was Gardner who had largely implemented the strategy that got them through the recession—behind the scenes of their fancy upscale image, she was dropping prices and tightening inventory, making sure that while J.Crew talked a good game about cashmere coats and exotic-skin clutches, what they were really moving were the bread-and-butter basics that had always paid the bills.

Back in '08, when crisis loomed, J.Crew had done deep research on what its customers really wanted. The answer was exactly what bloggers like Marika Casteel were raving about: Novelty. Specialness. Women especially didn't want to walk into J.Crew and find same-old, same-old basics. They wanted clothes that were still essentially conservative—clothes you could wear to work, or your kids' school recital—but that felt colorful, playful, a little escapist: skinny "Minnie" pants, "Tippi" sweaters, spangled tees, striped cardigans. They wanted J.Crew to be fun.

The more decorative J.Crew got, the more women seemed to love it. When they first introduced costume jewelry, "we started much more delicate and clean," Jenna says. "But every time we did something that was mildly more over-the-top, that's what sold." Only a handful of Emily-era survivors were around to savor the irony: the company whose employees once removed their bangle bracelets before walking into a meeting with the boss was now credited with inventing the big, gawdy "statement necklace"—ubiquitous by 2010—and egging on the stacks of "arm party" bracelets that clanked with every move a woman made. On *Oprah* in 2010, Jenna embodied the look: oversize stripe T-shirt, gold-spangled, drop-waist pants, a pair of swinging, navel-length necklaces, armful of bracelets—all, ostensibly, for a day of meetings at the office. Big picture, that meant that J.Crew has successfully pivoted again: It had been the essence of '80s prep, then '90s minimalism. And now it was synonymous with the extravagantly ornamental "personal style" of the late aughts.

Still, some of the higher-ups were already starting to fret: were they trying to be a fashion brand now? In an almost uncanny repeat of the Emily era, the business team was side-eyeing J.Crew Collection all over again. Mickey had identified the white space, but now Jenna, the true fashion fan—very high up the org chart—seemed to be pulling the brand ever further toward trendiness on the one hand, luxury on the other. Collection was envisioned as the pricey, pretty cherry on top of the J.Crew sundae. But some saw it as a distraction, both to the customer and to the company's own creatives. "It had started taking up too much energy, too much mind share," says a former exec. The design team increasingly seemed to believe that Collection *was* J.Crew. And who could blame them? An $800 Collection coat was a thing of beauty—a lot more fun to work on than the latest iteration of the trusty $175 stadium-cloth weekender.

As early as 2009—just as the Mickey-Jenna era was hitting its cultural peak—key merchants from that ex-Gap team saw the prices edging up, and the clothes getting trendier, and worried: where were they headed with all this? Mickey sometimes compared their product to that of Neiman Marcus, Saks, Bergdorf.[5] Fewer and fewer people on the inside had the stamina to keep reminding him and Jenna, *Um, we're a midtier mall brand . . . remember?* The Mickey Show had always been overpowering. Now, trying to steer the ballooning entity that was Jenna, too? Too much.

Which is to say, finding the right replacement for Tracy Gardner was critical. But Mickey seemed to know right away who he wanted.

Jenna was now entwined with the J.Crew name. She had transformed its look and identity. And while Jenna still acted like Jenna, more or less—demanding, but also jokey, self-deprecating—even among the people who watched her eat her takeout Cobb salad between back-to-back meetings every day, she had ceased to be regarded as a regular person. The reverence many long had for the merchant prince, with his Carnac-like predictions and his industry renown, they now had for Jenna—her taste, her instincts, her *fame*. She had become larger than life, the fashion star walking their hallways. Interns giggled and mock-fainted at the sight of her as they furtively peeked around the corner of her office door. To a degree, that feeling seeped all the way up the ranks: "We were in awe of Jenna, all of us," says a former executive. "No question. She'd walk in a room with an outfit, and you'd be like 'My god.' You wanted her approval, you did."

The combined presence of Jenna and Mickey gave working at J.Crew a sense of privilege, of specialness. They were the brand every other mass brand wished they could be. The one with the most famous dream team in American fashion.

Mickey loved design more than the average C.E.O. He saw it as the reason for J.Crew's success. Mickey had always been a bit of a fanboy around the creatives, who possessed a cool factor he never would. Many say he saw Jenna as a partner, one with real business instincts that could be honed over time. An eventual successor.

Did he see something of himself in her—like him, a creative genius who had transformed herself, rising from a bruising childhood to the top of the fashion heap; someone who loved the trappings of success but also deeply valued keeping it real; someone who shared both his obsessiveness and his X-ray vision, the ability to *see* a brand from the ground up? Or was it just that J.Crew was riding so high by 2010 that Mickey figured nothing—not even the departure of a practical, competent, seasoned business veteran like Gardner—could throw them off their game?

He pulled Jenna into a room and informed her, with little preamble: "Just want to let you know you're the president."[6] Not just of J.Crew, but of the whole company. Jenna leaned over and rested her head on the table. She took a few deep breaths, and sat back up. "Okay," she said. "Do I need to do anything different?"

"Just keep doing what you're doing," he told her. She later recalled the entire exchange as "a two-second conversation."

Mickey's not a secretive guy. For months, he'd been inviting Jenna to meetings and cc'ing her on emails that pointed in this direction. Still, she walked out of the room shell-shocked. "I hadn't really prepared for it. I never expected it to happen," she said later. "It was overwhelming—not what I ever expected for myself or dreamed of."[7]

She was forty-one. She now had a base salary of $1 million, plus millions in bonuses and other payouts to come. And the scope of her already-huge job had just tripled. The conversation might have been brief, but Jenna keenly felt the weight of this burden. "It's hard to imagine just how intense the job was," she says.

To industry insiders, Jenna's promotion was nothing short of shocking. Putting a designer at the helm of a $1.57 billion fashion company? It was like hiring a Harvard M.B.A. to design the clothes.

SOON ENOUGH, MICKEY WAS ON TO AN EVEN RISKIER, MORE CONTROVERSIAL decision. Not long after Jenna walked out of his office, gobsmacked, Mickey had breakfast with private equity player Jonathan Sokoloff. He was a partner at Leonard Green & Partners, one of several buyout firms that had been rushing in to prop up publicly traded retailers who continued to flounder in the wake of the recession. Leonard Green was a particularly prolific shopper: The firm would scoop up at least ten major American retailers, including the discount chain BJs, David's Bridal, and Sports Authority.

What did that have to do with J.Crew, which in 2010 appeared to be a roller coaster that only went up?

Sokoloff and Jim Coulter—the T.P.G. cofounder who'd brought Mickey into J.Crew in the first place—had been spitballing about an unlikely sequel: what if the two firms bought J.Crew, took it private, stoked its fires, and eventually went public all over again—for even more money?

Yes, that is déjà vu you're feeling. A second buyout by the same firm was unusual, even in those P.E.-heady days. But thanks to Mickey's turnaround of J.Crew, T.P.G.'s original leveraged buyout—so close to disaster in 2003 that the firm nearly threw in the towel—had ultimately turned out to be one of its greatest successes, paying off to the tune of $1.2 billion.[8] Coulter, in particular, was said to be a deep believer in Mickey himself, who was the main reason Coulter was willing to go in on a second buyout. The proposed deal valued J.Crew at $2.86 billion, five times what T.P.G. had paid for a majority stake in 1997.

Mickey would later frame his role in this scenario as that of innocent bystander: this was a deal cooked up by two freewheeling investment firms, and he worried from the jump that a new LBO would saddle J.Crew with a crippling amount of debt. (Which was exactly what happened.) That's a very different version of the story from the one that was widely reported in the press, and from the way the deal was perceived on Wall Street and, indeed, by many of Mickey's own employees. This second-time-around LBO, as far as most people were concerned, was Mickey Drexler's baby—his big bet on the power of the J.Crew brand, and on his own genius.

Why another buyout, why now? The logic offered up was that business was good but not great; with sales appearing to weaken, the freedom of the private market would give Mickey space to make necessary changes for growth. The stock had never fully recovered after the recession; if they went private and grew significantly, they could come back on the market at an appropriate value. Still that rationale didn't *totally* answer the question, why go private now? When Arthur and Emily sold a majority stake to T.P.G. in 1997, it was for reasons that were abundantly clear: Emily wanted to take over, Arthur had to be bought out, the company needed serious cash to open more stores. This time, the upside for J.Crew, the company, was less evident. What everyone knew was that Mickey had made a mint the first time J.Crew went public. Many simply assumed he was setting himself up to cash in; if he was able to pull the rabbit out of the hat again at J.Crew, this deal had the potential to land him in Don Fisher billionaire territory. One designer speculates, "Mickey figured he'd take the double-dip, and nobody would be the worse for it."

Plus, Mickey said it all the time: he hated running a public company. Like many C.E.O.s, he thought his company was undervalued. And he was arrogant. This was still the guy who fundamentally never liked having a boss. "He didn't like having shareholders to answer to, all the rigor," the same designer says, "people watching everything he did."

If you thought J.Crew's first wedding to T.P.G. was messy, well, it had nothing on round two. For starters, though Mickey entered talks with Sokoloff and Coulter in August, he did not inform J.Crew's board until October.[9] This timing mattered. Informing a corporate board of a buyout offer is what kicks off a "go shop" period—one or two months during which other investors can make competing offers. This is supposed to ensure that shareholders don't have to take the first deal they're offered; it gives the company a chance to attract a higher bidder. Mickey not only cut that period short, he also reportedly discussed his future employment at the company with the buyers (T.P.G. and Leonard Green). And, Mickey purportedly gave at least one potential buyer—Coulter himself, who sat on the board—access to confidential information.[10] All, unorthodox at best.

Then, when Mickey *did* finally discuss the deal with board members, he purportedly made it clear that his position on it was far from neutral: At the age of sixty-six, he reportedly said, he wasn't interested in working for a new boss. The implication: Take this deal—which was not seen as just T.P.G. and Leonard Green's deal, but rather *Mickey's* deal with the two firms—or risk losing your merchant prince. "A lesser executive might not have had such sway," *PitchBook* later noted, "but the industry consensus regarding Drexler's managerial brilliance provided him tremendous leverage over the J.Crew board."[11] (Mickey denies having pressured board members to take the deal.)

Eventually, these shenanigans landed Mickey and Co. in court. Shareholders balked at the short notice, not to mention Mickey's cozy relationship with Coulter, accusing the two of presenting a united front that had eliminated the possibility of any other offer.

A Delaware judge called it "icky kind of stuff"—bad corporate governance. The court approved a settlement requiring J.Crew to pay $16 million (at 0.5 percent of the transaction value, this amounted to a slap on the wrist) and to reopen the "go shop" window.[12] Still, in the end, Mickey got what he wanted. The deal would be notorious in the business press, but nonetheless, in March 2011, it went through. For just under $3 billion, J.Crew went private. Fifteen years after the T.P.G. buyout that almost broke the company, the brand was once again deeply in debt, on the hook for exorbitant fees and dividends to private equity keepers. Now, J.Crew would have to grow ever faster just to keep its head above water. But if anyone could rise to this challenge, it could. Right?

After the sale, Mickey's stake was up to $400 million. He rolled $100 million back into the company—an act of faith, or bravado, that surprised many in the finance world—restoring his ownership stake to 10 percent. If his handling of the deal had dinged his reputation, well, everyone knew that kind of damage is short-lived on Wall Street, as long as the company keeps making money. Shortly after the deal, Mickey was undaunted. "I would do it the same way [again]," he said. "I sleep well at night."[13]

At the time, "it felt like anything was possible," says a former menswear designer. "There was such momentum on the brand, with Jenna and with Mickey. It felt like anything was going to work—we could put out a line of cars and it would have sold."

So when Jenna decided next stop, Fashion Week, it seemed strangely doable. And when the most famous woman in the world showed up to the fashion show of a mall brand—it seemed not absurd, but rather a fitting testament to the unique power of J.Crew.

"*Ohmygod* I think I'm going to pass out," Jenna gasped. It was September 2011, six months after the buyout. Beyoncé—the woman whose voice had carried them through so many late nights in the J.Crew styling department—had just walked into their New York Fashion Week debut, wearing a gold sequin J.Crew Collection dress that discreetly hugged the curve of her belly. (Bey was awaiting a debut of her own: her first child, Blue Ivy Carter.)

Publicity SWAT teams spend months lining up this kind of appearance, paying stars up to $50,000 just to grace the front row.[14] Yet here was the shiniest star of all, free of charge, with zero wrangling. Because: Jenna.

Jenna had become friendly with Bey's hip younger sister, Solange, a fellow member of the Brooklyn glamourati. When Jenna invited Solange to the show, the younger Knowles had replied: "Sure. Can I bring my sister?" Recalls Jenna, "I said, 'Yeah, that's fine,' as my jaw dropped to the floor."

J.Crew at Fashion Week? Inconceivable at any other time in the company history. But by the fall of 2011, this was the house brand of the Obamas; a label sold on Net-a-Porter, right alongside Marni and Balenciaga; and a fashion kingmaker in itself—one In Good Company "collab" with J.Crew could restore life to a heritage label or put an indie brand on the map.

And besides, Jenna had just received the Nod. In 2011, she received a gilded invitation to the annual Costume Institute Gala at the Metropolitan Museum of Art, fashion event of the year. That May, she had ascended the museum's red carpeted stairs, rubbing elbows with pop stars and socialites, an exemplar of the imperfect-perfect mix she had by now made famous: she wore a slouchy cream-colored men's cashmere V-neck sweater—nothing like eveningwear—paired with a floor-length swirl of white feathers. In a Cinderella twist, her voluminous skirt left a trail of white fluff on the steps behind her. Jenna had become a *Vogue* girl.

Soon, she was a guest judge of the magazine's annual young designer competition. The magazine's fashion news editor was a good buddy who rented the garden apartment of Jenna's own famous Brooklyn brownstone. You couldn't get much closer to the inner sanctum. Imagine how that felt to a woman who once believed herself to be "officially gross."

So, Fashion Week? Not such a wild swing. After all, J.Crew wasn't planning a runway show, but rather a presentation—a tableau of models dressed in the new season's clothes. A modest affair, by Fashion Week standards. Still, it was the first time a mainstream retailer planted this sort of flag on the Fashion Week calendar. It was also Jenna's first big flex as J.Crew Group president.

That day, Beyoncé and every editor in New York were treated to the comfortingly familiar—preppy stripe coats, chambray shirts, tailored shorts—plus plenty of *extra*: splashes of brilliant green florals, wet-look sequin stripes, bubblegum-pink pants worn with shiny, fire-engine-red loafers (recalling the inaugural color combo of the youngest Obama). The collection was universally well received. But afterward, the thing that most people remarked on was not the clothes, but the models, with their tangerine-orange lipstick and slicked-back hair. You couldn't miss their resemblance to Jenna Lyons. Her own personal look—now indistinguishable from the "J.Crew look"—was the one even Fashion Week attendees aspired to achieve.

CHAPTER 21

Page Six on Line One

Six weeks after the triumph of the show, Jenna heard her name being paged over the office intercom. When she picked up the phone, it was Mickey, along with marketing-PR guru Margot Fooshee. They'd just gotten a call from the *New York Post*. "They're running a story that you're seeing a woman. Should we confirm or deny?" Staring at the wall, heart pounding, Jenna heard her voice say, "Confirm." After a long pause on the other end, someone said: "Okay. I think we need to talk."[1]

Jenna and her husband, Vincent Mazeau, were divorcing after thirteen years together. And at this moment, the *Post*, Mickey, and Margot Fooshee knew something that even Mazeau did not: Jenna was in the very early stages of a romance with a female friend. Nobody knew. Not Jenna's mother, not her friends. Certainly not her son. "I wasn't even totally sure what I was doing," she said later. "I was dipping my toe in the water." The call had come in at 4 P.M.; the story would go up online at midnight. Before Jenna herself had figured what this meant—which box her identity now checked—she was about to be outed in the city's most hotly read gossip rag.

Most of Jenna's colleagues learned the news when they opened their newspapers or emails the following morning. To them, the shock of learning that Jenna might be gay was nothing compared to the shock of realizing that their boss's sexuality had become tabloid fodder in the first place. "J.Crew exec in messy split," the headline blared on Page Six—the same gossip page Jenna sometimes read aloud with staffers, the way everyone else in New York did. What the hell? The personal lives of people who run mainstream fashion companies do not make it to Page Six. (Who *were* the executives of other mainstream fashion companies?)

It was a wakeup call. Jenna's public persona had reached a magnitude that people close to her—even the ones who had orchestrated her rise in the beginning—could not quite wrap their heads around. To make their newly quirky, polished prep feel *real* and desirable, J.Crew had offered up Jenna, the cool, great-looking woman with the dream job, the gorgeous home, the perfect family. That halo of domestic bliss—Jenna kissing Mazeau and toddler Beckett goodbye as she trotted off to the office, trailed by *Oprah*'s cameras—had been part of her perceived value. Now J.Crew's best marketing tool had taken on a life of its own, ricocheting well outside of the company's preppy soap bubble.

This wasn't Jenna's first run-in with the press in 2011. Months earlier, "Jenna's Picks" had included a photo of her with Beckett, both smiling adorably as she painted his toenails with hot-pink polish: "Lucky for me I ended up with a boy whose favorite color is pink," read the caption. It must have been a slow news day, because Fox News pounced. Jenna found that she had unwittingly stumbled into what was then new territory: the debate around gender identity.[2] A conservative media think tank called this happy photo "blatant propaganda celebrating transgendered children." Keith Ablow, psychiatrist and a Fox News talking head, felt compelled to weigh in. "It may be fun and games now, Jenna," he wrote, "but at least put some money aside for psychotherapy for the kid—and maybe a little for others who'll be affected by your 'innocent' pleasure."[3] Jon Stewart dubbed the drummed-up controversy "Toemageddon." Both J.Crew and Jenna declined to get involved, but Mickey's own wife, the psychologist Peggy Drexler, jumped to Jenna's defense on *Huffington Post*. "Full disclosure. I know Jenna. I know Beckett. And my husband runs the company," she wrote, lamenting the incident as evidence of yet another double standard mothers are held to: "Mothers doing anything that carries even a hint of crossing a line of gender correctness is viewed as another insidious step in the emasculation of American youth."[4]

Toemageddon blew up fast, but it also blew over relatively quickly. Most people seemed to have forgotten the "controversy" within a few weeks. But once Jenna's sexual orientation made headlines, the pink toenail photo got a second wind. This was 2011: the Supreme Court was still four years away from legalizing gay marriage in all fifty states; even most progressives had yet to consider concepts like gender fluidity and trans rights. In a rush of think pieces, Jenna was added to the short list of famous women who had left men for women, alongside Anne Heche and Cynthia Nixon. She and her girlfriend—whom the *Post* would soon identify as Courtney Crangi, sister and business manager of another New York fashion world denizen, jeweler Philip Crangi—were suddenly hailed and/or derided as a lesbian power couple. The column inches piled up.

"People seem stuck on this lesbian motif in a way that is especially jarring, since the whole tale is grounded in the fashion industry, where being gay is about as startling, interesting, or newsworthy as being thin," wrote *Washington Post* critic Robin Givhan. The "fashion gay," after all, was already a sitcom cliché—but that character was invariably male. It was hard to think of a famous lesbian fashion designer. Many of the commenters hinted that "fashion lesbian" was a contradiction in terms. Relatively few famous women had come out, and most who had—Ellen, Rosie—weren't exactly style stars. In a few years, we'd have Cara Delevingne, Kristen Stewart, Lena Waithe. But when the *Post* came calling for Jenna, Stewart was still the sweet *Twilight* girl besotted with her boyfriend, Robert Pattinson. Givhan pointed out the hypocrisy: "If this were the story of a male designer who was splitting from his wife and taking up with another man, it would not have taken over the internet the way this did."[5]

Keith Ablow resurfaced, of course, this time to suggest that while *he* certainly had no problem with homosexuality, he was concerned about the potential for Jenna—via photos in a catalogue—to convert little boys nationwide. "Ms. Lyons might be expressing her own discomfort with masculinity and projecting it onto her own son—and mine, and yours."[6] For what it's worth, Jenna's fellow New Yorkers didn't bat an eye at her sexuality. They were more worried about that Park Slope brownstone, with its cut-glass chandelier and charming front stoop. What would become of the real estate!? (After a bidding war, it sold for $4 million to a former member of Depeche Mode.[7])

Could the cult of Jenna Lyons survive this kind of hit?

If that worry reverberated around the offices of J.Crew, no one picked up on it. That's to Mickey's credit. Another C.E.O. with 266 stores in malls all over the country—in states red and blue—might have dialed back Jenna's public presence, but J.Crew did not. "I was treated with so much understanding, respect, acceptance," Jenna has said. "Had that not happened, it would have been much harder."[8]

Jenna kept her cool. You could discern her eye roll at the absurdity of it all, but she never explained herself. She and Crangi eventually began to appear together in person, Jenna towering like an exotic bird over her petite, tousled-blond girlfriend, looking thoroughly in love. "Even when the press was all over her, she owned it, she didn't hide it," says Gayle Spannaus. "She was unapologetic. I'm sure those things were difficult but she never really let it show."

That earned an extra measure of respect, not just around the office, but in the fashion world, too. Jenna had not turned out to be exactly what people presumed her to be—or even what she thought she was herself. But that did not knock her off her pedestal, or make her any less relatable.

If anything it made her an even more singular character: A woman who stood her ground—unafraid to be herself, even under intense scrutiny. The first queer woman ever to publicly rule the fashion space.

After she was outed, Jenna seemed to dial up her swagger even more. There was a quantum leap between the *Domino* Jenna of 2008—with her curled hair and apple pie approachability—and the woman who stepped out in the 2010s. Old Jenna had been stylish, but sweet. New Jenna was *chic:* she tossed her coats over her shoulders like she was playing the role of New York Fashion Designer on TV. In addition to the lipstick (now fire engine red) and the heavy, nerdy-chic glasses (the "Mensch" by Lower East Side eyewear brand Moscot)—totems now indivisible from J.Crew—Jenna scraped her hair into a severe bun and left her shirts unbuttoned to the sternum, or lower. Nip slips were a common sight in meetings, not that she seemed to care. (Someone once told her: whatever your assets are, exaggerate them. "I have good boobs, so my shirt's always unbuttoned too low," she told me.) Jenna still wore J.Crew—presumably?—but partnered with pieces by Marni and Dries, it didn't look like any J.Crew you or I could buy. Where was the girl who once turned down a job at Donna Karan because a $2,500 jacket was alienating to "real" people? Now, in interviews, she talked about Arnault, her regular salesperson at Céline's Paris boutique. This was not the preppy-with-a-twist girl of yore.

"We watched her change before our very eyes," marvels a former employee. "She turned into, like, *Jenna.* This fashion lesbian icon."

Later, Jenna described the metamorphosis she was going through. In a few short years she had gone from standing in her own backyard at her fortieth birthday party, wondering why, if her life looked so great on the outside (dream job, beautiful kid, gorgeous home) she still felt as if some indescribable *something* was missing—to finding herself rather unexpectedly in love with a woman, and growing into a new identity. Among other things, this changed her fashion sense. "I didn't realize how much I played to men," she said, "not just men in the workforce, but in the bedroom, in the way I dressed, in the way that I maneuvered." Old Jenna dressed for the male gaze. "I did what I thought they viewed as attractive or sexy. But the more I sat into myself, the better I felt."[9]

With "street style" at its peak, Jenna's amped-up look fit right in the moment. In the 2010s, fashion people who had once toiled behind the curtain—in clothes that were chic, but not usually showy—had begun to dress as if *they* were the big show everyone had come to see. In a way, they were: 2010 had brought the twin births of Instagram and the iPhone 4—the first smartphone equipped with a front-facing camera.[10] The selfie era was here. Now, fashion's armchair experts and its professionals alike didn't need the endorsement of street-style photographers. They could document and disseminate their "looks" themselves. As long as she was at J.Crew, Jenna steered clear of the Instagram game, perhaps protecting that remaining shred of privacy. Nevertheless she was among the most recognizable trendsetters of the era. "It was clear to me that Jenna became who Jenna always saw in her head," says a colleague from the '90s. "That's her power. No one gets to take that away from her."

CHAPTER 22

Cognitive Dissonance, Part Deux

When Jenna landed the cover of *Fast Company* in April 2013, in her signature black glasses and even a jaunty little bow tie, the cover read, "How J.Crew Stays White Hot." The *how* was implicit: This woman was the not-so-secret weapon. Jenna had gotten tons of press over the years, but this cover, on a business magazine, felt different: it seemed to say something not just about Jenna's ascent, but Mickey's faith in it. "Not since Steve Jobs and Jonathan Ive at Apple," the reporter raved, "has a creative pairing been as intriguing and fruitful as that of Drexler and Lyons."[1] Jenna *and* J.Crew were on top of the world; 2013 would be the company's best year ever, with $2.4 billion in revenue. By 2014, they'd have more than four hundred stores in the U.S., Canada, and the U.K. And the brand had caught the eye of one of the richest men in Japan.[2]

Tadashi Yanai had admired Mickey since the '80s, when he studied the Gap's winning formula as a model for his own company, Uniqlo, whose airy stores and rainbow of cheap yet well-made tees and sweats owed an obvious debt to the Mickey formula. At one point, the two men had met in Tokyo; Yanai referred to Mickey as "professor" and was said to have kept a photo from that meeting in his office for years. Now,

Yanai's corporation, Fast Retailing, aimed to make its biggest property, Uniqlo—then a $20 billion brand—the largest clothing company in the world, eclipsing even Zara. Would buying America's favorite preppy-with-a-twist retailer help it get there?

The response from T.P.G. and Leonard Green: Sure, Yanai could have J.Crew. For more than $5 billion. That was almost fourteen times EBITDA, nearly twice as much as the two investment firms had paid for the brand two years earlier.[3] But in 2013, J.Crew didn't *need* a Uniqlo deal. Why not roll the dice, see how high Yanai would go?

Yanai was said to be insulted by the bloated price tag. Talks of a buyout died there. Which didn't seem so tragic at the time: Coming on the heels of a $2.4 billion year, J.Crew had just tasked Goldman Sachs with starting the process of its second I.P.O. 2011's $3 billion dual buyout looked poised to pay off.

In hindsight, some see that squandered Uniqlo offer as the Hail Mary that might have saved J.Crew, both from a crashing wave of industry-wide change—and from its own not-insignificant internal issues. A new paradigm was emerging: J.Crew continued to be celebrated in the press, showered with one accolade after the next, while inside the company, a crisis was brewing. One that J.Crew had plenty of time to see coming.

Before Jenna ever posed for *Fast Company*, and long before Tadashi Yanai came calling, a new, steady drumbeat had taken hold within 770 Broadway: What was next, next, *next*? When Mickey first reinvented the company, there had been no corporate PowerPoint for what would become the J.Crew look. Yes, Mickey had his destination in mind—that white space between designer and mass. But so much of the aesthetic that eventually nestled them into that niche was less strategy than pure gut: Mickey, looking at Jenna, in her army pants and her navy blazer and her high heels, and thinking, *That's cool.* Todd Snyder, clocking the renaissance of butch, white-soled Red Wing boots and dark denim at Freemans and thinking, *Huh, cool.* Back then, J.Crew had no track record to beat. They were rising from the ashes, with only one way to go: up.

But with success had come a new overlord: *comps*. Retailspeak for a store's current sales, compared to those of the previous year. Comps are standard operating procedure: the quantity of an item you order for next fall is largely based on how many sold last fall. But comps can be a creativity killer. As early as 2012, "it was always, 'What sold well last year? How are we going to anniversary that?'" says a former designer. "It was 'L.Y. vs. T.Y.'"—last year vs. this year—"all that corporatespeak." Having to "anniversary" your own wins is a slippery slope. "They kept regurgitating," says a former creative. They had to keep giving the customer what she expected: "It was always, '*She* needs this kind of dress again, because *she* bought so many of them last year.'"

Success is "a beast," Jenna later told an interviewer. "How do you always top yourself? How is that possible?" She answered her own question: "You keep finding new avenues of growth, whatever that may be—whether it's going international, opening more stores, opening new divisions, throttling one division. It's what we talk about all the time."[4] When the interviewer suggested that it might not be possible to *always* top a best performance, Jenna's reply was unusually blunt: "Yeah, I don't live in that reality. I live in the reality that you do it again."

Now, every time J.Crew staffers walked out of 770 Broadway, they saw the windows of the nearby Ann Taylor plastered with eerily familiar, blown-up photos: red-lipped models laughing in front of clean white backdrops, their hair artfully mussed, their sweaters leopard print, their accessories aggressively sparkly. It was the J.Crew look, often shot on the same models J.Crew hired, by photographers J.Crew worked with. And it wasn't just Ann Taylor. Gap was awash in quirky prints, geek-chic glasses, bright color combos—all with a cheaper price tag. This look wasn't rocket science, after all; it was a trend, like any other, and could be copied. J.Crew heard rumors that on competitors' photo shoots, art directors didn't even try to hide where they were getting their ideas: they brazenly pinned up "swipe" from the J.Crew catalogue on their inspiration boards.

Copycats are all part of the game—J.Crew had done its fair share of "borrowing," too—and competitors had been churning out embellished tees and chunky costume jewels for years. But for a long stretch, no matter how many imitators there were, the J.Crew *brand* had felt iron-clad. No one could do J.Crew as well as J.Crew did. As long as that was the case, they were safe.

But by the time Jenna appeared on *Fast Company*, the women's look they pioneered was already starting to flame out. Pencil skirts and spangled cardigans, statement necklaces, candy-colored cashmere, glittery heels. It had once been so influential, so fresh. Then it had become predictable, but still good—still far more well executed than the competition. But now it was *everywhere,* almost like a costume, or a cliché, recognizable at fifty paces. The fashion-conscious shopper J.Crew had worked so hard to attract did not want to see herself coming and going. And for the less fashion-conscious, raising families and paying mortgages: with Gap and Ann Taylor serving up similar styles at much lower prices—and at far greater scale—it was a little like Mickey's revelation, back in 1991, when Target was selling Gap lite . . . why *wouldn't* you buy a slightly lesser version of the same look, if it was cheaper? J.Crew needed an answer to that question: What's next? But no one seemed to have one.

For years, Jenna and her team had stayed one step ahead of boredom with ever-more-inventive variations on a theme. They amped up the sequins, then got rid of them; cycled through ruffles, ribbons, layered necklaces, dangling earrings, pajama dressing, neon accents, camo; graduated from ballet flats to loafers; threw in ever more inventive "collabs." In the catalogue, Spannaus's styling team went from coral lips to bold red, then bright nail polish. When they experimented with a swipe of mint-green eyeliner and wet-look hair, the response was an unequivocal *no*. Too kooky! "Now, the feedback was 'Whoa, whoa, whoa,'" says a former copy editor. "We were fine when it was just about a sparkly ballet flat, but now you've gone completely fucking overboard."

What happened next? You guessed it. A pendulum swing.

Paris, 2012: Céline creative director Phoebe Philo—the true north of every fashion devotee, from Kanye to Jenna herself—unleashed $1,000 mink-lined faux Birkenstocks on her runway. *Furkenstocks!* In 2012 the humble orthopedic shoe now in every fashionista's closet was still an object of ridicule, widely considered a totem of total sartorial abnegation. But Philo's haute Birks delivered a devastating kick to the era of try-hard *Mad Men* dressiness and tricksy, highly decorative personal styling. They were a harbinger of the luxe, pragmatic minimalism that would soon take hold. Suddenly, *ease* was the thing. Soon, the same women who'd spent a decade-plus teetering around in lethal-looking Valentino Rockstud sandals would line up to catch the new limited-edition sneaker "drop."

Just as comfort footwear was trickling down from the runways of Paris, something not totally unrelated was bubbling up from the streets. The kids were calling it "normcore." The *New York Times* wasn't sure if it was "a fashion movement or a massive in-joke."[5] The word was a portmanteau of *normal* and *hardcore* that was originally birthed in a trend-forecasting report that described it as "a post-authenticity coolness that opts into sameness." Soon *Glamour* was doing fashion spreads on what appeared to be the wardrobe of a '90s suburban dad: unironic sweatshirts, ill-fitting jeans, clunky white sneakers. (The look owed a debt to the featureless clothes of Mickey-era Gap and indeed, sparked a trend for intentionally blasé Gap logo sweatshirts.) According to *New York* magazine, this was "fashion for those who realize they're one in 7 billion."[6] In other words, the latest fashion trend was all about a freedom from specialness. That would have been great news for the J.Crew of the '90s, or even of Y2K, when the *Dawson's Creek* kids were palling around in boxy sweaters and light-wash jeans. But the J.Crew of the 2010s had bet the farm on *special*. "When normcore came along, that killed us," says Spannaus.

Hang on, what was happening here? A $1,000 furry slipper from Paris, plus a trend so niche that the suburban dads whose closets it borrowed from have likely *still* never heard of it—these things had thrown a curveball at the mighty J.Crew? Absurd.

For decades, the trends from the street and the runways had occasionally aligned with J.Crew, but rarely because the company was chasing the whims of fashion. J.Crew wasn't *built* to chase trends, even if it had wanted to: trends moved too fast for their slow supply chain and yearlong development process. The schedule J.Crew followed worked well for timeless basics which, by definition, evolve slowly.

But by the 2010s, the trend cycle turned on a dime, spinning faster than ever as Zara, H&M, Topshop, Mango, and Forever 21 spotted looks on the runways and translated them to their shop floors, sometimes in a matter of weeks. These chains had changed consumer psychology: they retrained us to expect constant novelty. Now, it felt lame to walk into any store, or click on a site, and see the same stuff you saw yesterday. Instagram had only ratcheted things up further: Generation Selfie wanted a new look for every post. If an outfit only needed to last for a single photo, who cared about Mickey and Jenna's insistence that J.Crew clothes are better quality—built to last?

Today, it's easy to wonder: Why hadn't J.Crew just stayed in its lane, sticking with basics? Why had it tried to compete with this madness? But J.Crew's "specialness," its sparkle and ornamentation, its increasingly adventurous mixing and matching, wasn't just Jenna going bananas with a pile of sequins and a glue gun. It was the result of consumer research, which kept telling them: *Special. Festive. New. Fun.* That was what women expected of J.Crew.

In her 2013 fast fashion exposé, *Overdressed*, Elizabeth Cline—the Michael Pollan of the fashion industry—traces the start of the fast fashion mentality back to a curious source: one Millard "Mickey" Drexler.[7] Cline argues that Mickey's Gap was the O.G. fast fashion retailer, the first to convince shoppers—through a flood of high-end ads and high-profile appearances by, say, Sharon Stone—that low-price clothes were a viable alternative to higher-end fashion. Remember: Gap told us that mass clothing was good enough for people of any class. *Norma Jean wore khakis*. Gap got more Americans buying more inexpensive basics, more frequently, by consistently changing up store windows with each new color of the season's star sweater. Customers got hooked, buying Gap turtlenecks in every new hue. The fact that those turtlenecks cost $11? That recalibrated our expectations, too. Cline writes that fast fashion—not just at Gap—permanently changed what most people were willing to spend on clothes.

By 2014, those chickens had come home to roost, rather spectacularly: Everybody wanted constant novelty. And nobody wanted to pay much for it.

J.Crew was well aware that their exuberantly gaudy "bubble" necklaces had gone from played out to *over*. But they still kept pumping those necklaces into catalogues and stores and the website. Why? *Comps.* L.Y. vs. T.Y. They had sold a boatload of bubble necklaces last year, so they'd invested heavily in bubble necklaces for this year. That investment was made two full fashion seasons before the necklaces would hit stores. Betting on what people will want a year in advance had always been a gamble, but in a trend cycle that moves at hyperspeed, they were betting on an increasingly uncertain future. The bubble necklace was a look that J.Crew *owned*—one its customers expected to find. So they couldn't just not sell it anymore. Spannaus, whose job was to style these pieces to look fresh and current no matter how tired they got, remembers this moment with a groan: "Céline's got the fur-lined Birkenstocks, and we're still doing high heels with glitter? *No.*"

J.Crew wasn't standing there like a deer in the headlights. Jenna's team tried to pivot, veering from kooky to classic. They put out a catalogue awash in elegant grays and camels, dialed back almost to Emily-era minimalism. It flopped. "The customer who was still coming to us didn't want that either," says Spannaus. Kooky wasn't working anymore—that much was clear—but after years of fun exuberance, basic looked blah. That single, ill-fated catalogue seemed to resurface in every hindsight meeting, an illustration of the point at which things really went off the rails.

J.CREW WAS NOT A COMPANY THAT FAILED TO EVOLVE. THEY HAD rolled with the catalogue boom, the birth of specialty retail, the dawn of online shopping: remember Arthur Jr.'s 1997 race to get to the world wide web before Gap? But now almost every phone in the U.S. was a Wi-Fi equipped smartphone. People squinting at some four inches of screen couldn't see a lot of what J.Crew promised: the artful construction details and Italian silk were lost on a new consumer, who likely didn't care anyway. The younger customer "doesn't want to read an entire fucking essay about how their sweater got its name," says a copywriter. "She doesn't have the attention span for that."

J.Crew was falling behind. Could Mickey see it? "I don't think J.Crew understood how aggressively it needed to be digital in this new world," says one of his former deputies, clearly trying to be diplomatic.

In late 2011, Bain & Company retail consultant Darrell Rigby published a paper in the *Harvard Business Review* detailing the "start-from-scratch, across-the-board innovation" retailers urgently needed to undertake, not to thrive in the future of shopping, necessarily, but just to survive to see it.[8] The writing was on the wall, Rigby said: Amazon's market value was already up to $100 billion, roughly equivalent to Target, Best Buy, Staples, Nordstrom, J. C. Penney, Macy's, and Kohl's combined. But many great retail orgs were still permeated by a "technophobe culture," Rigby said. The retail execs in their corner offices knew everything there was to know about store lighting and layouts—they could tell you exactly why cherry red would sell better than tomato—but that kind of expertise wasn't enough anymore. In terms of computer literacy, these bosses were "shockingly subpar." Many had never personally ordered anything online; some still made their assistants print out their emails. "Knowledgeable young computer geeks shun [these companies] as places to work."

In some ways, this didn't describe J.Crew at all: Mickey's iPhone was surgically attached to his hand. He was almost *too* responsive to email. But if any of his employees had read this report, they might have seen other red flags. In website review meetings, it was clear Mickey wasn't used to navigating J.Crew's own site. Just as Arthur and Emily had once been catalogue people, Mickey was fundamentally a shopkeeper—forever stalking his stores, quizzing customers, answering their kvetching emails in the wee hours. The online world largely left him cold. In this, he was very much the type Rigby described.

On the face of things, J.Crew had a killer website; it looked gorgeous, won awards for visuals and tone. But they weren't putting in the back-end investment it would have taken to keep it on the leading edge. And by 2014, the site was only one piece of the digital puzzle. Facebook, Instagram, Twitter, Google, YouTube, Snapchat: each required a custom approach; each had a slightly different audience. (TikTok would dawn in 2016.) In the fast-paced, shoot-from-the-hip social media era, J.Crew was showing its age.

Social media had moved the goal posts of "authenticity" yet again.

Now, every communiqué from a brand had to feel intimate, immediate, and—crucially—spontaneous, transparent. "Real." The idea of being "real" online sounds like a joke today; we've wised up to just how auto-tuned most online personas have become. But in the early days of this revolution, social media was believed to be about a brand-new thing: unvarnished truth, in real time, from entities that had previously been walled-off, insular. Some old school fashion players were joyfully loosening the reins: Veteran stylist Carlyne Cerf de Dudzeele, newly besotted with Instagram in 2014, posted a shot from a recent shoot with the caption: "New World / No Retouching, No Assistant / No Budget, No Brainstorming, No Moodboard."[9] But how could a corporation throw caution to the wind? J.Crew had spent thirty-five years eking "real" out of every photo shoot via painstaking curation—indeed, that's arguably what they did best—and they didn't know another way to work. "It was a hangover of being a catalogue business," says an employee hired in 2012. "It's really hard to undo that machine." So though they did hire an in-house "social" team, they produced their feeds as carefully as catalogue pages, complete with location scouts and casting agents. Instead of setting an assistant loose to snap behind-the-scenes shots on someone's iPhone, J.Crew hired a professional to shoot "candids." And before any image was posted, it was highly edited by a creative director. By 2014, J.Crew had a very charming blog . . . on WordPress. It looked great, like everything else they did, but WordPress? It was the equivalent of a stone tablet. Says this source, "It was so embarrassing."

Now, preached Darrell Rigby, was the time for retail C.E.O.s to achieve "perfect integration of the digital and the physical." To make I.R.L. shopping utterly seamless, with quick, hassle-free returns. To mind the reviews of online "experts" on Facebook and Twitter. To recruit techies from Amazon and Google. But at J.Crew, employees were still working off Excel spreadsheets. The company infrastructure was inefficient, dated. Customers still waited a week to get the shorts they needed for vacation *and* they still paid for shipping. And most international customers were simply out of luck: Marika Casteel, the ardent J.Crew fan-blogger, took it upon herself to mail J.Crew shipments to a fellow aficionada in Australia. J.Crew didn't offer shipping Down Under, and Casteel didn't want any true believer to miss out. To fans who were watching closely, these were obvious, fixable problems: So why didn't J.Crew fix them?

Meanwhile, a new kind of competitor had arrived on the scene, one to whom all of this came naturally. These players had the new world order all figured out: understood how to navigate online reviews, social media marketing, free, fast delivery, multiplatform apps, instant checkout. These were digital natives, "disruptors"—Bonobos, Everlane, Reformation, Warby Parker—built to serve a new moment, and a new consumer that J.Crew had not reckoned with: one who cared more about digital-era convenience and "radical transparency" about where their clothes were manufactured (and of what, and by whom) than about J.Crew's halo of fashion insider-dom, or the old-world cred of "heritage" collabs. These companies were run not by merchant princes trained in the bowels of Bloomingdale's, but by Young Turks from outside of the fashion ecosystem. They were unencumbered by long store leases—in some cases, by any stores at all. Their playbook was based not on gut instinct, but on complex algorithms. Indeed, they were largely invented as a workaround to the problems posed by "old" retail—a category J.Crew suddenly found itself relegated to. The subscription shopping service Stitch Fix had been founded in 2011 by Harvard M.B.A. student Katrina Lake, who intuited her customers' personal tastes not by actually meeting them, but by gathering data from online surveys.[10] Lake's goal was for busy shoppers to never actually have to "shop" at all: new clothes magically showed up in a box on their doorstep several times a year. Fashion rental site Rent the Runway was founded in 2009 by two more Harvard M.B.A.s, who noted the skyrocketing price of designer clothes and wondered: why should a woman blow $500-plus on a formal dress she's only going to wear once?[11] When Mickey first envisioned the white space between designer and mass, these innovators didn't exist. Now, it seemed there was a new disruptor popping up the "better" space—with a fresher, tech-era spin—every day.

IN PUBLIC, MICKEY LAUGHED OFF THE COMPETITORS ENCROACHING from all sides. But behind the scenes, there were signs that he was feeling the heat. Bonobos, the menswear startup, had poached a series of designers from J.Crew's team. When a third designer, who happened to be a longtime Mickey favorite, defected to Bonobos, he was served with papers on his first day at the new job. J.Crew slapped him with a lawsuit for intellectual property theft of confidential business information. (The suit was dropped within a month, on undisclosed terms.)

To the man's former colleagues, this rang out as a shot across the bow—and not just to Bonobos. It was a wakeup call. If Mickey could go after *that* guy, one of his pets, what was he willing to do to any of them?

What was going through Mickey's mind by the time that issue of *Fast Company* came out, with Jenna on the cover? Sources close to him say Mickey had been instrumental in approving the cover, eager to position Jenna as his business equal—viable C.E.O. material, when the time came. But key players who had long questioned Mickey's fealty to Jenna now came to suspect he was starting to feel a little queasy about her ever-widening exposure. Perhaps even resentful of her being credited, almost single-handedly, with J.Crew's success. It's possible his *shpilkes* had kicked in: Was it a good idea to gloat about success when, privately, they all knew that a tsunami of challenges was on the doorstep—and that they had yet to answer that nagging question, *what's next?*

Whatever the reason, when *Fast Company* landed on newsstands across Manhattan, some believed Mickey was less than thrilled. A high-ranking J.Crew executive—either acting on Mickey's orders, or of his own accord—sent a team of employees out to scoop up every issue they could find. Why? As a staffer who was in on the mission told me, "They wanted to bury the issue."

Mickey has denied any knowledge of this. And it's true that the task was so covert, so ludicrous, it could have been done on his behalf without him ever knowing. Mickey was never short of yes-men happy to do his bidding, no matter how absurd. As far as the staffer I spoke with was concerned, it was clear that Mickey's problem with *Fast Company* was really a problem with Jenna.

Little by little, J.Crew had become the story of one woman. Their look reflected Jenna's personal style, her lifestyle, her . . . face. In catalogues and in fashion shows, she regularly cast the model Michèle Ouellet, a Jenna doppelgänger (on Instagram, the designer referred to her as "baby Jenna"). That kind of thing only served to wrap the brand more tightly around her.

It had long been a source of consternation among higher-ups that Mickey—their Carnac, their mystical seer—seemed to be the last to see the Jenna problem. Periodically, he got frustrated with some attention-seeking thing she did, but then he'd get over it. Mickey, as much as anybody, seemed to be under the spell of Jenna—her eye, her cool factor—she *was* that ineffable thing he had spent his career chasing. And of course he, more than anyone, had reaped the rewards of her talents: J.Crew had never done better than it did in the first years of Jenna's presidency. The company never won more praise, or earned more money, than it did between 2010 and 2013.

But, "the more Jenna started putting herself first in every decision, that trust started to erode," says a colleague of Mickey's. "A lot of second-guessing was happening."

JUDGING BY HER PUBLIC SCHEDULE IN 2014, JENNA EITHER NEVER caught wind of the *Fast Company* cleanout or she failed to heed the warning. That year she played an imperious GQ editor with a multi-episode arc on HBO's *Girls*, in a role written expressly for her by Lena Dunham.[12] ("I see you found the snack room," her character said snidely, in a perfect imitation of fashion bitchery.*) She also dug the famous white feathered skirt from the Met Ball out of her closet, plus a cropped fur jacket, to attend the New Orleans nuptials of Solange Knowles, after which her outfit was more widely documented than the bride's. She met her one-time personal style rival Kate Middleton, in New York on a royal visit.[13] The *Cut* reported that while the Duchess of Cambridge had been cool as a cucumber shaking the hand of Beyoncé, she "lost her mind when she met Jenna Lyons." And that Halloween, the slick-bunned, bespectacled character of "Jenna" was a go-to costume for the fashion-obsessed.[14] She was everywhere.

IT WAS NOT UNTIL DECEMBER 2014 THAT J.CREW'S DUAL identity—glowing success in public, increasing cause for worry in private—was made public. After eleven years of upward growth, and right on the heels of the company's single greatest year, Mickey found himself explaining bad news. J.Crew had plunged, in a single year, from a net income of more than $35 million to a loss of nearly $608 million.[15] Plans for a second I.P.O. were shelved—temporarily, they hoped.

---

* Mickey also got a TV moment in 2013, with a cameo on *Breaking Bad*.

It was pretty clear where the problem lay. It wasn't with Madewell. The little sister brand had taken five or six years to find her groove—losing millions a year in the beginning—but now it was finally taking off: in 2014 Madewell reported a 32 percent gain. And the problem wasn't the men's business, which was holding steady (for now). The problem was womenswear. The women's business had plummeted.

The plan, Mickey promised: back to basics. They'd refocus on well-styled, classic goods. Eliminate the perception—undeniable at this point—that the clothes were too expensive. And get on board with lower prices: J.Crew planned to open another twenty-one Factory stores the following year. "We are going to fight the fight and do better," Mickey promised.

But after the bad numbers hit, fashion site Racked was among the first to wonder: "Is the cult of Jenna Lyons eclipsing J.Crew?"[16] Mickey had reportedly pulled Jenna aside and asked her to dial back her public appearances. To Jenna's old friends at Page Six,[17] Mickey denied he ever said this: "Jenna is as good as it gets at being a voice for J.Crew." But today, Jenna confirms it's true: Mickey asked her to stand down.

CHAPTER 23

Knives Out

A guy, once he trusts the brand, he doesn't worry about the price," Mickey had said to the *New Yorker* back in the boom days of 2010. "We know there's a God of retail pricing looking over us all: 'They're worrying about price. But the only time I will strike is when they sell it at $98.50.'"[1]

In 2015, there was no denying it: the God of Retail Pricing had smote J.Crew.

The company was up against all the things that were ailing every other retailer of their ilk: the tsunami of fast fashion. Sale-addicted shoppers. The slow death of the mall. The tractor-beam pull of Amazon. And they weren't the only ones hurting. By 2015, Abercrombie & Fitch was trading at six-year lows; sales were down at Gap; Aéropostale was said to be fighting for survival. It was easy to assume that J.Crew was just one more car in a mounting pileup. "The hardest thing was having all of those elements happen at once," Jenna says today. "You can't all of a sudden compete with fast fashion, become Everlane, and get out of all of your mall stores. There's no way, when you're a large brand, to pivot that dramatically when you also make a product that has a nine- to twelve-month lead time."

So much of what J.Crew was up against was big and global. But many of its wounds were self-inflicted.

Take pricing, for instance. For years, every time the merchant team walked Mickey through their picks for a new collection, his first question was, "What are you selling this for?" If they planned to sell a men's shirt for $69.50, his response, invariably, was, "Can you do $72.50?" If they said yes, he might push further: "Can you go higher?"

"Those meetings were like a quiz show," says a former employee. "What should this cost? How much would you pay for this?" If someone said a dress was $59, he'd protest, "But that's a great dress! Charge $75—look how great it is!" "He just kept pushing it north," she says. "He so believed in the novelty and the appeal of the clothes." And he so believed that the J.Crew customer would stick with him.

Today, both Mickey and Jenna maintain the problem wasn't higher prices, but something more insidious: the *perception* of higher prices. A decade of marketing, come back to bite them. They say it wasn't the actual cost of the high-end, fashion-y stuff they had stirred into the mix—which actually made up a fraction of the bottom line: the luxe stuff was only about 6 to 10 percent of overall purchase, Jenna says, referring to the total amount the company spent on new goods—that was the issue. But rather that the fancy stuff hogged the spotlight, overshadowing the workaday basics. It made people think J.Crew was more expensive than it really was.

Perception, see? Likewise, a source close to Mickey argues that a nod from *Vogue* isn't always a good thing for a company like J.Crew. If the magazine ran a photo of a $400 sweater, "the perception is *Oh Jesus, J.Crew sweaters cost $400?*" he says. "That alienates more people than it attracts."

But to chalk up J.Crew's price problem to some kind of optical illusion—prices didn't go up, customers just *thought* they went up!—doesn't give those customers a lot of credit.

Especially since prices did inch up. The core-DNA products J.Crew people collected and relied on—the "secret wash" shirts, the toothpick jeans, the ballet flats—steadily rose. Why? It's simple, really. "It's a belief that they *can* go up," says a former executive. Mickey steadily raised prices until the retail gods struck—or until he hit a ceiling that customers weren't willing to go past. "That is a flawed idea," the exec continued. "Let's not forget Economics 101, the price elasticity of demand, which basically tells us the lower the price, the more you sell." Indeed, Mickey's strategy was not so different from that of the luxury houses whose price tags he ridiculed: the higher the price of the Birkin (or the Secret Wash shirt) the more people believe it's *worth*.

Key members of the original dream team who had stood beside Mickey on the New York Stock Exchange dais in 2006 had long been concerned that both price *and* perception were being pushed too high. By 2008, "I was starting to worry about it," says Jen Foyle, now arguably a merchant queen in her own right, as global brand president of American Eagle's wildly successful Aerie. Likewise, Tracy Gardner pushed vigilantly to keep J.Crew's image and price point in line. Both women had a gift for straight talk with Mickey. They knew how to manage him, or manage around him. "Not everyone knows how to interpret Mickey" is how Jen Foyle puts it. Another exec told me there was something I needed to understand: "He has to be surrounded by people who can do it with him. There's always a *right* group of people."

But by 2015, who was playing that role in Mickey's inner circle?

It was one of the great ironies of Mickey Drexler: he was a dogged interrogator, quizzing everyone on their opinion. But many of the people who worked with him felt he often failed to listen to the answers to his own questions. He was famous for plucking business ideas from assistants, and from two-second conversational asides, and running with them—a practice that made him sound like the most open-minded C.E.O. in the business. But when it came to something he didn't want to hear? Well. As one veteran put it, "He doesn't ask a question he doesn't already know the answer to."

Take Everlane, for example. A clothing business based on an algorithm? How soulless. Antithetical to the Mickey method. When one employee brought it up around 2013 as an example of an interesting new retail model, he shut her down and moved on. A witness recalls the scene with a laugh: J.Crew should have been paying *very* close attention to Everlane at that time.

Mickey's attention span was short, his patience shorter. "That's loser talk!" he'd snap, to shut down doubters. The takeaway: the only opinion that really mattered was his own.

So pricing was one self-inflicted wound. It had an equally problematic twin: quality. Talk to any longtime shopper and you'll hear the same story, in which there is a distinct *before*, when the quality of J.Crew's clothes was "amazing," and an *after*, when it "was never the same again." Several designers I spoke with swear up and down: never happened.

"No, I don't think we became cheaper at all," says Frank Muytjens. How *could* quality slip, he reasoned, when Mickey had pushed so hard to improve it, and continued to care so much about it? Muytjens says that during his tenure the cashmere—the focus of many such complaints—was never downgraded. "Mickey *loved* Italian cashmere."

But why, then, in the comments section of J.Crew's own site, did customers bemoan fraying fabrics, collapsing hems, pilled sweaters, and a boatload of problems with fit? For years, "we'd been screaming from the rooftops how well-made our stuff is," says a former copy editor. "Then you start to get tons of feedback: 'Well, I just washed this sweater once, and there's holes in it.'" J.Crew was supposed to be better than this. "If you buy something at H&M and it falls apart, you spent $12.99 on it, what did you expect?" she says. "If you bought a $225 cashmere sweater from J.Crew, people expect those to last. Because, at one point, they did."

Now, all these problems were piling up, all at once. Except . . . it wasn't all at once. A veritable Greek chorus had been wailing about all of this—price, fit, quality—unheeded, for years. "J.Crew should be reading this blog," one *J.Crew Aficionada* commenter wrote, "if they knew what was good for them."

Way back in '08, when the luxurious new Collection boutique on the Upper East Side was selling a $3,500 tortoise-print sequin jacket, the JCA crowd was skeptical. "There's a feeling they're turning away from their existing customers for these new customers," wrote a commenter. "Stuff like this is astronomically priced and not very practical. Like, who are you creating those sequin pants for?"

Over the years, the women of JCA had relatively little to say about Italian leather, Prince of Wales wool, Liberty of London prints—all those name-checked materials J.Crew was convinced kept its customer coming back. Price tags, though? A constant conversation. In 2012, when the Toothpick jean was inexplicably hiked from $108 to $125 midseason, an uproar ensued. And when the CeCe ballet flats hopscotched from $98, up to $110, and then to $125—with no apparent upgrade, other than the addition of new colors—a commenter knew just who to blame: "Does he think we don't notice?" (These people were very much aware of Mickey's *New Yorker* boast about the "gods.")

Now, JCAs were getting what they wanted, in one respect at least: after revenue dropped in 2014, the discounts Mickey had railed against so vociferously in his early days—"pull out the needle!"—became a permanent feature. Twenty percent off became 40, became 60. Everybody knew those Italian-made loafers would be half price sooner or later. "I don't even contemplate buying anything full price anymore," wrote a JCA. "Shopping at JC is almost like shopping for a house nowadays: The initial price is only the seller's asking price and bears no relation to what I pay eventually."

J.Crew was becoming Mickey's own worst nightmare: "a premium product customers were trained never to buy at full price," according to a top merchant at one of the brand's chief competitors. "That genie can't be put back in the bottle."

Was quality really sinking? Were the prices inflated? Did the clothes fit badly? At this point it didn't matter if it was true. J.Crew customers believed it was true. As Jenna puts it, "Perception is reality."

In March 2015, Oregon-based artist Tricia Louvar submitted an illustration to the feminist website The Hairpin. She called it, "An Open Letter to Jenna Lyons":[2]

> Dear Jenna, You are pretty dope . . . If only I, an ordinary mother on a modest income, could afford to wear a $400 cashmere skirt, silk barely-there blouse, + belt to a one-time business casual event.

Louvar tallied the cost of an "everyday" J.Crew outfit—top, jeans, blazer, booties—at $596. In working-mom dollars, she wrote, that was 298 school lunches. The "Open Letter" landed in The Hairpin's slush pile and could easily have languished there, never to be heard from again. Instead the website ran it, and the story blew up. The *New York Post* gave Louvar a ring. "I love her style," Louvar told them. "But can I relate to it?"

With J.Crew continuing to post dismal sales numbers, Jenna dissenters seemed to come out of the woodwork. For those who had begun to doubt J.Crew's queen bee—and, given the nature of the internet, for those who had never thought to hate on Jenna Lyons before but, given an opening, were more than happy to pile on—this was a call to arms: Women were sick of messy hair! Sequins for work? *WTF!*

It was all part of a massive tide that was beginning to turn: consumers were speaking truth to power, questioning both the corporations and the image-making machines that had long told them how they were supposed to look, act, and think. Back in 2008, when J.Crew started selling boots from a three-hundred-year-old workwear manufacturer, that kind of fake—or perhaps, *borrowed*—authenticity was all it took for a brand to *feel* real. But now that bar was set much higher: consumers wanted transparency about how brands were manufactured, whom they hired, where their materials came from, and whom they intended to serve. Authenticity wasn't about a great backstory; it was about ethics. Consumers were beginning to expect far more—*inclusion, representation, corporate responsibility*—than companies like J.Crew had ever been forced to worry about before.

In the clothing realm, a lot of these conversations were kicked off when people started questioning size ranges. In 2013, activists dressed in XXL T-shirts that said "#fitchplease" had stormed the Fifth Avenue flagship of Abercrombie & Fitch, demanding inclusionary sizing.[3] Two years later, former fashion journalist Alex Waldman founded size-inclusive clothing range Universal Standard, for the simple reason that she could not find clothes to fit her size 18 figure. "There's a lot of rage," Waldman has noted. "Women accepted what was given before. But now they're saying, 'It's not my fault. It's *your* fault I don't have clothes.'"[4]

Women had long been conditioned to believe that if a label went up to only size 12—as J.Crew did—the failure to fit into that brand's idea of an acceptable body was their own. Slowly, it was dawning on them:

companies that failed to offer inclusive sizing, and to show clothes in imagery that celebrated diverse types of beauty, were failing *them*. And leaving a lot of money on the table in the process.

And size was just one of the issues shoppers were raising. JCA types who had long loved J.Crew, bought it, and kept it afloat wanted to be listened to! They wanted less tricksy clothing, better quality, more reasonable prices. Yet from what they could see, after more than a year in crisis, nothing much had changed at J.Crew. The company had neither retreated from Fashion Week nor killed off Collection, the range that caused such consternation while adding so little to the bottom line. And in the meantime, other companies seemed to be paying increasing attention to women's actual lives and habits: Lululemon, Ann Taylor, and Old Navy had jumped on this new thing, athleisure, which accommodated both their gig-economy jobs and a wide range of bodies. Both Mickey and Jenna had turned up their noses at athleisure: so *not* J.Crew! And on the one memorable occasion when Mickey-era J.Crew attempted a catalogue shoot on "real" bodies, the whole thing ended up on the cutting-room floor: The verdict from on high was that the shoot was a fail. J.Crew clothes just didn't look all that magical when they weren't on woke-up-this-way gorgeous models. And as far as size ranges go, the only size-related headlines J.Crew generated in those years popped up after they expanded the size range *down*, adding sizes XXXS and triple-zero, to serve an expansion into Hong Kong stores. Meanwhile, 67 percent of American women could not shop J.Crew clothing at all because they were a size 14 or larger.[5]

From what the JCAs could tell, it appeared that J.Crew's big plan to get out of trouble was . . . more Fashion. The silhouettes seemed to just keep getting more experimental (and more unflattering). The luxury items were just as tone-deaf as ever. In 2015, more than a year into the downturn, a heather-gray cashmere hoodie made of fabric that, according to the caption, had been pulled apart by hand, then restitched together, cost $1,500.

That sweater was gorgeous! It might have played well at, say, Isabel Marant, which catered to a dedicated fashion follower with deep pockets. But it was too niche for a $2.4 billion brand that could succeed only by serving a wide swath of women. J.Crew was in an unfamiliar place: What had been the most *with-it* mass fashion brand maybe ever was creeping further and further into irrelevance.

For years, the company had catered to two different bases, like a purple state politician: fashion people and "real" people. Now, instead of hovering in a sweet spot between the two, the covetable "white space" they had conquered felt more like a no-man's-land middle. J.Crew was neither here nor there. The truth was that their bread-and-butter fan was *not* a fashion person. She was fairly . . . preppy. She dressed relatively conservatively, and in many cases probably voted conservatively, too. Her tastes were somewhat upscale, but they were also mainstream. And now she felt like her favorite brand no longer saw her.

"No, we're not hipsters," wrote an Aficionada named Violet. "We don't consume kale smoothies for meals. We can't wear sleeveless suits or metallic linen skorts to work. We do, however, want quality, flattering, well-made classics that are modern and fresh . . . We (and our money) are here for the taking."

Abra Belke, a former Washington lobbyist who runs the blog *Capitol Hill Style,* had this to say: "J.Crew is like the pretty, unpopular girl who ditched her old friends for the cool kids table and is struggling to stay there. Working women, prepsters, Basic Bettys, we were the J.Crew market base. We wanted good quality staples at a fair price with the occasional bit of flair."[6]

Was the pretty girl Belke had in mind J.Crew, the brand? Or was it the woman behind the brand—that rich, famous, liberal New Yorker who talked a good game about wanting to make clothes for "everybody" but kept turning up at Fashion Week hawking $2,000 snakeskin pencil skirts? Jenna had been a stellar ambassador when she walked that fine line between aspirational and relatable. But the TV-starring, breastbone-baring Jenna of 2015 had arguably evolved past the J.Crew base. It was getting harder to see what this fashion person had to do with the women who were buying her clothes.

On rare occasions, Jenna acknowledged the "emotional confusion" of navigating her public and private personae, almost with a Superman v. Clark Kent sense of dissociation. By day, she was trying to turn around an increasingly beleaguered brand; by night, she was a *Vogue* girl on the best guest lists in town. Never was that tension more acute than on the night of June 15, 2015, when Jenna stood in the East Room of the White House in a crowd that included Tyler Perry and Angela Bassett, listening to Prince and Stevie Wonder perform "Sign, Sealed, Delivered I'm Yours."[7] The scene was too good to be true, beyond her wildest dreams. Stevie Wonder *and* Prince? She burst into tears. Michelle Obama smiled and put an arm around her.

"It's hard," Jenna said later. "You get in your head too much. The most challenging thing was that I would go from—and I know it sounds crazy—literally having an incredible weekend at the White House, dancing with the president and the First Lady . . . and then come Monday morning, I'm sitting on the floor with someone who's three years out of college, negotiating about keeping a style on the line. It was a very hard balance."[8]

That June, "emotional confusion" might have been better described as whiplash. The hug from Mrs. Obama might have been partly motivated by concern. J.Crew's woes were no secret: same-store sales were down 10 percent from a year earlier. The company had just cut 175 jobs. And, four days before that concert, the *New York Times*—which two years earlier had anointed Jenna "the woman who dresses America"—had unequivocally called for her head: "Can a New Designer (Not Jenna Lyons) Fix J.Crew?"[9]

CUT TO MICKEY ON THE PHONE WITH SHAREHOLDERS, ANNOUNCING more bad news. This time, it wasn't the plunging sales figures that stopped the business press in its tracks, but rather the explanation he offered for those numbers. "We didn't have the right cardigan," he said, going deep into the weeds: the Tilly hadn't sold as well as expected; the Tippi had sold well, but they'd ordered too few. Sorry, what? EBITDA had sunk 31 percent from the same period in 2014. The company had written down $341 million in value. Inventory was backed up. And Mickey was talking about . . . Tillys?

Everyone from *Forbes* to *WSJ* picked up on that one: *What was* wrong *with this once golden brand?* But no one got as much mileage out of J.Crew in June 2015 as the Gray Lady. The *Times*' fashion pages might have been blaming Jenna for J.Crew's problems but in its business pages, columnist Steven Davidoff Solomon went after Mickey. J.Crew had a "'Great Man' dilemma," Solomon wrote, that was specific to the merchant prince.[10] If Mickey hadn't been Mr. Gap, then Mr. Old Navy, and now Mr. J.Crew, no one would have followed him down the garden path of 2011's messy $3 billion sale. That deal had only gone through because he was *the* Mickey Drexler. So, no, J.Crew's crippling problem was not sweaters. It was something Mickey had not elaborated on during that earnings call: $1.5 billion in debt.

It was the same old private equity story. J.Crew was paying T.P.G. and Leonard Green at least $2 million per quarter in consulting and management fees. Between 2011 and 2015, that reportedly tallied $685 million in dividends to the two firms, and $55 million to Mickey himself, so far, for his stake.

Now, in its darkest hour, J.Crew had no cushion. 2015 should have been their year to consolidate, retrench, beg their core customer to take them back. Maybe even decrease volume: Close some stores, reduce inventory. Pour some money into e-commerce. "If you don't have a lot of debt, you can get really defensive, circle the wagons," says analyst Richard Jaffe. "Pay your people, keep the lights on, and be unprofitable [for a while]. It's not an attractive way to run a business, but it means you live to fight another day. You don't go away." Then, after you've shored up the business and gotten the product back on track, "you roll the dice again." But servicing $1.5 billion in debt wiped out that margin of error. For J.Crew, not making money for a while was not an option.

Now the financial press was circling like buzzards, peering into the growing wreckage for clues. What was the word on Wall Street? "It really depends on whether you believe this is a fashion cycle and that they can reimagine themselves out of it," said Barclays analyst Hale Holden, "or whether they've created a tarnished brand and can't get the consumer back."[11]

CHAPTER 24

Three Horsewomen and an Apocalypse

Jenna!" chirps a black-clad fashion operative into her headset, ushering three women out of a shiny black vehicle and into the white tent that has been erected on the sidewalk along upper Fifth Avenue. "We have Jenna." Or is it, "We have . . . *Jennas*"?

May 2, 2016. The steps of the Metropolitan Museum of Art are carpeted in a strawberry shortcake swirl—lush pink, red, and cream—banked by stanchions disguised as faux privet, behind which photographers are banked six deep. The tent at the foot of the stairs, where the three women are deposited, is a holding tank for the most recognizable people on the planet. For attendees, the tent is a safe place to pause briefly, make sure there's no lipstick on your teeth and that your "naked dress" is revealing only the intended regions, before you're promenaded in front of the photographers. The tent also enables *Vogue* staffers to time each guest's release onto the carpet, meting out the fame drop by drop, so that every photo op is optimized, and monetized.

In the holding tent, the three women take it all in. Here's Lupita Nyong'o in shimmering, seafoam-green Calvin Klein, her hair conjured into a foot-high topiary in the shape of a joyful exclamation point: *Fashion!* Here's Lady Gaga, looking like she jumped right off the tour bus in a spangled bodysuit and six-inch platforms. Oh look, Sarah

Jessica Parker is wearing . . . pantaloons? And there goes Ivanka Trump, oozing '40s film star glam in GOP-red Ralph Lauren. (In a few weeks' time, most of the people in this tent will be stunned to learn her father has enough primary votes to become the presumptive Republican presidential nominee.) Oh cute, Marc Jacobs brought his mom! Wait, no, that's Bette Midler.

After a few moments, our trio of women gets the go sign: their turn has come. Taking a collective breath, they wrap their arms around each other, crank up their smiles, and step out. Now the photographers are shouting: *Lena! Jenna!*

At six feet tall plus a good four inches of stiletto, Jenna Lyons towers over Lena Dunham and Jenni Konner. With her arms draped around their shoulders in jokey hauteur, she perches over them like a very chic praying mantis.

The matching outfits had been Dunham's idea. It was ingenious: why go to the Met Gala dressed *by* Jenna, when they could go dressed *as* Jenna? So now Dunham, the writer/actor/cultural lightning rod; Konner, her co-showrunner on HBO's *Girls*; and Jenna all wear sleek black tuxedos, their white shirts unbuttoned to offer an unimpeded view of décolletage (the liberated nipple being a signature of Lyons and Dunham both), their hair slick and sharply parted. And, of course, they all wear the pièce de résistance: thick-framed black eyeglasses, the ultimate Jenna totem. Because by now *Jenna*, the archetype, is as recognizable as *Karl*, with his fingerless gloves and powdered wig, or *Anna*, with her sharp bob and dark glasses.

The night's theme is "Manus x Machina," a meditation on life and fashion in the age of technology. Much of the clothing on display evokes the kind of future we expected as kids, eating Lucky Charms in front of *The Jetsons*. There's a lot of silver and robot references: Pop star Zayn Malik has one arm encased in a metal sleeve reminiscent of

C-3PO. The clothes on display are costume-y, creative. Exceedingly shiny. But are they really . . . the future?

In the year of the Hillary Clinton pantsuit, with a woman almost certain to be elected president—sigh—you could argue that it is the three Jennas' fashion statement that is the most forward-thinking of the night. Dunham and Konner are two young women driving a bold, sometimes shocking, critically beloved TV show—they symbolize a new millennial feminism. And Jenna is roughly their fashion world equivalent. With Donna Karan, Vera Wang, and Diane von Furstenberg graduated into the roles of elder stateswomen, she is the most visible woman atop a major American label.

Their triple-threat fashion statement says, *We* are *the future*. Three powerful, clever women, dressed to please the female gaze, with enough combined clout to make a big, splashy in-joke at the fashion event of the year.

But more than anything, their look says: Jenna Lyons is a Big Fucking Deal. The designer of a mall brand is standing on fashion's grandest stage, making a splash equal to—or at least, far wittier than—those of the Pradas, Calvin Kleins, and Valentinos of the world. The hippest smart-girl duo in Hollywood is paying homage to *her*. What a coup for J.Crew. Right?

"If you had to caricature a New York fashion person, it would be a drawing of Jenna." Years earlier, Jenna's friend David Maupin, co-owner of Manhattan's Lehmann Maupin Gallery, said this to a reporter, intending it as a supreme compliment: she was "someone who touches every part of contemporary culture."[1] But by 2016, a similar line was being served up by Jenna's critics, with a chaser of Schadenfreude—Jenna, some said, had become a caricature of herself. The three Jennas was a great gag: it riffed on the surrealness of being the actual human inside of the meme—an experience that both Lyons and Dunham knew something about.

But in some corners of the company, as J.Crew continued to spiral, goodwill toward its leader had begun to ebb. It was increasingly unclear whether Jenna's PR antics were calculated to benefit the J.Crew brand . . . or her own. Her mannerisms, once benign, even endearing, had started to chafe. Coming from your boss—a fashion icon, raking in the dough, envy of women worldwide—constant self-deprecation and insistent modesty can feel like a threadbare performance. In meetings, Jenna might playfully put a hand over her mouth when a colleague was talking, as if to say, *Don't speak*. Wasn't that just a sugarcoated way of saying, *Shut up*?

Many at J.Crew say Jenna was working harder than ever to fix their problems. Others thought she was checked out. "After a certain time, she was unobtainable," says a designer. "Nothing got through to her. She didn't really give a shit about anything. She'd come to meetings and talk about who she saw that weekend, or some fabulous event. It was just like, who *are* you?"

So maybe the Three Jennas of the Met Gala was intended as a sly jab: *I'll show* you *a caricature*. Or maybe it was just a fabulous, one-night-only ticket out of an increasingly dark reality. As Frank Muytjens recalls with a sad chuckle, by 2016 working at J.Crew was "like dying a slow death." Who wouldn't need a night out?

FOR SO LONG, J.CREW HAD LOOKED AT THEIR NUMBERS GOING UP, UP, UP, AND asked themselves: who are we competing against, really? Now the sense of superiority that long had nestled inside J.Crew's breast pocket—secure and soigné as a pocket square—had been reduced to wounded pride. "We got a little bit full of ourselves," said a J.Crew V.P. "You know, we weren't high fashion—we obviously weren't Phillip Lim, or Céline. But we weren't the *Gap*." Now the reality check was harsh: "We were," she said, still a little stunned. "We *were* the Gap." And they were Banana

Republic, and they were Ann Taylor—those were their competitors. And yet, further complicating things, they also weren't: J.Crew was both more expensive and (no matter what the complainers said) higher-quality than companies like Gap or Uniqlo, and less so than the next rung up. They weren't able to pivot quickly like Zara. They weren't high fashion or fast fashion. That singularity—the white space they had consciously aimed to occupy, which had long been their greatest asset—was now a weakness.

Now, the blame game had begun in earnest. What had long been productive horse trading between creatives and merchants—that necessary tension between art and commerce—was strained. On the merchants' side, many felt Jenna had been too slow to pivot. She had refused to take the "Jenna" out of J.Crew, and instead wandered further off into her fashion fever dream. The creative side felt backed into a corner, forced to keep producing the same things over and over again to "meet the numbers." Any "specialness" they tried to inject into the clothes got slowly buried in an unfocused edit that revealed a simmering identity crisis.

It was an eerie repeat of the early T.P.G. years. In came the analytics, the roving bands of consultants trying to plug the leaks and find what's broken. AlixPartners and McKinsey did their high-priced stints. In "customer roadshows" they quizzed top shoppers on what they wanted next. The brand was used to having two crystal-clear voices at the top; now it was a cacophony, muddied with facts and figures and theories. "Here is where the arguing, the inner turmoil began—and the breakdown," says a source close to Jenna.

A new phrase crept into their conversations: who is *our girl*? It was a depressing question, one they had not needed to ask for at least twelve years. In Emily's day, and then again in Jenna's, "our girl" was easy to identify—she was *us*, the people who ate, drank, and breathed J.Crew. They made the clothes they wanted to wear. Now, in meetings, people were talking about "our girl" like she was some composite character they'd never actually met. And she seemed to swing in every direction. "Our girl" was super feminine. No, tomboyish. She wanted neutrals—no, colors. Not too many colors!

"That's where it got a little confusing," says Muytjens, a master of understatement. "People were on edge."

For the few who had been there pre-Mickey dark days, an overwhelming sense of déjà vu had set in. "They kept shuffling people around, saying, 'It's all going to be better now,'" says another designer. "And then, six months later, shuffling again . . . nothing was working."

MEANWHILE, ALL AROUND THEM, RETAILERS WERE IMPLODING. IN the six months between October 2016 and April 2017, American general merchandise stores laid off eighty thousand workers—more than the entire workforce of the much-mourned American coal industry.[2] Malls across the country were attempting to fill their empty acreage with trampoline parks and community colleges, or closing their doors altogether, giving rise to a new kind of doomscrolling: websites devoted to tours of "dead malls," these decaying, overgrown buildings—their fountains drained, acres of parking lot sitting empty. Mall buildings were too big to fill and too expensive to repair, or apparently even to bother knocking down. They had become symbolic of past excesses, and the ecological waste that a younger generation would be left to clean up: "Every video tour of an abandoned shopping center is a chance to gaze upon the wreck of our past selves," the writer Kate Folk would note in the *New York Times Magazine*.[3]

A new term had emerged to describe what was happening here: it was no longer just a downturn, it was a "retail apocalypse." In 2017, there were a record number of retail bankruptcies, even more than in the darkest hour of the Great Recession. At the same time, there was an inflection point in online shopping. According to a Pew survey, in

2017 Americans were "starting to shop online as often as [they] take out the trash."[4]

Among the paradoxes of Mickey—the guy with three Hamptons houses who was skeptical of the rich; the compulsive questioner who had a hard time listening—is the fact that he could not have missed that this was coming. Mickey had a front row seat to the digital revolution, sitting on the board of Apple for sixteen years. A former colleague says the first iPhone she ever saw was Mickey's own. He was an early investor in and advisor to direct-to-consumer eyewear company Warby Parker—whose clear-framed specs he'd worn for years—and the athleisure phenom Outdoor Voices. Both companies were leading the charge to disrupt his industry, and he was advising them on how to do it. And as early as 2014, Mickey was so devoted to SoulCycle—the stationary-bike chain that was toppling the traditional gym business model (and was later toppled by the pandemic Peloton)—they called him the "godfather of SoulCycle." At nearly seventy, he was known to show up first thing in the morning and climb aboard a bike in the front row, the spot usually occupied by the showiest athletes in class. "That's a specific kind of person," laughs a former employee. "He was *that guy*."

But in 2017, Mickey would sit onstage at Lincoln Center with *DealBook* columnist Andrew Ross Sorkin, pull his iPhone out of his inside pocket, and flash it at the crowd. This, he would proclaim—this was the thing he missed. "Every brand in the world," he said, "I can shop right now any brand, and check the prices." Sorkin said what you, reader, might be thinking: *This couldn't have come as a surprise! Hadn't Steve Jobs mentioned this was coming?* "We talked about it, for sure, and it was moving in this direction," Mickey said. "But the speed of it—I wasn't prepared for it."[5]

In February 2017, J.Crew seemed to demonstrate that it had, in fact, been listening to its customers' complaints, and was ready to make real changes. They showed the fall collection on "real" people. This did not reflect a newly expanded size range, but hey, it *looked* diverse on a hip, artsy bunch that spanned a wide range of ages, shapes, and races, including members of the company's own design team—none of whom especially looked like Jenna. Many of the models were dressed in what were described as "old friends" from the archives. That's right: they were back to rugbies and rollnecks, plus some greatest hits from the Jenna years, like low-slung camp pants and shiny pleated skirts.

Mickey genuinely believed in this reinvention. In an echo of the turnaround he worked slavishly to accomplish in his last months at Gap, he thought he'd done it: he had a lot of faith in the talent of their new head of womenswear, the J.Crew/Madewell vet Somsack Sikhounmuong, and in this new direction for J.Crew. Finally, they were delivering the back-to-basics revamp he'd been promising for nearly three years. But fashion critics, usually so laudatory of anything J.Crew put out, picked up on trouble in paradise. "One did catch an undercurrent of anxiety here . . . an identity crisis specific to J.Crew," Vogue.com noted. "What does the J.Crew customer want from this brand?"[6]

Two months later, in April 2017, another 150 full-time and 100 open positions were eliminated, mostly from corporate headquarters.

For Jenna, this job had always been rewarding, but relentless. The pace was brutal. She signed off on every look, catalogue page, store design, website home page, social media post, and customer email for three different brands—while constantly attending events and fielding breaking-news interview questions about her favorite brand of toothpaste. Mickey might have been the king of the working breakfast, but Jenna did not break for food. She favored tomato soup for lunch, specifically because it could be downed during meetings. She sometimes joked that she barely had time to use the bathroom. What she did do was sit in meetings for one thing, while answering emails about another. "I'm never where I am," she once said.

And now, when she did step outside, she was subject to a level of attention that felt borderline predatory. After her divorce had been splashed across the tabloids, she and Courtney Crangi had moved to a 3,500-square-foot loft on the fourth floor of a nineteenth-century cast-iron building in the heart of SoHo. The location had an ironic twist: it was around the corner from J.Crew's Prince Street store, then still located right where Emily and Dave DeMattei had planted it twenty years earlier, on the ground floor of André Balazs's Mercer Hotel. As Balazs had hoped, the Mercer had been a celeb magnet since day one, with paparazzi constantly staked out on its sidewalk. Now, the paps had taken to snapping local fashion celebrity Jenna Lyons. Whether she was going to a party or just running to the corner bodega for Ben & Jerry's, she was always on display. "I didn't want to leave the house without putting on makeup," she has said. "I was concerned about every little thing. I felt like I was under scrutiny."[7]

These photographers also snapped Crangi, Crangi's young daughter Coco, and Jenna's son Beckett. It was Gwyneth Paltrow who explained to Jenna that she had no legal recourse. As every celebrity must inevitably learn, photos taken in public, even of a child, are fair game.

For years now, she had been unable to reverse J.Crew's decline. In all respects, "the pressure was so heavy on her," says Gayle Spannaus, who saw her old friend beset on all sides by negative numbers and negative press. "I know it was deeply personal. Like Mickey at Gap: you created it, and then you're the one that's being blamed."

Jenna says that making decisions about J.Crew "used to feel really innate—like I knew exactly what I wanted, was charged to push through." But her foolproof sense of what *was* and *wasn't* J.Crew had started to fail her. "Now it was harder."

Her team felt this keenly. "Things started to fall apart," jokes a former creative. "Mommy wasn't in the house anymore." It began to feel as if Jenna had stopped pushing back on the merchant side—she wasn't fighting to make sure the creative was as important as the business anymore. Maybe because, in times like these, it wasn't.

Now Jenna walked into meetings fired up about a new idea, only to walk out later dissuaded, having caved to a totally different game plan. That never used to happen. More than once, Spannaus followed the boss back to her office: *What happened? You knew that was going to be amazing!* They had some "difficult conversations," Spannaus says. "Why aren't you fighting for us?"

But the fight was exhausting. Jenna had always shielded her teams from the brunt of J.Crew's business problems, trying not to hamper their creativity. But the numbers were dire, and these new consultants and analysts came at the problem armed not with instinct, but with data. How do you argue with facts? "I have nothing to go on but my opinion," she told Spannaus at one point. "And it's just not working."

In April 2017, a month after the latest round of layoffs, Jenna was on a much-needed beach vacation when someone overheard her talking about a plan to exit J.Crew. This made it to a reporter, who called J.Crew for comment. Many believed the designer was planning a more gradual exit down the line. But the leak fast-fowarded her timeline. Within days, J.Crew was forced to release the news: It was "time for a change." The decision was mutual, they said. Jenna Lyons was leaving J.Crew.

The press had a field day, naturally. The *New York Post* detailed "How Jenna Lyons got too big for J.Crew's britches." Within hours of the announcement, *Vogue* generated "9 Things to Remember About the Jenna Lyons Era at J.Crew."[8] On the list: sequins for day, neon-splashed color palettes, oversize baubles, and the fact that "she never feared the nipple." Despite J.Crew's current state, "the indelible mark she had made on defining American fashion for the past decade cannot go unacknowledged," said the industry site *Business of Fashion*.[9]

She'd been at J.Crew twenty-six years—eight years longer than Emily herself—through every phase: from catalogue company to mall retailer to omnichannel cultural phenom. She had remade the brand, embodied it; nobody knew its essence like she did. Which was probably part of the problem: back in the early 2000s, when it no longer worked for J.Crew to be "so Emily"—Emily had to go. And now, the same thing had happened with Jenna. She didn't have yet another J.Crew in her, because the J.Crew she had made *was* her: its aesthetic guardrails were her own. Most retailers agree that though twenty-six years sounds impressive, it was part of the problem. Fashion needs change, reinvention, fresh blood. Creative directors need term limits.

When the second woman to have been J.Crew's human embodiment left the company, she did not do it the Emily way. Of course not. The staff was by then so large, it had to be split into two large town hall meetings. Jenna offered everyone her thanks. Prosecco was clinked. "There was lots of tears, hugs, fear, and anxiety," she says. "I was grateful for being able to have a graceful exit." This might have been a long time coming, but it still hurt. "It's not like I didn't see it coming," Spannaus says. "But I cried. It blew my mind."

IN THE MIDST OF AN INDUSTRY-WIDE RECKONING THAT IS ACTUally referred to as an "apocalypse," how much blame can be laid at the feet of any one person? In the first six months of 2017, Payless, Limited, BCBG Max Azaria, and Wet Seal all declared bankruptcy. Stores were dying, fashion was flipping, a new consumer had arrived—and it was hitting every traditional retailer right where it hurt. Yet none of the C.E.O.s of these companies were taking heat quite the way Mickey Drexler was. Were Mickey's many vocal critics just happy to watch the great man fall on his face? Or were they correct to point out the parallels between Mickey's current predicament and his fall from grace at Gap?

"Mickey needs, but does not want, someone to put up guardrails," says retail analyst Richard Jaffe. Everybody knew Mickey didn't like having a boss—he'd said so himself. But by now it was clear to most that he needed one—or at least a powerful counterweight. In the postmortem on J.Crew, many industry insiders circle back to the moment Mickey gave the keys to the kingdom to Jenna, a creative with high-fashion aspirations and expensive taste. The move, they say, threw off the balance of church and state, art and commerce, essential to any fashion company, and especially one led by a larger-than-life creative. The most-cited example of an ideal yin-yang dynamic are Tom Ford and Domenico De Sole, who transformed Gucci from a sleepy leather goods firm to a fashion powerhouse in the '90s, before launching Ford's eponymous label together. Ford has always been the captivating frontman, the "defibrillator of fashion" who brought new meaning to the phrase *sex sells.* But De Sole's behind-the-scenes strategizing as C.E.O.—one who is happy to let Ford occupy the spotlight while he keeps the company on track—is seen as no less essential to their success.[10] The two forces are countervalent: the designer pulls for the most beautiful materials and the most forward-thinking ideas; the business mind looks after the bottom line, making sure they don't go offtrack. With the rise of Jenna's fame outside the company and her power within it, plus the cult of personality that had always surrounded Mickey, J.Crew arguably had two Toms. "Mickey and Jenna enabled each other," says a designer. "She gave him the aesthetic he needed to validate his genius. He gave her the space to be fully her own vision." No one was weighing down the other side of the seesaw.

Jenna and Mickey are, in a way, very alike: Both, brilliant, wildly charismatic, instinct-driven outsiders who rose from bruising childhoods to reinvent themselves and become the envy of their peers. Both, strivers who climbed their way into a world, and a lifestyle, they weren't born to—and found a way to market that possibility to others. Both, oversharers. Both, charmers. Both, perhaps, a little too keen to be the center of attention. Mickey had spent the previous fourteen years at J.Crew running mostly unchecked, which was not dissimilar from his latter years at Gap Inc.—when he was C.E.O. of three giant brands: Gap, Banana, and Old Navy. In his final stretch at J.Crew, T.P.G. and Leonard Green were technically his partners; the investment firms did have power over Mickey. "But they're quants, they're analysts, they're finance guys," says Jaffe. "They're all about the numbers. They've got twenty bets—one of them is J.Crew."

By the early summer of 2017, the comparisons to Gap were inevitable: J.Crew had been down eleven of the last twelve quarters. It wasn't enough for Jenna to leave. Mickey had to go, too. But unlike at Gap, there was no Don Fisher figure to hand Mickey an envelope and say, *See ya*. With a 10 percent stake in the company, he was J.Crew's largest individual shareholder, chairman of its board, and still emotionally and intellectually invested in the company. Mickey had decided to step down, but this time he was going to do it on his own terms. He believed he had set J.Crew on the right track with Somsack Sikhounmuong as creative director, creating solid, good-value style. All they needed now was a new C.E.O. to replace himself.

He was able to have a hand in picking his successor. But every person he interviewed, he rejected. J.Crew was back to that Emily-era problem: a great retail C.E.O. is hard to find. Finally, the headhunter sent in James Brett. As president of the interiors company West Elm, Brett had led twenty-four consecutive quarters of double-digit revenue growth.

Brett's detractors point out he had never been a C.E.O. before: West Elm was a brand within the Williams Sonoma conglomerate. He'd been C.M.O. of Urban Outfitters but had never run a major fashion company. Plus he and Mickey were oil and water. *No. Not this guy*, Mickey told Jon Sokoloff and Jim Coulter. *He's going to bankrupt the company.* This time, he was overruled. Brett was in.

That was it. In June, the announcement went out: Mickey Drexler was stepping down as C.E.O. There was a leaving party on the High Line, with a rock band. Mickey couldn't enjoy it. He knew J.Crew was in the wrong hands.

CHAPTER 25

The Cherry Pickers

As of this writing, Mickey's final day as C.E.O. of J.Crew was three head womenswear designers, three C.E.O.s, one strange period under the no-man's-land leadership of the "office of the C.E.O.," a new majority stakeholder, and one bankruptcy ago. And, oh yeah: a global pandemic, a Donald Trump presidency, a massive social justice reckoning, a global supply chain crash, and the worst spike in inflation in a generation. Who knows what else will have transpired by the time you read this?

Jim Brett's tenure was as disastrous as Mickey predicted. Brett took a wild swing, as if he believed all of J.Crew's problems could be fixed in one fell swoop: he cut prices, widened size ranges, launched feel-good charitable initiatives, built a fleet of new, lower-price ranges, and struck up a partnership with Amazon—and alienated a huge swath of the staff. Almost all of Brett's changes went live in one high-speed stretch in September 2018. Two months later, he was out after seventeen months. His successor, Jan Singer, lasted less than ten. Those years were as chaotic and, to the people inside the company, as dispiriting as the aftermath of T.P.G.'s first buyout had been some twenty years earlier. But according to the *Washington Post*, all that C-suite shuffling hardly mattered: with its debt up to nearly $2 billion, J.Crew was just "rearranging deck chairs on the *Titanic*."[1]

Then came March 2020, and the most devastating global pandemic in one hundred years. With brick-and-mortar ground to a halt, and store windows boarded up across the nation, industry-wide, the industry saw clothing sales plummet by half. J.Crew—treading water for five-plus years by that point—fell fast. Less than six weeks into the lockdown, J.Crew filed for Chapter 11 bankruptcy protection.[2]

Shocked J.Crew fans grieved loudly on Instagram. But in the business pages, the news was received with something like a shrug.

Of course, due lip service was paid: J.Crew was acknowledged as a venerable brand that had almost mystically claimed a spot in the fashion hierarchy. One that, for a certain swath of Americans, defined a new uniform, the look of the aughts. That, for women, broke rules that would never be rules again: even now, day dressing mingles with evening, sneakers pair with dresses, regular women fearlessly mix camo and leopard print—and nobody bats an eyelash. In the menswear press, J.Crew was eulogized as the brand that taught American men how to dress, outfitting flyover-state guys in a look that once belonged strictly to big-city cool kids.

But by the time of the bankruptcy, the days when J.Crew had set the pace for mainstream American fashion were a distant memory. After whipsawing through management teams with wildly different visions, the brand was in a far worse state than it had ever been under Mickey and Jenna, seemingly drained of any vision at all. The clothes were boring, the stores were a mess, the customers were dispirited—and it had been that way for a long time.

Beyond that, there was a certain willingness to bid adieu to J.Crew in the summer of 2020 that wasn't just about crisis fatigue. Weeks after the bankruptcy announcement, on May 25, in Minneapolis, a forty-six-year-old Black man named George Floyd went to buy a pack of cigarettes and ended up on the pavement, with a white police officer's knee on his neck. Floyd's dying words, "I can't breathe," were chanted by Black Lives Matter protestors in cities across the nation, in a long-overdue season of racial reckoning.

If J.Crew's second golden era had been born when the Obamas moved into the White House, it had also seemed to officially end when they moved out. Now that Mrs. Obama wasn't waving in a belted cardigan from the steps of Air Force One—and with no new, persuasive brand identity filling the gaping hole left by the twin first ladies of J.Crew, Michelle and Jenna—it was as if J.Crew's progressive associations went *poof,* and our cultural notion of the brand hit rewind, straight back to the original blueprint: East Coast prep.

That summer, I stumbled across a newspaper write-up about an event in Cape Cod in which the crowd was described as "very J.Crew." The mental image it conjured was the same one it would have twenty years earlier. No matter how hard J.Crew had worked to twist its version of prep, the brand was still synonymous with the word—and that word is tenaciously entwined, like ivy itself, in the bedrock of the American elite. In the summer of 2020, for the first time, even nonactivists were not flinching from calling the kind of privilege J.Crew had long conveyed exactly what it was: *white* privilege.

Late that June, most of us were still shut inside our houses spraying down the groceries with disinfectant when two married lawyers, Mark and Patricia McCloskey, made headlines for standing in front of their St. Louis manse wielding guns at peaceful Black Lives Matter protestors. As photos of the McCloskeys landed on front pages across the nation, the first thing anybody saw was his giant black AR-15 style rifle. But the second thing you noticed was their clothes. Patricia wore a bateau-striped T-shirt. Mark had on a pink Brooks Brothers polo and light khaki pants. They looked like the embodiment of the establishment. And the establishment looked like it had lost its ever-loving mind. Cintra Wilson, writing for *Town & Country*, said the McCloskeys had unwittingly pulled Brooks Brothers, "a 202-year-old symbol of American normcore, into a national polemic." It was now "the label of the un-woke."[3]

Within weeks Brooks Brothers, too, declared bankruptcy. This, of course, was not about the McCloskeys: it was about the "apocalypse," and an apocalyptic pandemic, and all the other reasons retailers had been laid low. Still, the timing did not seem entirely coincidental. Brooks Brothers symbolized an America that seemed to be fading fast into the rearview. Maybe it wasn't such a bad thing to let these preppy strongholds fade along with it?[4]

Wilson wrote that Brooks Brothers—and by extension, prep—had become a symbol of "what not to wear to the revolution." It felt like a direct echo of 1968 when protestors took to the streets, and civil rights leaders were being murdered in plain sight. To anyone who cared about being on the right side of history, the uniform of the establishment had a newly toxic undertone.

And meanwhile, fashion was tripping all over itself under a new kind of scrutiny. Anna Wintour apologized for *Vogue*'s long history of "publishing images or stories that have been hurtful or intolerant" of Black people. And on social media, some of harshest critiques were reserved not for old-world entities like *Vogue* but for next-gen brands that *defined* themselves by their progressive politics and stated goals of inclusion and diversity. Women's site Refinery 29; the luggage "unicorn" Away; the favorite millennial no-makeup makeup brand, Glossier; even the feminist workspace chain The Wing—all were outed for failing to practice what they preached. In response, Instagram was littered with a new art form: the corporate mea culpa, more abject than any in memory. "I've failed," wrote Yael Afalo, founder of hip fashion label Reformation, apologizing for "practicing diversity in the past through a 'white gaze' that falls too close to ignorance."[5] It was hard not to think you were damned if you did, damned if you didn't. If these young, progressive brands couldn't get it right, what hope did a Gen Xer like J.Crew—practically synonymous with "white gaze"—have?

Maybe "J.Crew didn't need to live forever," *New York Times* fashion critic Vanessa Friedman suggested in the wake of the bankruptcy. Her take on the situation was harsh, but as she saw it, in addition to a pandemic and a disastrous LBO, J.Crew was afflicted with "an inability to give urgent, desirable expression to who we are now."[6] Just because something was once great, did it *have* to be reinvented—particularly if its original foundation appeared to be disintegrating under pressure?

By 2021, shuttered J.Crew mall stores were being repurposed as COVID vaccine clinics.[7] If ever there was a death knell, that had to be it. Or so you would think. But in the 2020s, the only thing that's for sure is that nothing is for sure—in life and, yes, in retail.

The Future of Shopping had not turned out quite as expected. Between 2019 and 2021, online shopping spiked by more than 50 percent—no great surprise, since it had been headed in that direction, even before America got locked inside on our laptops.[8] What *was* surprising was that many of retail's digital wunderkinds, the upstarts who appeared to be sure bets at the end of the Mickey and Jenna era, had failed to deliver, so to speak. As of this writing, the clothing rental service Rent the Runway reportedly had "a long road ahead to profitability," with a net loss of $211.8 million in 2021.[9] Investors were likewise losing patience with secondhand giants the RealReal, Poshmark, and ThredUp, which all went public in splashy I.P.O.s—and all have yet to turn a profit.[10] Indeed, in mid-2022, the industry site *Business of Fashion* lamented disappointing returns from one-time "unicorns" ranging from FarFetch to Mytheresa: "The luxury dotcom pink cloud turned into a hail storm," *B.o.F.* declared.[11]

What *did* seem to be working? Real-life, in-person stores. Yes, really.

"The pendulum seems to be swinging back toward in-person retail," the *Atlantic* declared in 2022.[12] "As Americans have gradually returned to stores over the past year, people have rediscovered the intrinsic thrills of selecting a pristine tomato or feeling the luxe texture of a sweater while perusing through clothing racks." Even with the online boom, physical stores beat online shopping in 2021. "The future does not necessarily arrive in a straight line," noted *New York Times* tech columnist Shira Ovide, as shocked as anybody by this outcome.[13]

It's just as Mickey crowed to his staff back in the aughts: On a website, there is nothing to connect with, nothing to "belong" to. No dopamine high. Whereas in a store, people can see, hear, touch, and smell. And after being stuck at home waiting for dull brown boxes to land on our doorstep, we relished the very experience that Emily and Arthur Cinader first gave J.Crew shoppers back in 1989: immediate gratification. Walking out with that new sweater swinging from a (canvas!) shopping tote really can be mood altering. Retail therapy is real.

It's almost enough to give you whiplash, huh? The unicorns aren't soaring after all. Shoppers love brick and mortar. But the most curious about-face of the late-pandemic era is also maybe the most inevitable: "Preppy style is back with a vengeance!" shrieked the *Guardian*,[14] announcing that the sweater vest had staged a comeback. On TikTok, videos with the hashtag #oldmoneyaesthetic have been viewed, at last count, 375 million times. In a sea of hoodies and graphic tees, "it's now more shocking to see a Gen Z or millennial in a well-tailored suit than with tattoos on their face," a cultural trend researcher noted.

If there is one certainty this book should leave you with, it is that—like the indefatigable heroine in an action movie, or, depending on your point of view, the zombie in a horror flick—the sartorial traditions of the American aristocracy never die. Just when you think prep is done for good, it's *baaack*.

In its latest incarnation, the badge on prep's blazer is one of keen self-awareness and pointed inclusivity. It remixes strains of ye olde Princeton with beats from hip-hop, surf, skate culture. "It's as if the Ivy League uniform were worn for boardslides and visits to underground clubs in '90s downtown New York, rather than for Skull and Bones meetings," *Esquire* said.[15] In truth, this iteration had been brewing for a while, led in part by Jack Carlson, founder of cult label Rowing Blazers, purveyor of collegiate-print T-shirts, rugbies, and "dad hats," who has for years been on the forefront of a distinctly downtown version of prep that's about as far from establishment prep—picture, say, Jared Kushner's neatly combed schoolboy haircut and weekend polos—as you can get. In interviews, Carlson handles the P-word as gingerly as Emily Cinader did in the '90s. "It means so many things to so many people," he has said. "We even try to avoid the word." His aim is to achieve prep, sans baggage: take the good parts, leave the bad.[16]

Take the good, leave the bad. An apt distillation of the task J.Crew was up against after declaring bankruptcy: Could they cherry-pick the best parts of what this company stands for, and abandon the rest on the cutting-room floor?

If you were hoping I'd have an answer to that question, my apologies: your guess, after reading this book, is as good as mine. But as I put the final touches on these pages, J.Crew had at least two things going for it. The first, ironically, was the bankruptcy itself, which finally allowed the company to slough off its crippling debt—all $1.65 billion of it. T.P.G. and Leonard Green are finally out of the picture,* and J.Crew emerged from Chapter 11 with a new majority shareholder, New York–based hedge fund Anchorage Capital Partners, and a new, lighter debt

* T.P.G. helped strike the deal that eventually took J.Crew down. But after the bankruptcy, the *New York Post* reported that the firm, which put in $33 million up front in 2011, had managed to extract close to $100 million in fees from J.Crew on the deal—three times its original investment. T.P.G. disputes the "material misstatements and numerous incorrect assumptions about our investment and economic structure" in the *Post*'s account: "The company's bankruptcy resulted in significant losses for our investors."

load of $400 million, not due until 2027. With a break from the fees it was paying T.P.G. and Leonard Green, the company finally had the leeway to put the money it earned into its own renovation.

The second, most obvious sign of hope: new design talent. As of this printing, head of womenswear Olympia Gayot, a pre-Raphaelite blond and veteran of the Jenna era design squad, was earning plaudits for chic pieces that lightly reference Emily-era minimalism. But the louder applause was for Brendon Babenzien, who spent almost fifteen years as the creative director of Supreme, arguably the most influential streetwear company of all time. Babenzien's own brand, Noah, is not only one of the leaders of prep's downtown revival, but also gets props for its politics. Babenzien preaches "intelligent consumption," and checks all the boxes consumers now demand in exchange for their hard-earned dollars: He is transparent about production and supply chains; he informs his customers about the stress of pollution on the environment. *And* he has serious streetwear cred. His appointment made even jaded editors who had long washed their hands of J.Crew sit up and take notice. Many believe that if anyone can turn the tide, he can.

For a long time, I was certain that during the two-odd years I spent working on this book—stuck at home during COVID with two young kids, under an ever-present laptop, wearing the same motley assortment of pajama pants you were wearing, too—I had become almost monkish in my consumption habits. *Wow,* I marveled at myself, a little smugly, *you don't even shop anymore!* A closer review of my closet (and my credit card statement) reveals this to be just one of many lies I often tell myself. I still shop. I just stopped going *to* shops. Instead, I rent frivolous vacation dresses from Rent the Runway; buy secondhand Ulla Johnson from the RealReal; snap up tees at Target; reorder my preferred leggings from Lululemon. And experiment with a host of D.T.C.s—some of which had not even launched when Mickey and Jenna left J.Crew: I have ordered an exceedingly practical bag from Cuyana, a winter puffer from Everlane, jeans from AYR, a swimsuit from Summersalt, pajamas from Lake, bras from Negative.

Somehow, despite this prodigious consumption, and despite the fact that I was spending all day, every day, overthinking a certain preppy retailer, in those two years I bought next to nothing from J.Crew. Hard to believe, I know, considering the book you're now holding, or listening to, or that is being beamed into your brain via Amazon drone. But true nevertheless. J.Crew had been so untempting for so long, at some point I simply stopped looking.

But in the summer of 2022, I needed shoes. Specifically, a pair of shoes that were *not*: they had to be not boring, not wobbly, not strappy, not blister-giving, not dressy yet easy to dress up. In about three seconds Google divined that what I sought was a pair of espadrilles from J.Crew in a hue called "vivid flame." (For the record, I'd have called it "lobster.") There's nothing groundbreaking about espadrilles, to be sure, but staring at a photo of this pair, I experienced a shopping side effect I'd almost forgotten: the flood of a strong sense memory, the waft of an experience you've never actually had. These espadrilles were a Negroni chilled by a single, fat ice cube, on a dock overlooking limitless blue. They were the summer I wanted to have. I said J.Crew had two big things in its plus column, but here I was reminded of an even more potent third: the button inside of me that was first pushed by a J.Crew rollneck sweater in middle school—the one that had transported me to a place, a person, I longed to be—still functioned. You might call that button "Buy Now." And it took only one pair of shoes to push it.

When people ask if I think J.Crew can be great again, I think about those shoes. I'm no soothsayer—and as clearly stated in the previous pages, what I have learned, in these tumultuous years, is that nothing is certain—but my guess is that no, J.Crew will never again be quite what it was. Because consumers aren't what we were. Gone are the days when I kept my J.Crew shopping cart bookmarked on my laptop, ready to fill the moment I felt the first pang of need for some new thing, whether it was a new swimsuit or a winter coat. I can't imagine being faithful in that way to a single label anymore. There are too many new contenders popping up seductively in my feeds, night and day, on devices that never leave my hands. *Try me!* they demand. *Be me!* We are bombarded by *options*. Like something? You can find five cheaper versions online in ten minutes or less.

For that reason, I can't imagine how any single retailer could ever be *the* American brand again. And because there is no one idea of what it is to look "American" anymore. Nor is there one way to look cool, or *It*. Thank goodness.

But in my book—which, I suppose, is this book—J.Crew doesn't need to be *that* again to be indispensable again. What it needs are those fleeting moments when it makes us believe, when it makes us think, "*This!* This is what I want my life to look like." Even if just for a second, or for an evening, *this* is what I want.

I don't need an identity from J.Crew, after all. I just need a great vacation maillot. A pair of flattering shorts. A straw sunhat that, ideally, would make me look a little like Catherine Deneuve in *Je vous aime*. The perfect "not" shoes: exactly the ones I need, at exactly the moment I need them.

The espadrilles arrived three days later, by the way. They are great. I've yet to wear them on a dock with a matching cocktail in hand. But I haven't given up hope.

ACKNOWLEDGMENTS

I owe a tremendous debt to the designers, merchants, stylists, photographers, editors, accountants, models, copywriters, quants, techies, and sales associates of J.Crew past and present—more than one hundred of you in all—who shared your stories and your work with me. The education you gave me has been an M.B.A. in itself, covering everything from the science of catalogue prospecting to the back-end operation of a retail website. Who knew how many different "wales" of corduroy exist? I hope I've done justice to the company you built and believed in, and that *The Kingdom of Prep* will serve as a testament to the enormous skill, passion, and creativity you brought to the work of dressing America.

My greatest thanks to Carrie Thornton at Dey Street, for seeing the potential in this idea, but first and foremost for delivering unto me the steady, insightful Anna Montague—an editor capable of taking a mushy, half-baked manuscript and erecting the kind of scaffolding that can turn it into, well, this *book*. Thank you, amazing Anna! (Someday you will have to explain to me how you remain so unflappable.) Thanks, too, to endlessly patient researcher Jesse Dorris, who caught each of my boneheaded mistakes with such grace, and to Andrew Jacobs, for having my back as we brought this baby in for a landing.

This book would never have happened if not for my agents, Jen Marshall and Jane von Mehren. Jen, you were the very first to say, "Wait, that sounds like a book!" Jen and Jane, together you have been my cheering section, consiglieres, and spirit guides, jumping to my aid at every bend in the road of writing and publishing *KOP*. Every author—

every human—should have that kind of unflagging support and encouragement.

Speaking of encouragement. To my insightful and generous early readers: Sarah Haight and Jean Brownell, and members of my forever-*Elle* family, Robbie Myers (my longtime editor in chief, whose faith in me has fostered every major development of my career), and Laurie Abraham—the best editor out there, period—thank you. Each of you reassured me that I was onto something with this book: *Keep going.* Thank you to my Spread soul-sister, Rachel Baker, who had the temerity to found a Giant Media Empire with me while I was still half-witless with book duties, and thus became the official hand-holder in chief of this project.

Thank you to my family—in blood and in friendship. It wasn't easy being a mother of two young children writing a book in a global pandemic. But then, it also wasn't easy being the pit crew responsible for fueling and maintaining said mother: my parents, Bonnie and Bruce Julian, and Tony and Shelley Bullock; my ever-supportive in-laws, Stan and Kathy Cichanowski; Sorelle LaBerge Hynes; Sara Tyler; the women of "James-O"; the "ladies of the '80s"—it took all of you and more to supply the countless hours of childcare and bottomless moral support it took to get 'er done. Thank you.

To Nick: No one has ever helped and supported me the way you have. To you, Finn, and Max: The words *thank you* seem way too small for a feeling this big. Okay, my boys: What's next!?

NOTES

CHAPTER 1: "HOW TO BE REALLY TOP-DRAWER"

1. Lisa Birnbach, Jonathan Roberts, Carol McD.Wallace, and Mason Wiley, *The Official Preppy Handbook* (New York: Workman Publishing, 1980).
2. Birnbach et al., *Preppy Handbook*, 113, 103.
3. Molly Peterson, "*National Lampoon's Animal House*, Present at the Creation," NPR, July 29, 2002, https://seamus.npr.org/programs/morning/features/patc/animalhouse/index.html.
4. Liz Robbins, "A Cottage, So Preppy, Pops Up for Hilfiger," *New York Times*, May 5, 2011, https://www.nytimes.com/2011/05/05/nyregion/a-pop-up-pre-fab-preppy-house-for-tommy-hilfiger.html.
5. Dierdre Donahue, "Prep Rally," *Washington Post*, January 12, 1981, https://www.washingtonpost.com/archive/lifestyle/1981/01/12/prep-rally/c4d14e83-732e-4f81-8484-a51fa87aff19.
6. Birnbach et al., *Preppy Handbook*, 32.
7. Jenna Weissman Joselit, *A Perfect Fit* (New York: Owl Books, 2001), 79.
8. John William Cooke, *Brooks Brothers: Generations of Style* (New York: Brooks Brothers Group, 2003), 21, 33.
9. Jeffrey Banks and Doria de La Chapelle, *Preppy: Cultivating Ivy Style* (New York: Rizzoli, 2011), 4.
10. F. Scott Fitzgerald, *This Side of Paradise* (New York: Charles Scribner's Sons, 1920), 61.
11. Emily Spivack, "The Story Behind the Lacoste Crocodile Shirt," *Smithsonian Magazine*, June 4, 2013, https://www.smithsonianmag.com/arts-culture/the-story-behind-the-lacoste-crocodile-shirt-91276898/.
12. Baldassare Castiglione, *The Book of the Courtier* (New Delhi: Gyan Publishing House, 2019), 35.
13. Christian Chensvold, "The Rise and Fall of the Ivy League Look," *Ivy Style*, April 17, 2020, http://www.ivy-style.com/the-rise-and-fall-of-the-ivy-league-look.html.
14. Linda J. Bilmes and Cornell William Brooks, "The G.I. Bill Was One of the Worst Racial Injustices of the 20th Century. Congress Can Fix It," *Boston Globe*, February 23, 2022, https://www.bostonglobe.com/2022/02/23/opinion/gi-bill-was-one-worst-racial-injustices-20th-century-congress-can-fix-it/.
15. Edward W. Said, *Out of Place: A Memoir* (New York: Knopf Doubleday, 2012), 271.

16. Christian M. Chensvold, "Miles Ago," *Ivy Style*, January 26, 2020, http://www.ivy-style.com/miles-ago.html.
17. Jason Jules and Graham Marsh, *Black Ivy: A Revolt in Style* (London: Reel Art Press, 2021), 7.
18. Robin Givhan, "To Fight the Status Quo, the Activists of 1968 Harnessed the Power of Fashion," *Washington Post*, May 23, 2018, https://www.washingtonpost.com/lifestyle/style/to-fight-the-status-quo-the-activists-of-1968-harnessed-the-power-of-fashion/2018/05/23/1d2f2ad2-44dd-11e8-bba2-0976a82b05a2_story.html.
19. Chensvold, "Rise and Fall of the Ivy League Look."
20. Michael Gross, *Genuine Authentic: The Real Life of Ralph Lauren* (New York: HarperCollins, 2003), 82.
21. Jonathan Yardley, "Laurenization of America: How a Kid from the Bronx Labeled Us for What We Are," *Washington Post*, via *Orlando Sentinel*, January 3, 1987, https://www.orlandosentinel.com/news/os-xpm-1987-01-03-0100020120-story.html.
22. Rebecca C. Tuite, *Seven Sisters Style* (New York: Rizzoli, 2014).
23. Cooke, *Brooks Brothers: Generations of Style*, 83–84.

CHAPTER 2: COGNITIVE DISSONANCE

1. Martha McNeil Hamilton, "Montgomery Ward to Close All Stores," *Washington Post*, December 29, 2000, https://www.washingtonpost.com/archive/politics/2000/12/29/montgomery-ward-to-close-all-stores/c9f7f0f7-08d8-46b2-a63a-e20c92670b43/.
2. Tiffany Hsu, "When Sears Was Everywhere: Espionage, Politics and Fine Art," *New York Times*, October 15, 2018, https://www.nytimes.com/2018/10/15/business/sears-history-bankruptcy.html.
3. Holly Brubach, "Mail Order America," *New York Times*, November 21, 1993, https://www.nytimes.com/1993/11/21/magazine/mail-order-america.html.
4. Claudia Goldin, Lawence F. Katz, and Ilyana Kuziemko, "The Homecoming of American College Women: The Reversal of the College Gender Gap," *Journal of Economic Perspectives* 20, no. 4 (Fall 2006): 133–156. https://scholar.harvard.edu/files/lkatz/files/gkk_jep.20.4.133.pd
5. Quoted in Tony Long, "Dec. 26, 1982: *Time*'s Top Man? The Personal Computer," *Wired*, December 26, 2012, https://www.wired.com/2012/12/dec-26-1982-times-top-man-the-personal-computer/.
6. Michael J. Roberts, William A. Sahlman, and Lauren Barley, "Texas Pacific Group—J.Crew," case study, Harvard Business School Publishing, 2007.

CHAPTER 3: PUZZLE PIECES

1. Judith Schiff, "Yale After World War II," *Yale Alumni Magazine*, July–August 2016, https://yalealumnimagazine.org/articles/4312-yale-after-world-war-ii.

CHAPTER 4: GIRL, BOSS

1. Quoted in Rich Francis, "Zoran: The Serbian Fashion Designer You Should Know," The Culture Trip, January 9, 2017, https://theculturetrip.com/europe/serbia/articles/zoran-the-serbian-fashion-designer-you-should-know/.
2. Jacob Bernstein, Matthew Schneier, and Vanessa Friedman, "Male Models Say Mario Testino and Bruce Weber Sexually Exploited Them," *New York Times*, January 13, 2018, https://www.nytimes.com/2018/01/13/style/mario-testino-bruce-weber-harassment.html.
3. Gross, *Genuine Authentic*.

CHAPTER 5: HOOKED ON A FEELING

1. Louis Auchincloss, "There Was a Place for Style in Everything," *New York Times*, July 18, 1971, https://archive.nytimes.com/www.nytimes.com/books/98/05/24/specials/710718-review.html.
2. Matthew DeBord, "Texture and Taboo: The Tyranny of Texture and Ease in the J.Crew Catalogue," *Fashion Theory* 1, no. 3 (1997): 261–277, https://www.tandfonline.com/doi/abs/10.2752/136270497779640125.
3. Banks and de La Chapelle, *Preppy*.

CHAPTER 6: 625 SIXTH

1. Vanessa Friedman, "Fashion's Woman Problem," *New York Times*, May 20, 2018, https://www.nytimes.com/2018/05/20/fashion/glass-runway-no-female-ceos.html.
2. Warren St. John, "Emily Woods, Ultimate J.Crew Gal–Boss's Daughter Is Now the Boss," *New York Observer*, November 24, 1997, https://observer.com/1997/11/emily-woods-ultimate-j-crew-galboss-daughter-is-now-the-boss/.
3. Willy Staley, "Is Anna Wintour Really a Tyrant, or Something Else Entirely?" *New York Times*, April 30, 2022, https://www.nytimes.com/2022/04/30/books/review/anna-the-biography-amy-odell.html.
4. Carol Lynn Mithers, "The Captain of J.Crew," *Mirabella*, October 1991, 168–171.

CHAPTER 7: MALLS OF AMERICA

1. N. R. Kleinfield, "Even for J.Crew, the Mail Order Boom Days Are Over," *New York Times*, September 2, 1990, https://www.nytimes

.com/1990/09/02/business/even-for-j-crew-the-mail-order-boom-days-are-over.html.

2. Kleinfield, "Boom Days Are Over."
3. Wayne Curtis, "What's New in Mail Order: Struggling to Hook Shoppers—and Keep Them," *New York Times*, May 14, 1989, https://www.nytimes.com/1989/05/14/business/what-s-new-in-mail-order-struggling-to-hook-shoppers-and-keep-them.html.
4. Natasha Geiling, "The Death and Rebirth of the American Mall," *Smithsonian Magazine*, November 25, 2014, https://www.smithsonianmag.com/arts-culture/death-and-rebirth-american-mall-180953444/.
5. Steven Johnson, "The Strange, Surprisingly Radical Roots of the Shopping Mall," TED.com, November 29, 2016, https://ideas.ted.com/the-strange-surprisingly-radical-roots-of-the-shopping-mall/.
6. Joan Didion, "On the Mall," *Esquire*, December 1975, https://www.esquire.com/lifestyle/a38401618/joan-didion-shopping-center-essay/.
7. Ian Bogost, "When Malls Saved the Suburbs from Despair," *Atlantic*, February 17, 2018, https://www.theatlantic.com/technology/archive/2018/02/when-malls-saved-cities-from-capitalism/553610/.
8. William H. Meyers, "Rag Trade Revolutionary," *New York Times*, June 8, 1986, https://www.nytimes.com/1986/06/08/magazine/rag-trade-revolutionary.html.
9. Kleinfield, "Boom Days Are Over."

CHAPTER 8: CALIFORNIA GIRLS

1. Mimi Swartz, "Crew's Control," *Texas Monthly*, September 1992, https://www.texasmonthly.com/arts-entertainment/crews-control/.
2. Megan Garber, "Casual Friday and the 'End of the Office Dress Code,'" *Atlantic*, May 25, 2016, https://www.theatlantic.com/entertainment/archive/2016/05/casual-friday-and-the-end-of-the-office-dress-code/484334/.
3. Mithers, "Captain of J.Crew."
4. Debbie Millman, "Jenna Lyons," *Design Matters with Debbie Millman*, March 1, 2021, audio, https://podcasts.apple.com/us/podcast/jenna-lyons/id328074695?i=1000511123334.
5. Mark Holgate, "Measure of Success," *Vogue*, April 2006, 338–341.
6. Rosemary Feitelberg, "Jenna Lyons Talks New TV Show, Social Media Fears and Partying with the Obamas," *Women's Wear Daily*, via *Los Angeles Times*, December 21, 2018, https://www.latimes.com/fashion/la-ig-wwd-jenna-lyons-new-tv-show-20181221-story.html.
7. Mithers, "Captain of J.Crew."
8. Rene Chun, "Copy Catwalk," *New York*, December 16, 1996, 28–31.
9. Chun, "Copy Catwalk."
10. St. John, "Ultimate J.Crew Gal."

CHAPTER 9: GO BIG OR GO HOME

1. Benoit Denizet-Lewis, "The Man Behind Abercrombie & Fitch," *Salon*, January 24, 2006, https://www.salon.com/2006/01/24/jeffries/.
2. Quoted in Brad Tuttle, "8 Amazing Things People Said When Online Shopping Was Born 20 Years Ago," *Money*, August 15, 2014, https://money.com/online-shopping-history-anniversary/.
3. "Americans Going Online . . . Explosive Growth, Uncertain Destinations," Pew Research Center, October 16, 1995, https://www.pewresearch.org/politics/1995/10/16/americans-going-online-explosive-growth-uncertain-destinations/.
4. Edmund L. Andrews, "Accord Reached for Limiting Smut on the Internet," *New York Times*, December 2, 1995, https://www.nytimes.com/1995/12/02/us/accord-reached-for-limiting-smut-on-the-internet.html.
5. Nicholas Kulish and Rebecca R. Ruiz, "The Fortunes of MacKenzie Scott," *New York Times*, April 11, 2022, https://www.nytimes.com/2022/04/10/business/mackenzie-scott-charity.html.
6. Wendy Bounds, "Buttoned-Down J.Crew Arrives at a Management Crossroads," *Wall Street Journal*, August 22, 1997, https://www.wsj.com/articles/SB872202095855343000.
7. Justin Racz, *J.Crewd: A Parody* (New York: Doubleday, 1998).
8. "Boyz in the Designer Hoods: Crew," *Spy*, February 1995, 63–69.
9. Lisa Jones, *Bulletproof Diva* (New York: Random House, 1994), 145–148.
10. Mithers, "Captain of J.Crew."
11. "Captain of the Crew," *Esquire*, August 1997, 44.
12. Alix Browne, "From Main Street to Prince Street," *Harper's Bazaar*, November 1996, 250–254.

CHAPTER 10: FIVE . . . FOUR . . . THREE . . . TWO . . . ONE

1. David Moin and Sydney Rutberg, "The Book on J.Crew," *Women's Wear Daily*, December 11, 1997, https://wwd.com/fashion-news/fashion-features/article-1117338/.
2. Moin and Rutberg, "Book on J.Crew."
3. John Carney, "The Weird Love Affair Between TPG and J.Crew," CNBC, November 23, 2010, https://www.cnbc.com/2010/11/23/the-weird-love-affair-between-tpg-and-j-crew.html.
4. Katherine Fons, "Private Equity Pioneer! Helios CEO Tope Lawani on His Career Journey, the Future of Fintech, Impactful Investing, and So Much More," Walker & Dunlop, March 23, 2022, audio, http://www.walkerdunlop.com/insights/2022/03/23/invest-success-tope-lawani-co-founder-ceo-helios-investment-partners/.
5. Bloomberg Wire, "Buyout Giant TPG's Leaders Weigh In on Contrarian Dealmaking's Past, Present, and Future," *Dallas Morning News*, May 20, 2019, https://www.dallasnews.com/business/local

-companies/2019/05/20/buyout-giant-tpg-s-leaders-weigh-in-on-contrarian-dealmaking-s-past-present-and-future/.

6. Riva D. Atlas and Edward Wong, "Texas Pacific Goes Where Others Fear to Spend," *New York Times*, August 25, 2002, https://www.nytimes.com/2002/08/25/business/texas-pacific-goes-where-others-fear-to-spend.html.
7. Ellise Pierce, "Mondo Bondo," *Texas Monthly*, February 1996, https://www.texasmonthly.com/news-politics/mondo-bondo/.
8. "David Bonderman," *Forbes*, accessed June 16, 2022, https://www.forbes.com/profile/david-bonderman/?sh=3656ed5b2fce.
9. Atlas and Wong, "Texas Pacific Goes."
10. Jennifer Steinhauer, "J.Crew Caught in Messy World of Finance as It Sells Majority Stake," *New York Times*, October 18, 1997, https://www.nytimes.com/1997/10/18/business/j-crew-caught-in-messy-world-of-finance-as-it-sells-majority-stake.html.
11. Roberts et al., "Texas Pacific Group."
12. Joe Allen, "The UPS Strike, Two Decades Later," *Jacobin*, August 4, 2017, https://jacobin.com/2017/08/ups-strike-teamsters-logistics-labor-unions-work.
13. Steinhauer, "J.Crew Caught in Messy World."
14. Steinhauer, "J.Crew Caught in Messy World."
15. Moin and Rutberg, "Book on J.Crew."
16. Moin and Rutberg, "Book on J.Crew."
17. St. John, "Ultimate J.Crew Gal."
18. Roberts et al., "Texas Pacific Group."

CHAPTER 11: SWAN SONG

1. Leonora Epstein, "The Beautiful 1998 *Dawson's Creek* J.Crew Catalog," *Buzzfeed*, January 23, 2013, https://www.buzzfeed.com/leonoraepstein/the-beautiful-1998-dawsons-creek-j-crew-catalo.
2. Tracy Lomrantz Lester, "Um, the *Dawson's Creek* Cast Stars in this Vintage J.Crew Catalog," *Glamour*, January 28, 2013, https://www.glamour.com/story/um-the-dawsons-creek-cast-star.
3. David Moin, "Sources See Howard Socol Going to J.Crew as CEO," *Women's Wear Daily*, February 23, 1998, https://wwd.com/fashion-news/fashion-features/article-1093643/.
4. Vlonda Gault, "New Exec Tailors J.Crew Comeback," *Crain's*, April 27, 1998.
5. Bloomberg News, "Company News: Fingerhut to Acquire Popular Club Plan Unit of J.Crew," *New York Times*, November 4, 1998, http://www.nytimes.com/1998/11/04/business/company-news-fingerhut-to-acquire-popular-club-plan-unit-of-j-crew.html.
6. Gault, "New Exec Tailors."

7. Marc de Swaan Arons, "How Brands Were Born: A Brief History of Modern Marketing," *Atlantic*, October 3, 2011, https://www.theatlantic.com/business/archive/2011/10/how-brands-were-born-a-brief-history-of-modern-marketing/246012/.
8. Associated Press, "J.Crew's CEO Resigns After Less Than a Year," *Los Angeles Times*, January 5, 1999, https://www.latimes.com/archives/la-xpm-1999-jan-05-fi-60443-story.html.
9. Erin Kelly, "A Shift in Style," *Fortune*, via CNN Money, November 13, 2000, https://money.cnn.com/magazines/fortune/fortune_archive/2000/11/13/291575/.
10. Kelly, "Shift in Style."
11. Kelly, "Shift in Style."
12. Leslie Kaufman and Riva D. Atlas, "In a Race to the Mall, J.Crew Has Lost Its Way," *New York Times*, April 28, 2002, https://www.nytimes.com/2002/04/28/business/in-a-race-to-the-mall-j-crew-has-lost-its-way.html.
13. Roberts et al., "Texas Pacific Group."
14. Roberts et al., "Texas Pacific Group."
15. Meryl Gordon, "Mickey Drexler's Redemption," *New York*, November 19, 2004, https://nymag.com/nymetro/news/bizfinance/biz/features/10489/.

CHAPTER 12: ROCKET MAN

1. Cristina Alesci, "Why J.Crew's Mickey Drexler Succeeded: He Had Ants in His Pants," CNN Business, February 9, 2017, https://money.cnn.com/2017/02/03/news/companies/american-dream-mickey-drexler/index.html.
2. Arlene Alda, *Just Kids from the Bronx: Telling It the Way It Was* (New York: Henry Holt, 2015), 146–148.
3. Nick Paumgarten, "The Merchant," *New Yorker*, September 20, 2010, https://www.newyorker.com/magazine/2010/09/20/the-merchant.
4. Paumgarten, "The Merchant."
5. Alda, *Just Kids*.
6. Paumgarten, "The Merchant."
7. Paumgarten, "The Merchant."
8. Paumgarten, "The Merchant."
9. Joe Nocera, "A CEO Sells the Store," *New York Times*, March 1, 2008, https://www.nytimes.com/2008/03/01/business/01nocera.html.
10. Andrew Pollack, "At the Gap, a Bold New Look," *New York Times*, April 6, 1986, https://www.nytimes.com/1986/04/06/business/at-the-gap-a-bold-new-look.html.
11. Tina Gaudoin, "Retail Therapist," *WSJ: The Magazine from the Wall Street Journal*, June 2010, 48–55.

12. Greg Lawrence, "Jackie O, Working Girl," *Vanity Fair*, January 2011, https://www.vanityfair.com/culture/2011/01/jackie-o-working-girl-201101.
13. Pollack, "At the Gap, a Bold New Look."
14. Jonah Engel Bromwich, "Was the Gap Ever Cool? A Look at 50 Years in Denim and Khaki," *New York Times*, September 20, 2019, https://www.nytimes.com/2019/09/17/style/the-gap-jeans-history.html.
15. Bruce Weber, "Don Fisher, the Gap's Founder, Dies at 81," *New York Times*, September 28, 2009, https://www.nytimes.com/2009/09/29/business/29fisher.html.
16. Paumgarten, "The Merchant."
17. Jenny Strasburg, "Gap Inside Out: Founder Tells How It Was in 724-Page Tome," *San Francisco Chronicle*, February 15, 2004, https://www.sfgate.com/business/article/Gap-inside-out-Founder-tells-how-it-was-in-2796682.php.
18. Pollack, "At the Gap, a Bold New Look."
19. Genevieve Buck, "Gap Shows Us Who Wears the Pants," *Chicago Tribune*, November 20, 1994, https://www.chicagotribune.com/news/ct-xpm-1994-11-20-9411200368-story.html.
20. Buck, "Gap Shows Us Who Wears the Pants."
21. Naomi Campbell, "Sharon Stone on Dating Apps & Her New Tell-All Book," *No Filter with Naomi*, YouTube, April 2020, video, https://www.youtube.com/watch?v=P54bzdWTlII.
22. Paul Goldberger, "The Sameness of Things," *New York Times Magazine*, April 6, 1997, https://www.nytimes.com/1997/04/06/magazine/the-sameness-of-things.html.
23. Elizabeth L. Cline, *Overdressed: The Shockingly High Cost of Cheap Fashion* (New York: Portfolio/Penguin, 2012), 26–27.
24. Noah Briar and Colin Nagy, "The Monday Media Diet with Mickey Drexler," *Why Is This Interesting?* Substack, March 22, 2021, https://whyisthisinteresting.substack.com/p/the-monday-media-diet-with-mickey.
25. Stephanie Strom, "How Gap Inc. Spells Revenge," *New York Times*, April 24, 1994, https://www.nytimes.com/1994/04/24/business/how-gap-inc-spells-revenge.html.
26. Nina Munk and Michelle McGowan, "Gap Gets It," *Fortune*, August 3, 1998, https://archive.fortune.com/magazines/fortune/fortune_archive/1998/08/03/246286/index.htm.
27. Walter Isaacson, *Steve Jobs* (New York: Simon and Schuster, 2011), 371.
28. Matt Richtel, "Hip Joins Hip with Little Ado," *New York Times*, May 31, 1999, https://www.nytimes.com/1999/05/31/business/compressed-data-hip-joins-hip-with-little-ado.html.
29. John Chartier, "Gap Falls Deeper," CNN Money, February 20, 2002, https://money.cnn.com/2002/02/20/companies/gap/index.htm.

30. Justin Fox, "Telling Us to Go Shopping," *Time*, January 19, 2009, http://content.time.com/time/specials/packages/article/0,28804,1872229_1872230_1872236,00.html.
31. Dina ElBoghdady, "Gap Reports $8 Million Loss for Fiscal 2001," *Washington Post*, February 27, 2002, https://www.washingtonpost.com/archive/business/2002/02/27/gap-reports-8-million-loss-for-fiscal-2001/01456aa0-4c58-4137-8f92-2aac591d5dd7/.
32. Vanessa Friedman, "Lunch with the FT: Mickey Drexler," *Financial Times*, October 21, 2011, https://www.ft.com/content/bcf99a3e-fb01-11e0-bebe-00144feab49a.

CHAPTER 13: THIS IS YOUR CAPTAIN SPEAKING

1. Millman, "Jenna Lyons."
2. Joe Nocera, "A CEO Sells the Store."
3. Gaudoin, "Retail Therapist."
4. Paumgarten, "The Merchant."
5. Sarah Harris, "The Creative Force Behind J.Crew," *Guardian*, April 28, 2012, https://www.theguardian.com/fashion/2012/apr/29/j-crew-fashion-jenna-lyons.
6. Gaudoin, "Retail Therapist."
7. Danielle Sacks, "How Jenna Lyons Transformed J.Crew into a Cult Brand," *Fast Company*, April 15, 2013, https://www.fastcompany.com/3007843/how-jenna-lyons-transformed-jcrew-cult-brand.
8. Sacks, "How Jenna Lyons Transformed J.Crew."
9. Sacks, "How Jenna Lyons Transformed J.Crew."

CHAPTER 14: PANNING FOR GOLD

1. Susannah Conway, "The History of . . . Cashmere: The Golden Fleece," *Independent*, September 6, 1998, https://www.independent.co.uk/life-style/the-history-of-cashmere-the-golden-fleece-1196401.html.
2. "The Vanity Fair 100," *Vanity Fair*, October 2009, https://www.vanityfair.com/news/2009/10/new-establishment200910?currentPage=8.
3. "Ralph Lauren Announces End to the Rugby Line," *Menswear Market*, November 2, 2012, https://menswear-market.com/blog/ralph-lauren-ends-rugby/.
4. Tracie Rozhon, "Student Chic Is Remaking Itself, Trading Grunge for Cable Knit," *New York Times*, August 16, 2004, https://www.nytimes.com/2004/08/16/us/student-chic-is-remaking-itself-trading-grunge-for-cable-knit.html.
5. "The Jean Pool," *Forbes*, October 11, 1999, https://www.forbes.com/global/1999/1011/084_01.html.
6. Harriet Quick, "Loro Piana Preserves Its Heritage and Looks Forward to the Future," *Wall Street Journal*, December 3, 2015, https://www.wsj

.com/articles/loro-piana-preserves-its-heritage-and-looks-forward-to-the-future-1449157778.

7. Ellen Tien, "Hot Yarns, Cool Prices," *New York Times*, October 19, 2003, https://www.nytimes.com/2003/10/19/style/pulse-hot-yarns-cool-prices.html.
8. Christina Binkley, "What's in a Wool? The Secret of Loro Piana," *Wall Street Journal*, August 14, 2009, https://www.wsj.com/articles/SB10001424052970204908604574332472424083020.
9. Rozhon, "Student Chic Is Remaking Itself."

CHAPTER 15: REDEMPTION DAY

1. Suzanne Kapner, "Big Crew Debut—CEO Drexler Srikes [*sic*] It Rich in IPO Comeback," *New York Post*, June 29, 2006, https://nypost.com/2006/06/29/big-crew-debut-ceo-drexler-srikes-it-rich-in-ipo-comeback/.
2. Kapner, "Big Crew Debut."
3. Associated Press, "J.Crew Directors Resign," *New York Times*, September 30, 2006, https://www.nytimes.com/2006/09/30/business/today-in-business-j-crew-directors-resign.html.
4. Tony Dokoupil, "Retail: Is the American Shopping Mall Dead?" *Newsweek*, November 11, 2008, https://www.newsweek.com/retail-american-shopping-mall-dead-84829.
5. Cline, *Overdressed*, chapter 3.
6. Suzy Hansen, "How Zara Grew into the World's Largest Fashion Retailer," *New York Times*, November 9, 2012, https://www.nytimes.com/2012/11/11/magazine/how-zara-grew-into-the-worlds-largest-fashion-retailer.html.
7. Louise R. Morgan and Grete Birtwistle, "An Investigation of Young Fashion Consumers' Disposal Habits," *International Journal of Consumer Studies* 33, no. 2 (March 2009): 190–198, https://onlinelibrary.wiley.com/doi/abs/10.1111/j.1470-6431.2009.00756.x.
8. Dan Nosowitz, "Something Borrowed, Something Blue," *Buzzfeed*, September 28, 2014, https://www.buzzfeed.com/dannosowitz/how-madewell-bought-and-sold-my-familys-history.
9. Nosowitz, "Something Borrowed."

CHAPTER 16: THE TAO OF JENNA

1. Jenna Lyons [credited as Hairston], "The Watermelon Skirt," *Lenny Letter*, December 8, 2017, https://www.lennyletter.com/story/the-watermelon-skirt.
2. Holgate, "Measure of Success."
3. Lyons, "Watermelon Skirt."
4. Yasmin Nouri, "Fashion Icon Jenna Lyons Opens Up About Her J.Crew Exit," Behind Her Empire, September 8, 2021, https://dot

.la/jenna-lyons-jcrew-exit-to-loveseen-beginnings-2654930334.html. This article features the audio "How to Reinvent Yourself & Start Over with Jenna Lyons, Fashion Icon & Founder of Love-Seen."
5. Millman, "Jenna Lyons."
6. Millman, "Jenna Lyons."
7. Millman, "Jenna Lyons."
8. Holgate, "Measure of Success."
9. Millman, "Jenna Lyons."
10. "Jenna Lyons," *Into the Gloss*, August 2014, https://intothegloss.com/2014/08/jenna-lyons-j-crew/.
11. Chensvold, "Rise and Fall of the Ivy League Look."

CHAPTER 17: MAD MEN AND BROOKLYN LOGGERS

1. Sam Schube, "The Man Who Taught Men to Love Clothes," GQ, February 6, 2018, https://www.gq.com/story/todd-snyder-taught-men-to-loves-clothes.
2. Alex Pappademas, "Designer of the Year: The Incredible Suit-Shrinking Man," GQ, October 31, 2008, https://www.gq.com/story/designer-of-the-year-thom-browne-menswear.
3. Sarah Nassauer, "A Hard-Working Suit," *Wall Street Journal*, April 14, 2011, https://www.wsj.com/articles/SB10001424052748703385404576258671135584478.
4. Alexandria Symonds, "Ludlow Calling! J.Crew Déjà-Vu," *New York Observer*, September 13, 2011, https://observer.com/2011/09/ludlow-calling-j-crew-deja-vu/.
5. Jonathan Evans, "Prince Harry Wore His Go-To J.Crew Suit Again to Sit Down With Oprah," *Esquire*, March 5, 2021, https://www.esquire.com/style/mens-fashion/a35745777/prince-harry-oprah-interview-gray-jcrew-ludlow-suit/.
6. Amy Larocca, "The Spades' New Bag," *New York*, February 10, 2010, https://nymag.com/fashion/10/spring/63806/.
7. Roger Bennett, "Where J.Crew Shops for Ideas," *Bloomberg*, October 13, 2011, https://www.bloomberg.com/news/articles/2011-10-13/where-j-dot-crew-shops-for-ideas.

CHAPTER 18: THE *J* IN J.CREW

1. Jeanne Cummings, "RNC Shells Out $150K for Palin Fashion," *Politico*, October 21, 2008, https://www.politico.com/story/2008/10/rnc-shells-out-150k-for-palin-fashion-014805.
2. Stephanie Clifford, "J.Crew Benefits as Mrs. Obama Wears the Brand," *New York Times*, November 15, 2008, https://www.nytimes.com/2008/11/17/business/media/17crew.html.

3. *J.Crew Aficionada*, "Jenna Lyons + Oprah (in Studio)," clip from *The Oprah Winfrey Show*, Facebook, April 22, 2010, video, https://www.facebook.com/JCrew-Aficionada-107015039335269/videos/jenna-lyons-oprah-in-studio/1342637538019/.
4. Gaudoin, "Retail Therapist."
5. Mike Albo, "A Package Store for Preppies," *New York Times*, September 15, 2008, https://www.nytimes.com/2008/09/18/fashion/18CRITIC.html.
6. Eric Wilson, "J.Crew Gets Uppity," *New York Times*, October 15, 2008, https://www.nytimes.com/2008/10/16/fashion/thursdaystyles/16ROW.html.
7. Michael Rock, "Human Emotion: The One Thing the Internet Can't Buy," *T: The New York Times Style Magazine*, October 14, 2015, https://www.nytimes.com/2015/10/14/t-magazine/human-emotion-the-one-thing-the-internet-cant-buy.html.
8. Joan Didion, "The Promises Martha Stewart Made—and Why We Wanted to Believe Them," *New Yorker*, February 21 & 28, 2000, https://www.newyorker.com/magazine/2021/09/06/magazine 20000221everywoman-com.
9. Nicole Phelps, "Ikram Goldman Finally Speaks About Dressing Michelle Obama During the 2008 Campaign and Her Early Days in the White House," *Vogue*, November 18, 2016, https://www.vogue.com/article/michelle-obama-ikram-goldman.
10. Phelps, "Ikram Goldman Speaks."
11. Cathy Horyn and Eric Wilson, "Behind the First Lady, a Shadow Stylist," *New York Times*, November 2, 2009, https://www.nytimes.com/2009/02/12/style/12iht-12ikram.20136429.html.
12. Andrew Clark, "Website Crashes as First Family Cuts a Dash in DC," *Guardian*, January 22, 2009, https://www.theguardian.com/world/2009/jan/23/obama-endorse-j-crew.
13. Vanessa Friedman, "What Michelle Obama Wore and Why It Mattered," *New York Times*, January 14, 2017, https://www.nytimes.com/2017/01/14/fashion/michelle-obama-first-lady-fashion.html.
14. David Yermack, "Vision Statement: How This First Lady Moves Markets," *Harvard Business Review*, November 2010, https://hbr.org/2010/11/vision-statement-how-this-first-lady-moves-markets.
15. Jones, *Bulletproof Diva*.
16. Lauren Sandler, "Totally Modern Timelessness," *Domino*, November 2008, 102–111.
17. Muriel Rukeyser, "Käthe Kollwitz," in *The Speed of Darkness* (New York: Random House, 1968); "Käthe Kollwitz," Muriel Rukeyser: A Living Archive, http://murielrukeyser.emuenglish.org/2018/12/07/kathe-kollwitz/.
18. Holgate, "Measure of Success."
19. "My Stuff: Jenna Lyons," *Vanity Fair*, November 21, 2011, https://www.vanityfair.com/culture/photos/2011/11/my-stuff-slide-show.

CHAPTER 19: EVERYONE'S AN EXPERT

1. Alice Pfeiffer, "Young Bloggers Have Ear of Fashion Heavyweights," *New York Times*, September 13, 2019, https://www.nytimes.com/2009/09/14/technology/14youth.html.
2. Eve Wiseman, "One-Click Wonder: The Rise of Net-a-Porter," *Guardian*, July 10, 2010, https://www.theguardian.com/lifeandstyle/2010/jul/11/natalie-massenet-net-a-porter-internet-fashion.
3. Rock, "Human Emotion."
4. Sacks, "How Jenna Lyons Transformed J.Crew."
5. Sacks, "How Jenna Lyons Transformed J.Crew."
6. Leanne Shimabukuro, "Customers' Service: The Fan Blogs Behind the Companies," Ozy, May 8, 2014, https://www.ozy.com/good-sht/customers-service-the-fan-blogs-behind-the-companies/31294/.
7. Chavie Lieber, "Meet the Bloggers Tracking J.Crew, Anthro and Lulu's Every Move," Racked, July 9, 2014, https://www.racked.com/2014/7/9/7587517/bloggers-ikea-anthropologie-lululemon-jcrew-net-a-porter-fashion.

CHAPTER 20: LET'S MAKE A DEAL

1. Gaudoin, "Retail Therapist."
2. Gaudoin, "Retail Therapist."
3. Gaudoin, "Retail Therapist."
4. Paumgarten, "The Merchant."
5. "Interview with Alexis of *J.Crew Aficionada*," Feather Factor, July 6, 2012, https://www.featherfactor.com/2012/07/interview-with-alexis-of-j-crew-aficionada.html.
6. Millman, "Jenna Lyons."
7. Millman, "Jenna Lyons."
8. Julie Creswell, "J.Crew Flounders in Fashion's Shifting Tides," *New York Times*, June 10, 2015, https://www.nytimes.com/2015/06/11/business/j-crew-flounders-in-fashions-shifting-tides.html.
9. Anupreeta Das and Gina Chon, "J.Crew Board Didn't Have Many Details Ahead of Bid," *Wall Street Journal*, December 7, 2010, https://www.wsj.com/articles/SB10001424052748703471904576003911260873464.
10. Das and Chon, "J.Crew Board Didn't Have Many Details."
11. Kevin Dowd, "This Day in Buyout History: On March 7, 2011, J.Crew's Private Equity Saga Begins," *PitchBook*, March 7, 2017, https://pitchbook.com/news/articles/this-day-in-buyout-history-on-march-7-2011-j-crews-private-equity-saga-begins.
12. Steven Davidoff Solomon, "For Wall Street Deal Makers, Sometimes It Pays to Be Bad," *DealBook* (blog), *New York Times*, December 17, 2011, https://dealbook.nytimes.com/2011/12/27/for-wall-street-deal-makers-sometimes-it-pays-to-be-bad/.

13. "Mickey Drexler on Taking J.Crew Private: 'I Would Do It the Same Way,'" NBC New York, April 13, 2011, https://www.nbcnewyork.com/local/thread-mickey-drexler-on-taking-jcrew-private-i-would-do-it-the-same-way/1943120/.
14. Hitha Prabhaker, "Price of Admission," *Forbes*, February 2, 2007.

CHAPTER 21: PAGE SIX ON LINE ONE

1. Millman, "Jenna Lyons."
2. "New J.Crew Ad Sparks Debate on Gender Identity Confusion," CBS News New York, April 13, 2011, https://www.cbsnews.com/newyork/news/new-j-crew-ad-sparks-debate-on-gender-identity-confusion/.
3. Keith Ablow, "J.Crew Plants the Seeds for Gender Identity," Fox News, November 27, 2015, https://www.foxnews.com/health/j-crew-plants-the-seeds-for-gender-identity.
4. Dr. Peggy Drexler, "Do Painted Toes Make the Man?" *Huffington Post*, April 16, 2011, https://www.huffpost.com/entry/do-painted-toes-make-the_b_850104.
5. Robin Givhan, "Jenna Lyons Divorce and Alleged New Girlfriend: Why We Care," *Daily Beast*, October 29, 2011, https://www.thedailybeast.com/jenna-lyons-divorce-and-alleged-new-girlfriend-why-we-care.
6. Keith Ablow, "Jenna Lyons, You and J.Crew Wanted Your Son to Stop Being Such a Boy," Fox News, November 27, 2015, https://www.foxnews.com/opinion/jenna-lyons-you-and-j-crew-wanted-your-son-to-stop-being-such-a-boy.
7. Hilary Moss, "Jenna Lyons's Park Slope Townhouse Sold to Former Depeche Mode Bandmember [Updated]," *Cut*, March 27, 2012, https://www.thecut.com/2012/03/jenna-lyons-park-slope-townhouse-goes-for-4m.html.
8. Millman, "Jenna Lyons."
9. "Jenna Lyons Live!" *Dyking Out*, episode 214, December 14, 2021, audio, 17:00, https://dykingout.com/jenna-lyons-live-ep-214/.
10. Elizabeth Day, "How Selfies Became a Global Phenomenon," *Guardian*, July 13, 2013, https://www.theguardian.com/technology/2013/jul/14/how-selfies-became-a-global-phenomenon.

CHAPTER 22: COGNITIVE DISSONANCE, PART DEUX

1. Sacks, "How Jenna Lyons Transformed J.Crew."
2. Jian Deleon, "Uniqlo Reportedly in Talks to Buy J.Crew," GQ, February 28, 2014, https://www.gq.com/story/uniqlo-might-buy-j-crew-stores.
3. Evan Clark, Amanda Kaiser, and Vicki M. Young, "Fast Retailing Setting Sights on J.Crew," *Women's Wear Daily*, March 3, 2014, https://wwd.com/business-news/mergers-acquisitions/fast-retailing-setting-sights-on-j-crew-7540780/.

4. The Information, "Lyons L.A.D.'s Founder Jenna Lyons in Conversation with The Information's Jessica Lessin," YouTube, September 18, 2020, video, https://www.youtube.com/watch?v=YFoFlubeqFw.
5. Alex Williams, "The New Normal," *New York Times*, April 2, 2014, https://www.nytimes.com/2014/04/03/fashion/normcore-fashion-movement-or-massive-in-joke.html.
6. Fiona Duncan, "Normcore: Fashion For Those Who Realize They're One in 7 Billion," *Cut*, February 16, 2014, https://www.thecut.com/2014/02/normcore-fashion-trend.html.
7. Cline, *Overdressed*, 17–21.
8. Darrell Rigby, "The Future of Shopping," *Harvard Business Review*, December 2011, https://hbr.org/2011/12/the-future-of-shopping.
9. Ruth La Ferla, "Carlyn Cerf de Dudzeele: A Legend Who's Unafraid to Say So," *New York Times*, November 13, 2013, http://www.nytimes.com/2013/11/14/fashion/carlyn-cerf-de-dudzeele-a-legend-whos-unafraid-to-say-so.html.
10. Jeff Bercovici, "How This Millennial Founder Created a $730 Million Fashion Startup—With the Help of an Algorithm," *Inc.*, October 2017, https://www.inc.com/magazine/201710/jeff-bercovici/stitch-fix-katrina-lake.html.
11. Sapna Maheshwari, "Rent the Runway, a Secondhand Fashion Site, Makes Its Trading Debut," *New York Times*, October 27, 2021, https://www.nytimes.com/2021/10/27/business/rent-the-runway-ipo.html.
12. Darla Murray, "Q&A Jenna Lyons on Her *Girls* Cameo, Befriending Lena Dunham, and More," *Cut*, February 9, 2014, https://www.thecut.com/2014/02/qa-jenna-lyons-on-her-girls-cameo-fedoras.html.
13. Véronique Hyland, "Jenna Lyons on Her Solange Wedding Outfit, Getting Promoted, and Sequins," *Cut*, March 2, 2015, https://www.thecut.com/2015/02/jenna-lyons-on-career-advice-sequins-and-more.html.
14. Allison P. Davis, "Kate Middleton Lost Her Mind When She Met Jenna Lyons," *Cut*, December 9, 2014, https://www.thecut.com/2014/12/kmidd-freaked-out-when-she-met-jenna-lyons.html.
15. Form 8-K, J.Crew Group, Inc., United States Securities and Exchange Commission, December 4, 2014, https://investors.jcrew.com/static-files/e36c95dc-94d6-4871-b45b-2aa1927d8b68.
16. Adele Chapin, "Is the Cult of Jenna Lyons Eclipsing J.Crew?" Racked, December 22, 2014, https://www.racked.com/2014/12/22/7563399/jcrew-jenna-lyons-self-promotion.
17. Emily Smith, "J.Crew's Jenna Lyons Told to 'Cut Back on Self-Promotion,'" Page Six, December 21, 2014, https://pagesix.com/2014/12/21/j-crews-jenna-lyons-told-to-cut-back-on-self-promotion/.

CHAPTER 23: KNIVES OUT

1. Paumgarten, "The Merchant."
2. Tricia Louvar, "An Open Letter to Jenna Lyons," The Hairpin, March 25, 2015, https://www.thehairpin.com/2015/03/an-open-letter-to-jenna-lyons/.
3. Beth Strebner, "Nonprofit Group Storms Abercrombie & Fitch, Demands It Make Plus-Size Clothes," *Daily News* (New York), June 7, 2013, https://www.nydailynews.com/new-york/group-storms-f-flagship-demanding-extended-sizing-article-1.1365546.
4. Aimee Levitt, "Protest Fashion Is All the Rage," *Chicago Reader*, December 6, 2017, https://chicagoreader.com/arts-culture/protest-fashion-is-all-the-rage/.
5. John Hockenberry, "Closing the Representation Gap for Plus-Size Women," *The Takeaway*, September 28, 2016, audio, https://www.wnycstudios.org/podcasts/takeaway/segments/closing-representation-gap-plus-size-women.
6. Abra Belke, "Why J.Crew Is Faltering, and How It Can Recover," *Capitol Hill Style* (blog), March 24, 2015, https://caphillstyle.com/capitol/2015/03/24/why-j-crew-is-faltering-and-how-it-can-recover.html.
7. Bangshowbiz.com, "Prince Performs at White House," *Washington Post*, June 15, 2015, https://www.washingtonpost.com/entertainment/prince-performs-at-white-house/2015/06/15/75bc4406-1334-11e5-8457-4b431bf7ed4c_story.html.
8. Millman, "Jenna Lyons."
9. Vanessa Friedman, "Can a New Designer (Not Jenna Lyons) Fix J.Crew?" *New York Times*, June 11, 2015, https://www.nytimes.com/2015/06/12/fashion/somsack-sikhounmuong-of-madewell-becomes-womens-wear-designer-at-j-crew.html.
10. Steven Davidoff Solomon, "J.Crew Struggles with Its 'Great Man' Dilemma," *DealBook* (blog), *New York Times*, June 10, 2015, https://www.nytimes.com/2015/06/11/business/dealbook/j-crew-struggles-with-its-great-man-dilemma.html.
11. Creswell, "J.Crew Flounders."

CHAPTER 24: THREE HORSEWOMEN AND AN APOCALYPSE

1. Holgate, "Measure of Success."
2. Derek Thompson, "The Silent Crisis of Retail Employment," *Atlantic*, April 18, 2017, https://www.theatlantic.com/business/archive/2017/04/the-silent-crisis-of-retail-employment/523428/.
3. Kate Folk, "Letter of Recommendation: Dead Malls," *New York Times Magazine*, July 25, 2018, https://www.nytimes.com/2018/07/25/magazine/letter-of-recommendation-dead-malls.html.

4. Danielle Paquette, "We're Starting to Shop Online as Often as We Take Out the Trash," *Washington Post*, July 13, 2017, https://www.washingtonpost.com/news/wonk/wp/2017/07/13/how-your-shopping-habits-are-hurting-american-jobs-especially-today/.
5. "Mickey Drexler: Things Have Been 'Miserable' In Retail," CNBC, November 9, 2017, video, https://www.cnbc.com/video/2017/11/09/mickey-drexler-things-have-been-miserable-in-retail.html.
6. Maya Singer, "J.Crew Fall 2017 Ready-to-Wear," *Vogue Runway*, February 13, 2017, https://www.vogue.com/fashion-shows/fall-2017-ready-to-wear/j-crew.
7. Millman, "Jenna Lyons."
8. Nicole Phelps and Steff Yotka, "9 Things to Remember About the Jenna Lyons Era at J.Crew," *Vogue*, April 3, 2017, https://www.vogue.com/article/jenna-lyons-out-at-jcrew.
9. Lauren Sherman, "Jenna Lyons Exits J.Crew," *Business of Fashion*, April 3, 2017, https://www.businessoffashion.com/articles/retail/jenna-lyons-exits-j-crew/.
10. Kali Hays, "When Tom and Dom Left Gucci Group," *Women's Wear Daily*, December 22, 2017, https://wwd.com/fashion-news/designer-luxury/when-tom-ford-and-domenico-de-sole-left-gucci-group-ysl-11079847/.

CHAPTER 25: THE CHERRY PICKERS

1. Abha Bhattarai, "'Rearranging Deck Chairs on the *Titanic*': J.Crew, Mired in Debt, Is Trying to Turn Around Its Business," *Washington Post*, June 21, 2018, https://www.washingtonpost.com/news/business/wp/2018/06/21/rearranging-deck-chairs-on-the-titanic-j-crew-mired-in-debt-is-trying-to-turn-around-its-business/.
2. Vanessa Friedman, Sapna Maheshwari, and Michael J. de la Merced, "J.Crew Files for Bankruptcy in Virus's First Big Retail Casualty," *New York Times*, May 3, 2020, https://www.nytimes.com/2020/05/03/business/j-crew-bankruptcy-coronavirus.html.
3. Cintra Wilson, "How Brooks Brothers Became a Symbol of What Not to Wear to the Revolution," *Town & Country*, July 26, 2020, https://www.townandcountrymag.com/style/fashion-trends/a33415887/brooks-brothers-mccloskeys-controversy/.
4. Dominic-Madori Davis, "The End of an Era: Brooks Brothers, J.Crew, and Other Emblems of Upper-Class America are Going Bankrupt Because of the New Uprising," *Insider*, August 4, 2020, https://www.businessinsider.com/brooks-brothers-j-crew-black-lives-matter-white-america-uprising-2020-8.
5. Priya Elan, "'Woke' Fashion Brands Face Backlash for Not Practicing What They Preach," *Guardian*, June 13, 2020, https://www.theguardian.com/fashion/2020/jun/13/fashion-brands-culture-george-floyd.

6. Vanessa Friedman, "J.Crew Didn't Need to Live Forever," *New York Times*, May 4, 2020, https://www.nytimes.com/2020/05/04/style/j-crew-bankruptcy.html.
7. Carly Haynes, "New Vaccination Site in Former J.Crew Location Opens," CBS19 News, June 28, 2021, https://www.cbs19news.com/story/44199977/new-vaccination-site-in-former-j-crew-location-opens-monday.
8. Allie Volpe, "The Resurrection of Retail," *Atlantic*, April 6, 2022, https://www.theatlantic.com/culture/archive/2022/04/online-shopping-decline-pandemic/629482/.
9. Cathaleen Chen, "Rent the Runway's Long Road Ahead to Profitability," *Business of Fashion*, April 14, 2022, https://www.businessoffashion.com/articles/retail/rent-the-runways-long-road-ahead-to-profitability/.
10. Cathaleen Chen,"Can Fashion Resale Ever Be a Profitable Business?" *Business of Fashion*, April 4, 2022, https://www.businessoffashion.com/articles/retail/can-fashion-resale-ever-be-a-profitable-business/.
11. Pierre Mallevays, "Luxury E-Commerce: Crash or Correction?" *Business of Fashion*, June 8, 2022, https://www.businessoffashion.com/opinions/finance/luxury-e-commerce-crash-or-correction/.
12. Volpe, "Resurrection of Retail."
13. Shira Ovide, "A Comeback for Physical Stores," *New York Times*, February 23, 2022, https://www.nytimes.com/2022/02/23/technology/physical-stores-ecommerce.html.
14. Lauren Cochrane, "Step Aside Streetwear, Preppy Style Is Back with a Vengeance," *Guardian*, August 27, 2021, https://www.theguardian.com/fashion/2021/aug/27/step-aside-streetwear-preppy-style-is-back-with-a-vengeance.
15. Scott Christian, "Prep Is Back—But It's Completely Different Than You Remember," *Esquire*, June 19, 2019, https://www.esquire.com/style/mens-fashion/a28068830/prep-preppy-fashion-style-comeback/.
16. Christian, "Prep Is Back."

INDEX

ABOUT THE AUTHOR

Maggie Bullock started her career as an editor at *Vogue* and spent thirteen years as an editor at *Elle*, covering culture, style, and beauty. As a freelance writer she contributes to publications including *The Economist, Vanity Fair, The Atlantic, Vogue, Elle, New York* magazine, and *T: The New York Times Style Magazine,* and is co-creator of the cult women's-media newsletter The Spread (www.thespread.media). She lives in Amherst, Massachusetts, with her husband, Nick, and their sons, Finn and Max.